Victorian Popular Dramatists

Twayne's English Authors Series

Herbert Sussman, Editor

Northeastern University

TEAS 440

Victorian Popular Dramatists

By Victor Emeljanow

University of Newcastle, Australia

Twayne Publishers
A Division of G.K. Hall & Co. • Boston

Victorian Popular Dramatists

Victor Emeljanow

Copyright © 1987 by G.K. Hall & Co.
All Rights Reserved
Published by Twayne Publishers
A Division of G.K. Hall & Co.
70 Lincoln Street
Boston, Massachusetts 02111

Copyediting supervised by Lewis DeSimone
Book production by Elizabeth Todesco
Book design by Barbara Anderson

Typeset in 11 pt. Garamond
by P&M Typesetting, Inc., Waterbury, Connecticut

Printed on permanent/durable acid-free paper
and bound in the United States of America

Library of Congress Cataloging in Publication Data

Emeljanow, Victor.
    Victorian popular dramatists.

    (Twayne's English authors; TEAS 440)
    Bibliography: p. 171
    Includes index.
    1. English drama—19th century—History and
criticism.   2. Popular literature—Great Britain—
History and criticism.   I. Title.   II. Series.
PR734.P65E54   1987   822'.8'09   86-19450
ISBN 0-8057-6935-8

Contents

About the Author

Victor Emeljanow is chairman of the Department of Drama, University of Newcastle, Australia. He received his B.A. and M.A. at the University of Auckland, New Zealand, and Ph.D. at Stanford University, California. His scholarly interests and publications are in popular theater, Chekhov, the productions of Theodore Komisarjevsky, and nineteenth-century theater audiences. He is as well a professional director and actor with credits in live theater and television.

Preface

The Victorian period saw the last manifestation of a universally popular dramatic form on the live stage. It saw the remarkable phenomenon of a play in English being performed to audiences everywhere the language was spoken, and obtaining a similar response. This suggests a degree of uniformity of dramatic taste that enabled plays and their performers to move fluidly between England, America, Australia, New Zealand, South Africa, and the Far East. The plays were written by dramatists as popular as Dickens, Hardy, Thackeray, Eliot, and Trollope, yet their names have been largely forgotten and have only become prominent again with the recent interest in popular drama. To understand the nature and extent of Victorian popular drama, therefore, we need to become familiar with names that include William Moncrieff, Edward Fitzball, J. B. Buckstone, Douglas Jerrold, Edward Bulwer-Lytton, Tom Taylor, Tom Robertson, and Dion Boucicault.

Popular drama, a drama directed at and reflecting the aspirations of a broadly based, heterogeneous audience, is not new. Its serious investigation by scholars and its general appreciation, however, have been somewhat belated. Since the mid-1960s popular drama has come under increasing scrutiny not only by theater scholars but also by cultural historians. Since World War II, inherited conceptions about dramatic form have been progressively eroded. It was not until the 1960s, however, that the political and social radicalization of theater brought a new perspective to such issues as differences between "medium" (form) and "message" (content), theater as affirmation and theater as confrontation, theater for the many and theater for the few. The result of social upheaval was an aesthetic redistribution of light and shade on the various components of the theatrical experience, the most important of which was the nature of the theatrical performance as distinct from the dramatic text. When performers and historians looked backward for a tradition and an historical vindication for this renewed interest, they rediscovered the Renascence world of *commedia dell'arte,* the world of circus and pantomime, and the theater of the nineteenth century. Part of the 1960s legacy has been the readiness to identify the interests of popular drama with those of the economically or socially disadvantaged in society. The result has been a tendency to give any discussion of popular drama a Marxist coloring, as narrow and dogmatic as the old, Aristotelian-based principles of dramatic criticism. More fruitful discussions, however, have involved the comparison of the techniques of popular drama as seen on stage with those on screen and television, the investigation of the role and influence of popular audiences, the important shaping process of theatrical conditions upon dramatic writing, and, in particular, the historical evolution of popular dramatic tastes in the light of the industrial revolution and the consequent development of the modern urban society.

The problem since the 1960s has been a question of definition. In attempting to define popular drama, David Mayer in 1974 suggested criteria that may prove useful for an understanding of the works and dramatists we will consider:

> Several affirmative answers to the following queries are enough to indicate that the work in question is popular drama. Is the author unknown? Is the piece of work of more than one author? Is the playwright indifferent to his reputation as a poet? Is the author's identity of little importance to those who announce and present the play? If the author is known, is he known for a style of drama, for sensational scenes, for the use of character types who are amusing in their own right irrespective of the overall unity of the piece? Are plays of this sort favoured over situations that deal with immediate moral and social values in a meaningful way? Does theatrical effect take precedence over literary and artistic conventions? . . . Is the piece intended for a large general audience rather than a select group of spectators? Does the piece give the undiscriminating spectator "what he wants" at the expense of meeting the tastes and predilections of an educated class? Is the dramatic plot embellished with actions and displays offered as much for their own effect as for their relevance to the plot? Does the piece reassure the audience in the validity of traditional values and in the continuity of belief rather than reinterpret traditional attitudes, accepted facts, or mythologies? Is the piece traditional, or is much of the material in the piece of a traditional nature?[1]

All four authors examined in this study fit easily under the umbrella as suggested by Mayer of popular drama. Nevertheless, there are perceptible differences in attitudes contained within their plays that reflect changes in audience tastes at various periods of the nineteenth century, and changing perceptions of the role of the dramatist in his society. All four dramatists wrote plays that were imitated, indeed even copied, and performed extensively throughout the English-

Preface

speaking world. The transmission of the plays was inextricably tied to their actors. This study, therefore, makes reference to the theatrical reception of the plays and to the connections between the dramatic texts and their performances. Finally, the thrust of this study, is to provide some understanding of the nature of popular dramatic writing, its themes and techniques, with reference to the period between about 1820 to 1900, and also to illustrate the movement in the Victorian period from a drama based on the principle of the widest popular appeal, to a drama in which the theatrical respectability of its audience militated against the very principle that had insured its popularity.

Victor Emeljanow

University of Newcastle, Australia

Acknowledgments

The selection from "Towards a Definition of Popular Theatre," by David Mayer in *Western Popular Theatre*, edited by David Mayer and Kenneth Richards (London: Methuen, 1977), is reprinted by permission of the publisher. The selections from *The Life and Letters of Henry Arthur Jones*, by Doris Arthur Jones (London: Victor Gollancz, 1930), are reprinted by permission of the publisher. I have been unable to trace the holder of additional rights.

I would like to record my deep gratitude to Professor Michael Booth, Department of Theatre, University of Victoria, Canada, for his personal and scholarly generosity, and to my family for their love and tolerance.

Chronology

1802   13 November, Holcroft's *A Tale of Mystery* introduces melodrama to the English stage.

1803   3 January, Douglas Jerrold born in London.

1814   Edmund Kean makes his debut at Drury Lane.

1817   19 October, Tom Taylor born in Bishop-Wearmouth, Sunderland. Patent theaters lit by gas for the first time. John Philip Kemble retires.

1820   17 May, James Sheridan Knowles's *Virginius* with Macready.

1821   30 April, Jerrold's first play *More Frightened than Hurt*.

1822   Dion Boucicault born in Dublin.

1827   Debut of Charles Kean.

1828   6 October, Jerrold's first domestic melodrama *Ambrose Gwinett;* 24 November, first temperance play, *Fifteen Years of a Drunkard's Life*.

1829   9 January, T. W. Robertson born at Newark-upon-Trent. 8 June, Jerrold's *Black Eyed Susan;* 30 November, *Thomas à Becket*.

1830   Madame Vestris begins her management of the Olympic Theatre. 7 July, Jerrold's *Mutiny at the Nore;* 15 December, Byron's *Werner*.

1832   25 January, Jerrold's *The Rent Day*. Report of the Select Committee on Dramatic Literature.

1833   Edmund Kean dies. Passing of the Dramatic Copyright Act.

1837   Macready begins management of Covent Garden. Benjamin Webster takes over the Haymarket Theatre.

1838   Henry Irving born in Somerset. 15 February, Bulwer-Lytton's *The Lady of Lyons*.

1840   8 December, Lytton's *Money*.

1841   Jerrold writes his first contribution for *Punch*. Macready takes over the management of Drury Lane. 4 March, Boucicault's *London Assurance*.

1842 25 February, Jerrold's *Bubbles of the Day;* 1 March, *Prisoner of War.*

1843 Theatre Regulation Act passed ending patent theater monopoly.

1844 14 November, Taylor's first play *A Trip to Kissengen.* Samuel Phelps begins management of Sadler's Wells Theatre.

1845 26 April, Jerrold's *Time Works Wonders.*

1846 14 September, Taylor's first success, *To Parents and Guardians.*

1847 Madame Vestris and her husband, Charles Mathews, start their management of the Lyceum Theatre.

1848 Queen Victoria initiates regular theatrical performances at Windsor.

1849 Ellen Terry born in Coventry.

1850 Charles Kean begins management of Princess's Theatre.

1851 3 May, Jerrold's *Retired from Business.* 20 September, Henry Arthur Jones born at Grandborough. Charles Morton opens the Canterbury Hall, the first London music hall.

1852 Jerrold begins editing *Lloyd's Weekly Newspaper.* 20 November, Taylor and Reade collaborate in *Masks and Faces.*

1853 Buckstone takes over from Webster as manager of the Haymarket. Alfred Wigan begins his management of the Olympic Theatre.

1854 Robertson works for the Vestris management at the Lyceum. 9 October, Jerrold's last produced play, *A Heart of Gold.*

1855 14 May, Taylor's *Still Waters Run Deep.*

1856 Madame Vestris dies.

1857 8 January, Douglas Jerrold dies in London.

1858 18 October, Taylor's *Our American Cousin* in New York.

1859 18 October, Taylor's *The Fool's Revenge.* Charles Kean relinquishes the Princess's Theatre.

1860 23 February, Taylor's *The Overland Route.* 16 September, Boucicault's *The Collen Bawn.*

1861 14 February, Robertson's *The Cantab,* the first play to bring him London notices. 16 November, Taylor's *Our American Cousin* in London.

1862 Phelps retires from Sadler's Wells.

1863 27 May, Taylor's *The Ticket of Leave Man.*

1864 30 April, Robertson's first London success, *David Garrick.*

1865 4 March, Taylor's *The Settling Day.* 4 September, Joseph Jefferson introduces *Rip Van Winkle* to English audiences. Marie Wilton begins her management of the Prince of Wales Theatre; 11 November, she produces Robertson's *Society.*

1866 15 September, Robertson's *Ours.* Report of Select Committee on Theatrical Licenses and Regulations. 29 December, Gilbert's first play, *Dulcamara.*

1867 6 April, Robertson's *Caste.*

1868 15 February, Robertson's *Play.* Charles Kean dies. John Hollingshead opens the Gaiety Theatre.

1869 14 January, Robertson's *Home;* 16 January, and *School.* 25 October, Taylor's *New Men and Old Acres.* 18 September, Robertson's *Progress.*

1871 16 January, Robertson's last play, *War.* 3 February, Robertson dies in London. 25 November, Irving appears in *The Bells.* 26 December, Gilbert and Sullivan first collaborate in *Thespis.*

1873 Macready dies.

1874 Taylor becomes editor of *Punch.*

1878 Irving assumes sole control of the Lyceum.

1879 29 May, Jones's first produced play, *Hearts of Oak* at Exeter. Wilson Barrett takes over as manager of Court Theatre.

1880 12 July, Taylor dies in London. The Bancrofts take over the Haymarket. Irving starts to darken the auditorium of the Lyceum consistently.

1881 16 November, Jones's *The Silver King* establishes his reputation. William Archer publishes *English Dramatists of Today.*

1883 Irving's first American tour.

1884 25 September, Jones's *Saints and Sinners.*

1885 21 March, Pinero's *The Magistrate.*

1887 International Copyright Act passed. Beerbohm Tree takes over management of the Haymarket.

1889   27 August, Jones's *The Middleman*. First English production of Ibsen's *A Doll's House*.

1890   21 May, Jones's *Judah*.

1891   George Alexander begins management of the St. James's Theatre. 15 January, Jones's *The Dancing Girl*. American Copyright Act passed. The Independent Stage Society formed by Jacob Grein.

1892   9 December, Shaw's *Widower's Houses*.

1893   19 April, Wilde's *A Woman of No Importance*. 27 May, Pinero's *The Second Mrs. Tanqueray*. 30 September, Jones's *The Tempter*.

1894   3 October, Jones's *The Case of Rebellious Susan*.

1895   Henry Irving knighted. 14 February, Wilde's *The Importance of being Earnest*. Jones publishes *The Renascence of English Drama*.

1896   15 January, Jones's *Michael and his Lost Angel*.

1897   6 October, Jones's *The Liars*. 17 November, Shaw's *The Devil's Disciple*. Tree opens Her Majesty's Theatre. Squire Bancroft knighted.

1898   The Irish Literary Theatre formed in Dublin.

1900   2 May, Shaw's *You Never Can Tell*. 9 October, Jones's *Mrs. Dane's Defence*.

1929   7 January, Henry Arthur Jones dies in London.

Chapter One

Dramatic Forms and Their Theatrical Context

Although all four writers whom we will consider wrote plays during the reign of Queen Victoria, the form as well as the content of those plays extend backward to at least the eighteenth century and forward to the modern manifestations of popular drama, the melodramas and situation comedies of television. When we consider the careers of our representative dramatists and their output we cannot help but be astonished at the scope and variety of their writing. If we look at Allardyce Nicoll's handlists of plays by these authors we might well be bewildered by a catalog that enumerates melodramas, farces, domestic dramas, comedies, comedy dramas, burlesques, extravaganzas, burlettas, tragedies, comediettas, romantic dramas, and so on.[1] We may be further bewildered to discover that among them these four men wrote about 255 plays. All this serves to emphasize their prolific energy and the presence of a very considerable consumer demand.

The Audience

The variety of dramatic forms suggests a dynamic, changing audience composition and that this audience responded to and demanded novelty. The audience of the nineteenth was very different from that of the eighteenth century. In London, the eighteenth-century repertoire reflected the presence in the theater of an educated middle-class and aristocratic audience. Lower classes, though present, formed a minority of playgoers. The division of the theater itself into boxes, pit, and gallery preserved clearly differentiated social classes which lasted into the following century. In defining the composition of a theater audience in 1809, John Dallas in a preface to his play *Not at Home* could speak of "that cultivated Company who usually occupy the circle of dress boxes; . . . those judicious Critics who take their station in the Pit; . . . my worthy friend John Bull, who is to be found in either Gallery."[2] By 1800, however, the sense of a comfortable club housing equals was rapidly dissipating. The population of London was increasing phenomenally. It had already reached nearly one million, and by 1850 it would treble. The old patent theater system that limited the licensed theaters in London to three—Drury Lane, Covent Garden, and a special summer license for the Haymarket—was totally inadequate to cater for the theatrical needs of immigrant farm workers, artisans, people involved in servicing the import and export of goods through the Port of London, domestic servants, and soldiers and sailors on leave from the Napoleonic Wars, let alone the proliferation of shop owners and their assistants who provided the goods and services for an urban population. As the population of London grew, so did its perimeters, as large new districts populated by the new working classes established themselves particularly in the East End and the area south of the Thames. It was natural that living and working in the same neighborhood would suggest a demand for a neighborhood theater that reflected its concerns as well as the variety in social origins and working patterns of its inhabitants.

"Major" and "Minor" Theaters

The result of the demand for increasing theatrical entertainment after 1800 was the emergence of the "minor" theaters and a concomitant division of dramatic fare into "legitimate" (reflecting the legal and aesthetic apartness of the patent theaters) and "illegitimate" (reflecting the legal suffrance and informality of the minor theaters). As early as 1782 the Royal Circus on the south bank of the Thames had set itself up as a venue for equestrian displays, and even before that, Sadler's Wells, on the northern perimeter of London, had been providing a bill of fare that included recitations and performing animals. This "illegitimate" kind of entertainment was soon to be augmented by the formal introduction of melodrama to the English stage in Thomas Holcroft's *A Tale of Mystery* at Covent Garden in November 1802. That the play should have been produced at one of the patent theaters is significant. It is an admission that by the turn of the century the "legitimate" fare of tragedy, comedy, and the plays of Shakespeare was insufficient to cater for the tastes of the new audience.

As theaters proliferated, the dichotomy between "major" and "minor" theaters widened, and the first forty-three years of the nineteenth century saw the battle for the new audience's patronage joined between the entrenched interests of the patent theaters and the new breed of actor/manager/showman prepared to give the audience whatever it wanted.[3] In part this explains the huge variety of entertainments offered by theaters in the first part of the century. Managements were battling to discover and define the tastes of their particular audiences. At the same time they were trying to circumvent the restrictive legal conditions of performance. This was the context in which Douglas Jerrold was writing.

By the end of Jerrold's creative life circumstances had changed considerably. In 1843 the Theatre Regulation Act had abolished the patent theater monopoly and "major" and "minor" theater terminology became anachronistic. The huge theaters of Drury Lane and Covent Garden had become prestigious liabilities to their managers while the remainder were trying to define their own particular identities. At this, many were successful, and from the 1830s the history of nineteenth-century theater is the history of specific theaters and their managements: the Adelphi under Yates and then Madame Celeste (1825–58) for a special brand of sensational melodrama; the Olympic under Madame Vestris noted for genteel burlesque, extravaganza, and light comedy (1830–38); Sadler's Wells under Samuel Phelps (1844–62) and the Princess's under Charles Kean (1850–59) for their Shakespeare revivals and literary melodrama; the Prince of Wales under the Bancrofts (1865–79) for its comedies; and the Lyceum for Irving's spectacular melodramas and Shakespearean revivals (1878 to the end of the century). What is significant in this catalog is the persistence of melodrama, raised from illegitimacy to respectability.

"The Decline of the Drama"

Before examining the various manifestations of dramatic writing we need to look at a generalization that permeates the criticism of nineteenth-century drama: that, until at least the 1850s, the drama demonstrated a process of decline and degeneration. The statement was largely the responsibility of the English romantic writers, their followers among the Victorian poets, and literary critics. It incorporated also a nostalgic response to the vanished club atmosphere of the eighteenth-century theater and its established conception of repertoire. The causes for this alleged decline were many. The first of these was the failure of the established writers and poets to involve themselves in the theater. Though Coleridge, Wordsworth, Byron, Keats, and Shelley all wrote plays, their success in the theater was very limited.

Coleridge's play *Remorse* was performed at Drury Lane in 1813 and Byron's *Werner* and *Sardanapalus* became successes when Macready or Charles Kean produced them after Byron's death. The failure, however, on the part of these poets to provide a dramaturgic leadership of the kind that Goethe, Schiller, and Hugo provided on the Continent stemmed from their unwillingness to come to terms with the dramatic marketplace. All of them wished for dramatic success but felt unwilling to entrust their work to others. They were, furthermore, abnormally diffident about allowing their work to be scrutinized by a random aggregate of spectators. It was as much as anything a terror of the new audience that held them back and even dissuaded them from attending theatrical performances.

The result was a failure to learn the essentials of dramatic structure and characterization which no amount of historical adherence to Shakespearean or Jacobean dramatic principles could rectify. Byron's relative success came from providing a role in Werner with which an actor/manager's ego might identify and, in *Sardanapalus,* spectacular scenes which would assault the playgoer's senses. Because he could not provide even these, Browning's hopes as a dramatist remained unrealized. On the other hand, Tennyson's hopes to a limited extent, were realized. In *Becket* and *Queen Mary* he provided vehicles for spectacular costumed recreations, and in Becket and Philip of Spain, two suitable roles for Henry Irving. The element that constantly recurs in the limited success of the poets in the theater is the failure to provide opportunities for actors and audiences. To provide these required a degree of self-abnegation which the poets, like their heroes, were unprepared to tolerate. Most of the successful writers in the new popular forms were prepared to accept the absence of personal fame, and they remained unknown while they focused their attention on gratifying the wishes of an actor or the supposed wishes of an audience.[4]

To discover the wishes of actor and audience, however, was no easy task. Already in 1792 and 1794 the two patent theaters had increased their capacity to over 3,000 to cope with the influx of audiences made up of the new components of London society. Their tastes were unpredictable except in their response to spectacle. To this was attributed the second major cause of the drama's decline. Again the objection to spectacle proceeded from the writings of nineteenth-century literary critics. Spectacle, they argued, was a product of theatrical machinery or a scene painter's ingenuity or an actor/manager's sense of mass organization. Though suggestions for spectacular effects might indeed reside in the text, these could be ignored or minimized if the attention of the text's interpreters was on its characterization or thematic development. Conversely, the constant demand for spectacular moments, suggested their detractors, inevitably led to episodic plays that flouted the rules of conventional dramaturgy. Even more destructive was the diminished importance of the spoken line in favor of visual impressiveness which the size of the new theaters tended to require. The taste for spectacle, however, was not limited to the major theaters; it preoccupied the managements of the minors as well. Thus theatrical conditions and dramatic responses to them collaborated in diminishing the drama's textual basis. Spectacle was to remain, despite literary protest, a constant factor throughout the century, in the elaborate revivals of Shakespeare, the sensation dramas of Boucicault, in the doctrine of meticulous realism as demonstrated in the authenticity of Taylor's *Ticket of Leave Man* and the Bancroft productions of Robertson in the 1860s, and in the pantomimes of Augustus Harris at Drury Lane in the 1880s and 1890s.[5]

The last important reason to which the drama's decline was attributed was the position of the actor and manager vis-à-vis the dramatist. In 1807 Leigh Hunt was able to say that a play's effectiveness had little to do with the contribution of the dramatic author: "[the spectator] will find that his chief entertainment has arisen from the actors totally abstracted from the author."[6] With few exceptions this was to remain a rule throughout the century and to have a profound effect on dramatic authors' opinion of themselves and their craft. Until the 1860s authors were poorly paid and could not subsist on their dramatic writing alone. Some, like Jerrold, Robertson, and Taylor were practicing journalists, others resorted to writing as much as possible for as many managements as they could for a maximum fee of fifty pounds per play, while others tried to carve a niche for themselves as resident playwrights with a particular theater. Nevertheless, some outstanding authors were well paid for individual plays. Colman's comedy *John Bull* in 1803 brought him 1,200 pounds; Frederick Reynolds could average 500 pounds for his plays between 1805 and 1810. It is little wonder, however, that Thackeray and Dickens preferred to entrust themselves to the more lucrative and regular means of earning their incomes, the serialization of their novels and their printing in popular editions for the rapidly expanding reading public. Nevertheless, plays were needed, and to accommodate the demand many dramatists turned to German and then French sources for their plots and characters, and to the dramatization of successful novels by Walter Scott, Dickens, Harrison Ainsworth, or Mrs. Braddon. Again the persona of the dramatist was obscured by the more notable original. It also helped to maintain the dramatist's relative poverty, as managers needed to pay little for translation or adaptation.

By the 1850s a dramatic author without a track record could expect no more than fifty pounds per act. In 1860, however, Boucicault began an arrangement that would radically change the position of dramatic authors. He asked Webster, the manager of the Adelphi Theatre, to share receipts from his play *The Colleen Bawn*. The arrangement did not become the norm until the 1880s but after the passing of the international copyright agreement in 1887 and the American Copyright Act in 1891, literary men were again to return to the theater. They were by then guaranteed of adequate returns both from the box office and from the publication of their plays for the benefit of a wide reading public in England and America.[7] Adequate reward and personal renown brought with it not only respectability but also a change in the nature of the drama offered. The theaters were now in the hands of an audience that believed itself to be discriminating and wished to see on stage a demonstration of its own moral and social values. Plots were discussed by critics in terms of originality of conception and condemned for any actions or situations that were irrelevant. Late-nineteenth-century drama had started to lose its popular basis and to become the preserve of a coterie.

Melodrama

The most characteristic form of popular drama throughout the nineteenth century was melodrama.[8] Like the term "Victorian," however, its definition is not a watertight one. There are melodramatic elements in Shakespeare, in Jacobean drama, and in an eighteenth-century bourgeois tragedy like Lillo's *The London Merchant*. The application of the term "mélodrame" to the English stage merely emphasized the importance of those elements that had hitherto been integrated into the fabric of a play, and the fact that its immediate source was French.

Gothic melodrama. Though the romantic writers made a negligible contribution to the English stage, romanticism provided a storehouse of atmosphere, situation, and theme in its Gothic manifestation. Horace Walpole had written his archetypal Gothic novel *The Castle of Otranto* in 1764 and a tragedy *The Mysterious Mother* in 1768. This resulted in the immediate popularity of the Gothic novel and Gothic play not only in England but also in France. Its most successful exponent in England from 1797 to 1810 was "Monk" Lewis with plays like *The Castle Spectre* (1797) and *The Wood Daemon* (1807). In France supernaturalism was domesticated somewhat by Pixérécourt. His was the drama of the Revolution seeking at once to please and instruct the new citizenry. It proved immediately attractive to the English minor houses. From the turn of the century Gothic romanticism was supplemented rapidly by adaptations of the novels and poetic romances of Walter Scott, the first adaptation of which was Dibdin's *The Lady of the Lake* at the Surrey Theatre in 1810. One of the most successful of Scott's adaptors was Isaac Pocock who in 1813 wrote *The Miller and his Men,* and shifted the focus of Gothic melodrama from the dungeon to what Michael Booth calls "the bandit-cottage-forest" type.[9] As the dominant mode of melodrama, the Gothic remained in force until the mid-1820s when it was supplanted by the nautical and the domestic. Its impression, however, was indelible. Theatrically, it used the advances in technology to the fullest to assault the senses of the audience, as the ending of act 1 of Fitzball's *The Flying Dutchman* (1827) suggests: "Music—Peter attempts to snatch the letter, when it explodes—a sailor is about to seize Vanderdecken, who eludes his grasp, and vanishes through the deck. . . . Vanderdecken, with a demoniac laugh, rises from the sea in blue fire, amidst violent thunder—at that instant the Phantom Ship appears in the sky behind. . . ."[10]

Thematically, it introduced to the stage the resourceful and complex melodramatic villain, often tortured by guilt and remorse, but sensual, cruel, and ruthless. So powerful was this stage creation and so able to flout normal convention and morality that dramatists found, as did the romantics, their own positions to be curiously ambivalent. To audiences, the audacious outlaw able to transcend the restrictions of society through intellect and emotional strength, was an attractive, anarchic figure. At both major and minor theaters, Gothic melodrama was the epitome of escapism. Its supernaturalism and dynamic emotional range were the stuff of dreams. Its characters were identified with actors like O. B. Smith and T. P. Cooke who were lionized for their creations. As the century wore on, Gothicism retained its fascination. Gothic fiction flourished in the works of Ste-

venson, Edgar Allan Poe, and Bram Stoker, and on stage it appeared
in a more internalized form: in the psychological torture of Mathias
in *The Bells* or in the hypnotic dominance of Svengali in *Trilby,* or as
the incarnation of evil of Irving's Mephistopheles in his production of
Faust.

Nautical melodrama.   The form of nautical drama is no different to that of the Gothic. The villains are no longer earls maundering
in their decaying castles or despotic Eastern potentates but smugglers
and pirates. If they are aristocratic their status is reduced to baronets
and the basis of their power is money, while the object of their desire
is the wife or fiancée of the sailor hero. The hero, however, is a common sailor and not an officer, thus again emphasizing the drama's plebeian appeal. He is courageous, more resourceful than the villain, and
unswervingly patriotic. The heyday of nautical drama covers the period 1825–35 starting with Fitzball's *The Pilot* which he followed by
The Inchcape Bell; or, The Dumb Sailor Boy (1828) and *The Red Rover;
or The Mutiny of the Dolphin* (1829). It ends with J. T. Haines's *My
Poll and My Partner Joe,* performed at the Surrey Theatre in 1835.
Both of the last plays were performed at the Surrey which, under its
name of the Royal Circus, had been largely responsible for the minor
theater's fascination with nautical drama since the 1790s.

From the end of the eighteenth century and during the early years
of the nineteenth, nautical melodrama had taken the form of exciting
confrontations between pirates and sailors, augmented by shows intended to glorify the achievements of English sailors in the war
against Napoleon. Thus Sadler's Wells re-created *The Battle of Tra-
falgar* in 1806 and *The Battle of the Nile* in 1815 using model ships
and children as the sailors. In essence they are no different to the
modern filmic re-creations of *The Charge of the Light Brigade* or *Waterloo*. In the first twenty years of the century these spectacles served a
patriotic and socially cohesive function. They demonstrated the superiority of the British navy and the determination of Britain to keep
the sea lanes of commerce free from marauders. In the 1820s the focus
changed. By then the wars were over and interest centered not on the
navy but on the individual British tar who had made up that navy or
who was at that moment safeguarding the livelihood of those who saw
him on stage.

After 1835, nautical drama continued as long as its writers like
Haines, Fitzball, and Edward Stirling were prepared to respond to the
demand of the local seafaring audiences of the Victoria and Surrey

theaters. As late as 1847 Fitzball wrote *The Wreck and the Reef* for the
Surrey and Stirling *The Anchor of Hope; or, the Seaman's Star.* Though
nautical melodrama was replaced by a prevailing interest in the domestic, the fascination with the sea and sailors remained. The common sailor was still the hero in Seymour Hicks and Fred Latham's
With Flying Colors at the Adelphi in 1899, while the success of films
like *Captain Blood, The Crimson Pirate,* and *The Mutiny on the Bounty*
attest to the continuing popular appeal of Gothic-inspired outlaws
and the anti-aristocratic, anti-authoritarian values of early nineteenth-
century nautical melodrama.

   Domestic melodrama.   Such was the appeal of the sailor hero
that he figured in plays that had little to do with the sea. Buckstone's
Luke the Labourer in 1826 is often regarded as the first domestic melodrama. Its setting is a village and its focus is on domestic values.
Here the sailor figures as a returning serviceman who rescues a heroine
persecuted by a villainous country squire and his henchman Luke.
The term "domestic," however, suggests a particular ambiance, that
of the home with its concomitant set of values. It transcends economic and social barriers and reflects directly the everyday concerns
of its spectators. Whereas Gothic and nautical spectacle indulged the
spectator's desire for vicarious excitement through a world of fantasy,
domestic melodrama prompted the immediate recognition of familiar
environments and motives upon which could be grafted the elements
of wish fulfillment and dramatic engineering. At first the settings of
domestic melodrama were humble: the village, the cottage, the humble aspirations of country living. It accorded well with the nostalgic
memories of former agricultural laborers and with the wishful thinking of a city-born proletariat. When the setting shifted to the city,
the countryside became a symbol of lost innocence, and the country-
man shown to be an innocent more than susceptible to the viciousness
of his new world. Martha Willis in Jerrold's play of the same name
arrives in search of her village sweetheart and is dragged into a world
of theft and murder. In Taylor's *Ticket of Leave Man* in 1863, the
hero, Bob Brierly, is a Lancashire lad in London with no money and
no prospects. In Jones's *The Dancing Girl* in 1891, the world weary
Duke of Guisebury is corrupted by the superficial values of London
society and gives it up for a life of hard work in a remote part of
Cornwall.

   The most frequently used catalyst of domestic melodrama becomes
the preoccupation with money, its acquisition or its loss. In the pe-

riod up to 1850 money was seen to be the root of all evil. The desire
for its acquisition led to gambling and to inevitable criminality. Its
absence led to hardship, drink, and the dissolution of the family. In
this period melodrama was at its most socially engaged. It demonstrated on stage not only the consequences of drunkenness as in Jerrold's *Fifteen Years of a Drunkard's Life* (1828) or T. P. Taylor's *The
Bottle* (1847) but also industrial strife as in John Walker's *The Factory
Lad* (1834) and J. T. Haines's *The Factory Boy* (1840).

After 1850 attitudes to money changed perceptibly as more affluent
audiences influenced the nature of the dramatic repertoire. Domestic
melodrama, now more often than not simply styled as "drama," introduced the world of banking, of stocks and shares, and of the men
of commerce and those whose job it was to protect this financial
world, the police. It was a world of cause and effect, the application
of reason and of progress. Not unnaturally audiences familiar with
this world wished to recognize their own experiences and to see cor-
roborated on stage the belief in their growing sophistication and
taste. This necessitated a change in the older form of melodrama,
though the provision for visual gratification remained. Audiences responded to plot organization and character development that was independent of spectacular effects.

Sensation drama.   From the 1860s audiences were able to combine visual gratification with sophisticated plot contrivance in the
new "sensation drama" in which apartment blocks burned, ships
sank, trains crashed, and heroines were rescued from rivers or the sea.
Boucicault set the fashion for sensation in *The Colleen Bawn* in 1860
and repeated his success in plays like *The Flying Scud* (1866) and *After
Dark* (1868). In these the resources of the theater converged to present a culminating thrill: the excitement of a "real" horserace or the
impending arrival of an underground train. It marks the beginning
of a fascination with the mechanics of realism that found its culmina-
tion in *Ben Hur* in 1902 with real chariot races performed on stage.[11]
But by then the new technological marvel of film was in the wings
prepared to realize the visual sensationalism far more successfully.

While the sensation drama of Boucicault—domestic melodrama
with isolated and climactic moments of surprise and wonder—bred
a kind of melodrama that perpetuated the popular craving for visual
stimulation and large-scale effects, the craving for authenticity of
detail and the precise delineation of character was satisfied by the realistic settings and minutiae of physical detail in the plays of Tom

Taylor, Grundy, and Henry Arthur Jones. When authors like these rejected melodrama's episodic structure and quickly sketched, functional character drawing for an integrated organic plot and characters with particular accents, idiosyncrasies, and forms of dress, the term "melodrama" came to describe not a form but a coloring.

Though on the West End the term *melodrama* might have assumed a perjorative connotation by the end of the nineteenth century, as a form it was by no means dead. The theaters of the East End of London and south of the Thames provided the same fare that Moncrieff and Fitzball had offered in the first half of the century. Even the West End theater had merely responded to the structural advances suggested by the French theater of Scribe, Dumas, and Augier and had adjusted the contents of its plays to accommodate the interests of its more fashion-conscious audience. Its actors behaved on stage in immediately recognizable ways in settings that reflected both a reality for some and the realization of fantasy for others. These differences, however, "distinguish late century West End melodrama from the popular variety, but one must again emphasize that the differences are superficial, not fundamental. Fundamental emotions, situations, moralities, and character types changed not a jot; the clothes were new, but not the wearers."[12]

Tragedy and Verse Drama

Neither tragedy nor verse drama can strictly speaking be regarded as popular forms of drama. Yet the lure of both was a potent one for any dramatist seeking to be taken seriously and to be involved in raising the dramatic author's status. Three of the four writers we are considering wrote tragedies: Jerrold wrote *Thomas à Becket* (1829), Taylor wrote *Jeanne d'Arc* (1871), and Jones wrote *The Tempter* (1893). Jerrold and Jones were also heavily involved in improving the dramatist's position by arguing for adequate copyright provisions.

Tragedy was the most "legitimate" of forms involving a five-act structure and a theme based on Graeco-Roman mythology or history, the Italian Renaissance, or pre-Elizabethan English history. Its form until the end of the eighteenth century was also heavily influenced by French neoclassical models. Nevertheless, the figures of the solitary hero or heroine at odds with natural forces, the gods, society, or themselves were bound to attract romantic sensibilities as well. Dur-

ing the early decades of the century, the poets tried to write tragedies. Wordsworth wrote *The Borderers* in 1795 (it remained
unproduced until 1842), Coleridge wrote *Remorse* and had it produced
at Drury Lane in 1813, Browning had *Strafford* produced in 1837,
Keats wrote *Otho,* and Shelley, *The Cenci,* of which the latter was produced only in 1886. What is remarkable is the general lack of success
of all these attempts.

Though Byron's *Werner* offered a role to Macready, in its ruined
palace and malevolent villain, Stralenheim, the play harked back to a
dramatic model that did prove successful, the Gothic mode of romanticism so influential upon melodrama in the early years of the century.
Writers other than the poets did try to accommodate tragedy to the
new taste for extravagant Gothic emotionalism. The best-known example is Maturin's *Bertram; or, The Castle of St. Aldobrand* which the
histrionic rage of Edmund Kean turned into a personal triumph at
Drury Lane in 1816. More enduring, however, were tragedies based
on classical subjects. Kean suggested a Roman subject to the young
playwright James Sheridan Knowles. Knowles had tried his hand at
tragedy in 1815 with *Caius Gracchus,* which though esteemed had little popular appeal. Kean's idea he turned into *Virginius* and it was
played not by Kean but by Macready in 1820 at Covent Garden. Its
success was immediate and the play continued in the repertoire until
the end of the century performed by tragedians like Forrest and Dil-
lon, and even Wilson Barrett as late as 1897. The success of the play
caught critics unawares. Knowles seemed to have inherited the mantle
of Shakespeare, but the secret of the play's attraction, apart from its
histrionic opportunities, lay not in the rediscovery of tragic form but
rather in its adherence to nineteenth-century domestic values. The
play's strength came from the depiction of the relationship between
Virginius and his daughter, Virginia, and the affection and pride
which they feel.[13]

It was again Macready's encouragement that brought temporary
fame to writers like Talfourd and Westland Marston. Talfourd's *Ion*
(1836) was written under the influence of Addison's *Cato* and adhered
strictly to neoclassical ideas about the unities. Marston, on the other
hand, tried to integrate modern themes into a traditional form in *The
Patrician's Daughter* (1842) in which Macready played the role of a
politician, Mordaunt. Marston tried again to introduce the contemporary themes of money and social status in *Anne Blake* (1852) but with-

out success. As with most nineteenth-century attempts at tragic writing, the artistic tension between immediately relevant contemporary concerns and pseudo-Elizabethan fustian remained unresolvable. Jerrold's *Thomas à Becket,* which was written in prose, suggested at least a partial, formal resolution.

Though the poets remained unsuccessful, verse drama continued to appear from time to time, and even to be revived on the stage. Knowles wrote verse plays like *William Tell* (1825), *The Hunchback* (1832), and *The Daughter* (1836), but the most enduring writer was Bulwer Lytton who was the only example of a successful novelist in the nineteenth century able to transfer his reputation to the stage. He began his career with *The Duchess de la Vallière* (1837) and followed this up in two plays written in close collaboration with Macready, *The Lady of Lyons; or, Love and Pride* (1838) and *Richelieu; or, the Conspiracy* (1839), both produced at Covent Garden. The role of Richelieu was played subsequently by Phelps and then finally by Irving in 1892. As with the role of Becket, its attractions to a star actor are obvious, particularly when set in a world of intrigue and gorgeous costume. *The Lady of Lyons,* on the other hand, is a play about wish fulfillment, and depicts the growing love and respect felt by its heroine for the low born but upwardly mobile hero, who achieves heroic status through his personal bravery rather than aristocratic origins. Lytton was able to negotiate the line between popular melodrama with its basis of democratic values, and a literary form based on heroic values. Moreover, he could write unassuming and actable verse. After Lytton, however, instances of genuine popularity are few. Taylor's *The Fool's Revenge* (1859), based on Hugo and *Rigoletto,* is one such example, once more assisted by the playing of an established star actor, Samuel Phelps. Lytton's example was not repeated until W. G. Wills provided his successful verse plays for Irving in *Charles the First* (1872), *Eugene Aram* (1873), and *Faust* (1885). With the last, the nineteenth-century tradition comes full circle back to a German-derived romanticism augmented by Gothic malevolence.

Comedy

A perennial complaint of critics during the first half of the nineteenth century was the absence of genuine comic writers who would assume the mantle of Goldsmith, Cumberland, and Sheridan and thus provide the times with a comic study of its manners. When we consider the constant shifts in the make up of urban society in the early years of the century, it is hardly surprising that comic writing should be the most susceptible to uncertainty as regards either its audience or its artistic intentions. It is very difficult to write "universal" comedy. Comedy depends largely on the dramatist's grasp of prevailing taste, on common experience, and on a sense of established "milieu." Farce, on the other hand, depends little on these but rather on both performers and spectators sharing an experience that demolishes social barriers and sets educational background at nought. Comedy is therefore less "popular" than farce. Once again, however, we are confronted by the way in which dramatic forms become more and more imprecise in the nineteenth century. Melodrama constantly used comic elements to undercut or counterpoint its seriousness. Similarly comedy could employ pathetic or dramatic elements, the seriousness of which might be suppressed by a happy resolution of the plot or by comic ingenuity that triumphed over adversity or setback.

The first twenty years of the century saw comedy at its most diverse, exemplified by the plays of Thomas Morton and Frederick Reynolds. In plays like Reynold's *Folly as it Flies* (1801) or Morton's *Education* (1813) there is as much melodrama and villainy as comedy, with exaggerated eccentric characters providing the latter. The plays are curious mixtures of inherited eighteenth-century paradigms, with a nineteenth-century sentimentality about home and simple country virtues. After 1820, however, the attraction of discovering a basic common denominator asserted itself in an increase in low-comedy elements and farce. Nevertheless, side by side with this should be placed the emergence of elegant extravaganzas based on French models with which are associated the names of Planché and Charles Dance. They are sui generis and look forward to the comedies of Robertson rather than to the prevailing popular taste. Sheridan Knowles tried his hand at writing comedies as well as tragedies and emulated the examples of Shakespearean comedies like *Much Ado about Nothing* and *The Taming of the Shrew*. It once more demonstrates the search for form as well as content. If the "legitimate" playwrights looked back to Shakespeare, the "illegitimate" found a source in history, albeit aristocratic history. Thus we find Jerrold and Moncrieff locating comedies in the reign of Charles II in *Nell Gwynne; or, The Prologue* (1833) and *The "Tobit's Dog!"* (1838). It was their attempt to graft themselves onto a comic tradition.

After 1840 the tensions caused by trying to relate an inherited form to contemporary issues started to resolve themselves. In 1841 Boucicault scored an enormous success with *London Assurance* which won favor with literary critics for its reminiscences of eighteenth-century form. Its popularity, however, owed itself to the creation of individual character types like Lady Gay Spanker who looks forward to Georgiana Tidman in Pinero's *Dandy Dick,* and Dazzle, whose dextrous, "off the cuff" humor suggested a new acting style at variance with the techniques of low comedy.[14] This last aspect had already been anticipated somewhat in Bulwer Lytton's comedy *Money* which in 1840 effectively ushered in the major preoccupations of the mid-Victorian period: wealth, its acquisition and loss, privilege, and social position. Macready had played the hero, Alfred Evelyn, in a restrained, realistic manner. In *Money* and the comedies of Jerrold these themes are treated satirically in a world where virtues should be, but are no longer, simple, or have been corrupted by commercial values. In keeping with these themes, the focus becomes the middle-class home and the battleground, marriage, exemplified in Jerrold's *Retired from Business* (1851), Taylor's *Still Waters Run Deep* (1855), and Falconer's *Extremes* (1858).

The plays of Robertson are traditionally regarded as marking the beginning of a new era. There is little evidence to support this but rather more to support the generalization that Robertson caught in his comic writing for the first time the exact temper of his audience that had eluded his predecessors. So impressive was his achievement that it rapidly became a yardstick for future writing as well as a landmark in its own right. The influence of Robertson on subsequent comedy was great. He was directly imitated by Taylor in *New Men and Old Acres* (1869) and Albery in *Two Roses* (1870). H. J. Byron imitated the conflict between commercial wealth and aristocratic pretension of Robertson's *Birth,* and *Progress* in *Our Boys* (1875), which had a phenomenal run of over four years, much to the fury of the "new critics" like William Archer, who despised Byron's pot pourri of burlesque elements, low-comedy characters, and personal style of eccentric playing. Some of these elements had also been present in Robertson, but by the mid-1870s comic tastes were again changing. The last period of the nineteenth century was dominated by the comedies of Pinero and Henry Arthur Jones. By this stage their audiences had been established as a fashion conscious, middle class defined by money rather than by birth.

Farce

Farce is the most democratic of dramatic forms because it levels pretensions. No amount of social status will prevent a man from slipping on a banana skin. No amount of dignity will compensate for the horror of being caught with one's trousers down in unlikely but perfectly logical circumstances. It was a form well attuned to theatrical circumstances of nineteenth-century theater. It was performed as a curtain raiser to whet the audience's appetite or to satisfy the demands of that portion of the audience in the early part of the century that either arrived at 9:00 P.M. and paid half price after a lengthy dinner or could not afford to pay the full price of a ticket. Farce's physicality compensated for the problems caused by the size of the patent theaters, the distance from the stage, or the inattention of audiences coming to be seen rather than to watch.

Farce remained perennially popular throughout the century. Like French farce, the English variety based its situations on domestic complications, on physical defects, and on the constant attempts by characters to justify and rationalize their self-delusions. Like comedy, however, nineteenth-century farce was also susceptible to change. Eighteenth-century farce reflected the milieu of its theater's audience: more aristocratic, more refined. Its core was the ingenuity with which two lovers outwitted the constraints imposed by a narrow-minded and stupid older generation. This form carried over into the nineteenth century in farces like James Kenney's *Raising the Wind* (1803) and Samson Penley's *The Sleeping Draught* (1818), both produced at the patent theaters. The first thirty years of the century, however, saw the proliferation of minor theaters and differing perceptions of audience taste. Farce reflects this variety accurately though, as with other forms in the century, its definition becomes increasingly imprecise. With the addition of sentimentality there is often little to choose between comedy with farcical elements like Buckstone's *Married Life* (1834) and *Single Life* (1839), and a farce with domestic sentimentality and even elements of villainy like Jerrold's *Wives by Advertisement* (1828), Charles Mathews's *My Wife's Mother* (1833), or Taylor's *To Oblige Benson* (1854).[15]

We have seen the extent to which popular authors were at the mercy of and dependent on the talents of the actor in the presentation of melodrama. The same is true of farce written to accommodate a Tyrone Power as the most typical of stage Irishmen, a Charles Mathews's elegant weariness, or a Liston as a gormless booby. After 1840 theaters like the Haymarket and the Strand became identified with farce and low comedy and their success depended less on individual actors than on their collective idiosyncrasies within a company.

Of the dramatists who specialized in farce during the period 1845 to 1870, the most representative were Stirling Coyne and John Maddison Morton, in farces like *Did You Ever Send Your Wife to Camberwell* (1846), *Box and Cox* (1847), and *My Wife's Bonnet* (1864). What they share is the depiction of a world of shop assistants, journeymen, domestic servants, and retired small-time merchants. It is the world of daily business and its frustrations, and the attempts of its inhabitants to overcome the intransigence of boarding-house keepers, irritating lodgers, and incompetent tradesmen. It is a lower-class world that predominates in this period, and though its values are domestic its basis is impermanence and instability.

From the 1870s the impermanence was reflected in the farcical depiction of marriage, an antidote to the increasingly straitjacketed idealism about marriage that was appearing on the serious and even comic stages. In this it was much influenced by adaptations from the French of writers like Labiche and Delacour. Farce's dramatic engine becomes the familiar attempts to circumvent matrimonial respectability by the delusions of extramarital sex, best exemplified in the last quarter of the century by Boucicault's *Forbidden Fruit* (1876) and James Albery's *Pink Dominoes* (1877). More directly typical of the English tradition of farce, however, are the full-length plays by Pinero in which eminently respectable magistrates like Posket in *The Magistrate* (1885), headmistresses like Miss Dyott in *The Schoolmistress* (1886), or churchmen like Dr. Jedd in *Dandy Dick* (1887) find their respectability attacked and dragged through the mud by circumstance and the vagaries of a cruel world. The humor nonetheless is good hearted, indulgent, and lacking in any sexual innuendo. The plays manage to combine romance, disguise, idealism, physical knockabout, and satirical tilts at the symbols of Victorian respectability without losing their Victorian demureness.

Burlesque, Extravaganza, and Pantomime

Burlesque and extravaganza were of particular attraction to audiences that were able to contrast adaptation or parody with a known original, be they an opera, a fairy story, a Greek myth, or a familiar play. Pantomime was of universal attraction, and thus, suggests Michael Booth, the most "popular" theatrical form of the nineteenth century.[16]

The tradition of pantomime looks back to the popular booth theater of the Italian *commedia dell'arte* filtered through its French modifications and eighteenth-century English additions. Pantomimes appeared at the patent theaters at Christmas and Easter and at the minor theaters at Easter and during the summer when the major houses were closed. They were characterized in the first thirty years of the century by elaborate fairy-story openings, low-comedy harlequinades composed entirely of mimed action, spectacular scenic transformations, and an extensive use of music. Like farce and the later Gilbertian "topsyturvydom," pantomime delighted in its inversion of accepted moral codes and in its ridicule of hallowed institutions. Its identification with religious festivity gave to pantomime the sense of an entertainment licensed for a period of misrule. With farce, pantomime shared its cruelty toward the inept and the aged and its battle between human beings and a hostile mechanistic world. At the same time, pantomime acted as a social safety valve releasing the frustrations felt by young people with the older generation, and the older generation with politics, technology, or the urban environment.

From the 1840s the structure of the pantomime changed. Whereas the earlier pantomime emphasized the harlequinade with its knockabout and often savage humor at the expense of the opening dramatic setting, this process was reversed until by the 1870s the harlequinade was virtually superfluous. The opening had become a dramatic entity in its own right but imbued with the farcical elements of the harlequinade. In keeping with other dramatic developments in the same period, pantomime's moral stance hardened. Instead of a safety value it became a spectacular visual confirmation of domestic and social values. The transformation scenes were used to show the triumph of good over evil, idleness, or the seven deadly sins. Victorians, however, were obsessed by the visual and the pictorial. Transformation scenes lent themselves therefore to the expression of the spectacular with little direct dramatic connection or moral implication. If the history of the pantomime shows a deterioration of the traditional Harlequin and Colombine component, it also offers a showcase of the developing theatrical technology. The history culminates in the massively impressive pantomimes in the 1880s and 1890s of Augustus Harris at Drury Lane like *Mother Goose* (1880), *Aladdin* (1885),

Humpty-Dumpty (1891), and *Dick Whittington* (1894). These required huge numbers of extras for processions of fairy-tale characters, or ball guests dressed as flowers or kings and queens, and huge sums of money spent on lighting and costume. By the early 1890s the production costs of one pantomime at Drury Lane were between 16,000 and 20,000 pounds with a single performance cost of 290 pounds.[17] It is little wonder that pantomime was a particular target for literary critics, who ascribed to its spectacle one of the principal causes for the dichotomy in the century between drama and the theater.

If pantomime shared with sensation and spectacular melodrama a common emphasis on visual display, it was particularly influenced by the popularity of extravaganza that came into prominence in the 1830s. As a form extravaganza was identified with the work of J. R. Planché, who gave it its primary meaning: "distinguishing the whimsical treatment of a poetical subject from the broad caricature of a tragedy . . . correctly described as a burlesque."[18] In this he collaborated with Madame Vestris during her management of the Olympic Theatre. His formula of reducing to absurdity the world of classical mythology was itself a derivation from Fielding's burlesques of the previous century and the *féeries* of the Parisian stage. The latter gave rise to the fairy extravaganzas which Planché wrote from 1836 to 1856 and include *Ricquet in the Tuft* (1836), *The Sleeping Beauty in the Wood* (1840), and *The Golden Branch* (1847). By 1856 the extravaganza had absorbed considerable influences from pantomime and had in turn contributed to the latter's element of romance, and by 1870 extravaganza had fractured into its various components: music hall turns and chorus numbers, burlesque, comic sketches, and revue routines.

Even in Planché's earliest extravaganzas like *Olympic Devils* (1831) burlesque had been its basis, the reduction of a known fairy story or myth to its most absurd. Earlier than Planché, burlesque meant the parody of a dramatic form, in particular, verse tragedy, its situations and characters. This form of burlesque remained popular throughout the nineteenth century but its target shifted to melodrama and opera. Lawler and Poole's *The Earls of Hammersmith* (1811) parodies Gothic melodrama; Cooper's *Black Eyed Sukey; or, All in the Dumps* (1829) began an enduring series of parodies of nautical drama exemplified by Jerrold's play, of which the best known was F. C. Burnand's *Black Ey'd Susan; or, The Little Bill that was Taken Up* (1866); and Lester Buckingham wrote *Virginius; or, The Trials of a Fond Papa* (1859) as a parody of Sheridan Knowles's tragedy. There were even travesties of Shakespeare like William and Robert Brough's *The Enchanted Isle; or "Raising the Wind" on the Most Approved Principles* (1848) which parodied *The Tempest*. The connection with extravaganza in these is obvious, and by the 1860s the nature and style of burlesque had been defined as "a compound of music hall, minstrel show, extravaganza, legs and limelight, puns, topical songs, and gaudy irreverence."[19]

The 1870s saw a trend that moved burlesque toward musical comedy. It began with the increasing popularity of Offenbach's opera bouffe that had been launched in the mid-1860s and was supplemented by English opera bouffe with Gilbert and Sullivan's *Thespis* in 1871. Through the 1870s and 1880s the Gaiety Theatre became the center for burlesque under John Hollingshead's management. Pantomime and music-hall performers like Kate Vaughan and Nellie Farren appeared on its boards, blurring further any formal definition between pantomime, burlesque, and music hall as separate popular forms. By 1886, however, when Hollingshead retired, the signs of burlesque decay were already in evidence. The Savoy operas had supplanted French opera bouffe and had absorbed many of the intrinsic elements of burlesque as well. The low comedy turns were to be found at the music hall while dramatic three-act farces like those of Pinero at the Court Theatre were proving more popular. The effective end to dramatic burlesque came when the Gaiety Theatre turned wholly to musical comedy after 1890.

Chapter Two
Douglas Jerrold

"The author of a good play is quite a different person from the author of a good poem; yet it is always expected that a great poet should produce a good play. Acting under this impression, Scott, Byron, Moore, and perhaps Campbell have tried and failed. Whereas such a writer, or rather doer, as Mr. Jerrold, has carried the whole town before him." With this comment by the *Westminster Review* of 1833 we are immediately confronted with the failure of the romantic writers to come to terms with the theater and with Jerrold's popularity. The secret of his appeal lay in his ability to identify with the experience of large sections of his audiences. As a midshipman for two years during the Napoleonic Wars, he could speak directly to the sailors and their wives who frequented theaters like the Coburg, the Surrey, or the Pavilion. As the son of a failed theater manager and reduced to living in grinding poverty in the center of London, he had firsthand knowledge of the worker's daily struggle for survival. As a friend of Dickens and an associate of Thackeray, he was determined to document that struggle on stage and in print. Jerrold's personal outrage at the failure of society to remedy quickly its own inequities drove him to satirical journalism and the employment of an increasingly acerbic wit. When he died, therefore, he might have been detested by Queen Victoria and Charles Kean, but his editorship of *Lloyd's Weekly Newspaper* had insured him a weekly following of 182,000 readers.[1]

Jerrold's Life and Career

Jerrold was born in London 3 January 1803. Like T. W. Robertson who came after him, his parents were involved in the day to day business of running a theater company. In 1807 his father Samuel took over the lease of a theater in Sheerness, a coastal town at the entrance to the Thames estuary and a center of naval activity during the Napoleonic Wars. This is where Douglas obtained his first taste of the theater and the navy which he would put into good effect in his nautical melodramas. Between 1813 and 1815 he in fact served as a midshipman on the *Namur* under the command of Charles Austen, the brother of Jane Austen. Austen was a cultured scholarly man who encouraged Douglas to read and to be involved in amateur theatricals on board. At the end of his period of duty, he was transferred to a ship ferrying supplies to Ostend and carrying back wounded after the Battle of Waterloo. After demobilization he returned to Sheerness to discover that peace had removed the sources of income of a population geared to the war effort. The theater was faring badly. Douglas's father had lost heavily on a summer season at the theater in Southend, and had unwisely undertaken rebuilding of the Sheerness Theatre. Financially the results were disastrous and the Jerrold family decided to move back to London.

After the family moved to Bow Street in 1816, Douglas, his mother and two sisters worked to keep the family together, he, as apprentice to a printer, and they as actresses. Though working long hours, he read as widely as possible, went to the theater to see Edmund Kean, and started to write short pieces for submission to various journals. In 1818 he wrote his first play, *The Duellist,* which, renamed *More Frightened than Hurt,* was performed at Sadler's Wells in 1821. It did little to establish Jerrold's reputation but it did encourage him to continue writing for the stage.[2] He wrote four more plays in the period to 1823 for Sadler's Wells, including his adaptation of Scott's *Guy Mannering* called *The Gypsy of Derncleuch.* For these he received a total of twenty pounds. At the same time his essays and articles were appearing in papers like *Mirror of the Stage.* Although there was little at this point to suggest personal success or even stability, Jerrold married Mary Swann in 1824, and in order to provide for his family, he became the resident dramatist for the Coburg Theatre under George Davidge. He continued to write for journals and anticipated future developments by becoming editor of the *Weekly Times* at the beginning of 1828. The years to 1829 formed Jerrold's period of apprenticeship. He wrote Gothic-influenced melodramas like *Descart, the French Buccaneer* and *The Tower of Lochlain,* as well as vaudevilles and burlettas to order. At the end of 1828, however, he wrote two plays that attracted more than passing notice, *Ambrose Gwinnett; or, a Sea Side Story* and *Fifteen Years of a Drunkard's Life,* both of which can lay claim to being regarded as the first example of developed domestic melodrama.[3] The latter certainly is the first example of a temperance play on the English stage. The success of these two plays brought a festering antagonism between Jerrold and Davidge to a head. Jerrold left the Coburg and joined R. W. Elliston at the Surrey, and it was there in 1829 that he scored his biggest success with *Black Eyed Susan*. It made a fortune both for Elliston and T. P. Cooke who played William; it netted Jerrold a mere sixty pounds.[4] The success of this play was phenomenal. Cooke played William at both the Surrey and Covent Garden theaters simultaneously, rushing from one theater in order to play *Black Eyed Susan* as an afterpiece at the other. Even if Cooke's success added nothing to Jerrold's income, it did familiarize his name among the patrons of the patent theaters. It also encouraged him to be even more ambitious. On 30 November he saw his own full-length tragedy, *Thomas à Becket*, produced at the Surrey. It was a *succès d'estime* that lasted only six performances but enhanced the reputations both of Jerrold and Elliston. Jerrold was also confident enough to make much of the fact that the source of his story was English rather than French and to argue for the cultivation of a national drama. With this his critics fully agreed: "We feel a double satisfaction in announcing the success of any of Mr. Jerrold's writings: for he is not one of those recreant bards, who glean the vile refuse of a Gallic stage. All his dreams are true English, from top to toe; so that his very failures are entitled to respect."[5]

The years 1830 to 1841 were years of consolidation. As a journalist Jerrold wrote for the *Athenaeum* from 1831 to 1833 and started a short-lived predecessor to *Punch* with *Punch in London* in 1832. In 1835 he begin to write short stories for *Blackwood's Magazine* and in the same year in France met Thackeray, who was at the time Paris correspondent for the *Constitutional and Public Ledger*. Jerrold further consolidated his position from 1837 as an author of short fiction by writing comic sketches for the *New Monthly Magazine*. But in this period his reputation grew more as a result of his playwriting. It was not until 1841 that Jerrold's name would come to be closely identified with journalism through his contributions to *Punch*. In the 1830s Jerrold found an outlet in playwriting for both his sense of the ridiculous and his sense of social injustice. Until 1832 he continued to write mainly melodramas with a strong element of social criticism in them: *The Mutiny at the Nore*, *Martha Willis, the Servant Maid*, *The Rent Day*, and *The Factory Girl*. After 1832, he turned progressively toward comedy, in part influenced by the readily accessible market for comedies, farces, and burlettas. Embittered by his experiences with rapacious theater managers, and constantly in financial difficulties, Jerrold sought to improve the status of dramatic authors by founding, along with Buckstone and Sheridan Knowles, the Dramatic Authors' Society in 1833. This move was the beginning of a struggle for adequate remuneration on the part of dramatists that would not end until Dion Boucicault was successfully to negotiate percentage agreements in the 1860s and Henry Arthur Jones was to reap the benefits of copyright laws in the 1890s. Jerrold's efforts, however, brought little reward to Jerrold who was forced to elude his creditors by periodic sojourns in France.

As a member of literary clubs that numbered Thackeray, Dickens, and the self-consciously serious actor Macready, Jerrold would have been very aware of the demand for a "literary comedy" which might rival Sheridan and Goldsmith. His comedies of the 1830s, therefore, saw him attempting comedies of manners set within a seventeenth- or eighteenth-century context. The titles of *Nell Gwynne; or, The Prologue* and *Beau Nash, the King of Bath* suggest the preoccupation with notoriously flamboyant figures set within a mannered courtly or socially pretentious milieu. In 1836 Jerrold, in collaboration with his sister and her husband, James Hammond, took over the management of the Strand Theatre. The theater had been the focus of legal battles between the patent and minor theaters since its opening in 1832. Jerrold was able to obtain a license for it as a minor theater and wrote a number of burlettas. Though he brought to the venture much journalistic goodwill, Jerrold found the strain of writing, managing, and acting a burden, and was forced to give up the management at the end of 1837. Even by 1835, when Dickens first met him, Jerrold was subject to crippling bouts of rheumatism. In any case he was preparing for the publication in 1838 of his first volume of collected sketches called *Men of Character* which Thackeray had illustrated. His abandonment of the Strand led to an absence from theater of three years.

By the end of the 1830s, Jerrold was respected as a notable contributor to the theater. His stress on English subjects and English manners differentiated him from the translators and adaptors of the French dramas of Pixérécourt or the German dramas of Kotzebue. His engagement with social issues endeared him equally to the Young Turks of the journalistic world and to the audiences whose language he spoke and whose experiences he had shared. Nevertheless, it is hardly surprising that from 1840 until his death he should have concentrated on journalism—it elicited a more lasting response and was more lucrative.

In 1841 Jerrold began writing for *Punch* and his contributions continued undiminished until 1849. His most notable pieces in the period were "Mrs. Caudle's Curtain Lectures," "Punch's Letters to his Son," and the "Q Papers." They made both his name and that of the newly founded journal.[6] At the same time he founded and edited magazines like the *Illuminated Magazine* and *Douglas Jerrold's Shilling Magazine,* short lived but permeated by the same radical sentiments he had espoused in his earlier years and in his satirical articles for *Punch:* anti-aristocratic, anticapitalist, and, above all, humane. This would culminate in his editorship of *Lloyd's Weekly Newspaper,* a journal intended for the rapidly expanding working-class public. He assumed this responsibility in 1852 and maintained it until his death. As a playwright, Jerrold's output diminished. He wrote only one more drama, and for the remainder of his fifteen plays produced between 1841 and 1853, confined himself to comedies. The best of these were *Bubbles of the Day,* produced at Covent Garden in February 1842, *The Prisoner of War* which was produced by Macready in February of the same year at Drury Lane, *Time Works Wonders* with Benjamin Webster at the Haymarket in April 1845, and, under the same management, *Retired from Business* in May 1851. That Jerrold had "arrived" was unquestionable. His plays were being performed by the major theater companies, and in 1853 his *St. Cupid; or, Dorothy's Fortune* was performed at Windsor Castle. But there was little venom in the plays and little of what Allardyce Nicoll calls "genuine laughter" in their cumbersome five-act structures or collections of verbal sparring matches.[7] The end of Jerrold's career as a playwright was marked by bitterness and journalistic invective. He had attacked Charles Kean's Shakespearean revivals at the Princess's Theatre in *Punch* and thought little of his acting abilities. Kean in return mounted in 1854 a production of *The Heart of Gold,* a play he had bought in 1850 from Jerrold, with what appeared to be deliberate miscasting of the four principal roles and little attention to physical setting. This apparent vindictiveness was too much for Jerrold who felt that he had emancipated himself from the ruthlessness of managers like Davidge and Elliston.[8] The events also enabled Jerrold to dissociate himself formally from a stage that had little to say in the wake of disappointment at the promise of the 1832 Reform Bill and the suppression of the Chartists in 1848. He would be able henceforth from his position as an influential editor to offer practical assistance to Chartists like Thomas Cooper by finding publishers for their works.

Jerrold died suddenly on 8 June 1857 at the age of fifty-four. He died beggared by his own generosity; his family were only saved from penury by Charles Dickens's organization of benefit performances that raised 2,000 pounds. At his death, Jerrold was remembered by obituary writers primarily as a comic dramatist in the tradition of the "literary art" of Goldsmith and Sheridan.[9] Far more accurate, if nostalgic, was the poetic assessment, spoken by Jerrold's successor, Tom Taylor, at the benefit performance held at the Adelphi Theatre on 29 July 1857:

> He had a sailor's heart: 'twas thus he drew
> The sailor's character with touch so true:
> The first that gave our stage its British tar,
> Impulsive, strenuous, both in love and war;
> With English instinct, using still his blade
> Against the strong, the weaker cause to aid.
> While Dibdin's song on English decks is sung,
> While Nelson's name lives on the sailor's tongue,
> Still Susan's tenderness and William's faith
> Shall weave for Jerrold's tomb a lasting wreath.

The Apprenticeship Years to 1829

As part of his training Jerrold in his early years looked to existing models for his inspiration. He found them in the writings of Scott and Byron and in the contemporary repertoire. *Guy Mannering* had originally appeared in 1815 and was quickly adapted by Daniel Terry for the Covent Garden stage in 1816. Planché had produced a further version called *The Witch of Derncleuch* in 1821. Jerrold's version capitalized on the popularity of the character of Meg Merrilies that had been a great success at Covent Garden in 1815. *Paul Pry,* which he wrote for Davidge in 1827, was itself an attempt on the part of the manager to undercut the great success the actor Liston had scored at the Haymarket two years before in an identically named play by John Poole. For the rest, Jerrold's preference was for originality, though he was quite prepared to cater for the prevailing audience interest in Scottish themes in plays like *The Tower of Lochlain; or, The Idiot Son* (Coburg, September 1828) or exotic locations in the Africa of *Descart, the French Buccaneer; or, The Rock of Annaboa* which appeared on the same bill.

In 1828, however, came suggestions of future developments. *Wives by Advertisement; or, Courting in the Newspapers* appeared at the Coburg on 8 September. The play is called a dramatic satire and is built round two scenes, the first poking fun at people who advertise for suitable mates in the columns of newspapers, and the second showing the ludicrous consequences of taking these advertisements seriously. A month after this one act trifle Davidge put on Jerrold's *Ambrose Gwinett; or, a Sea Side Story* on 6 October. The play is usually bracketed with *Black Eyed Susan; or, All in the Downs* in their insistence on the family unit.

Fifteen Years of a Drunkard's Life. This was the first of Jerrold's plays to be an overt investigation of a social problem. In 1825 the duty on spirits had been reduced in England and the year marked the beginning of the era of the gin palace. But attitudes toward drink were divergent and often contradictory. Middle-class-based temperance and teetotal movements might campaign against what they took to be a threat against the work ethic, but the provision of drink was tied to upper-class interests and an increasingly strong lobby group. When hotels were able to provide a drink as cheap as tea or coffee and an environment with heat, companionship, and reading matter, they formed a considerable attraction for the working classes.[10] It is hardly surprising, therefore, that Jerrold in the play makes little of drink as a social evil or even the product of urban poverty. Neither Davidge, who supplemented the theater's takings from the selling of alcohol, nor the powerful representatives of the Licensed Victuallers, nor, for that matter, the costermongers who thronged the galeries of the Coburg and Surrey theaters would have tolerated a blanket denunciation of alcohol.

Jerrold tells his story through two interlocking narrative threads charting the effects of alcoholism on men of contrasting backgrounds. Vernon is young and wealthy, happily married to Alicia and with a sister who is about to be married to his friend Franklin. Copsewood is a member of the yeomanry, with a sister Patty, and two aged parents for whom he cares. The villain is Vernon's false friend Glanville, who uses forgery and gambling to beggar Vernon. Vernon is a compulsive alcoholic, as is Copsewood. Alicia is compelled to take shelter in the house of Franklin and Vernon's sister. Glanville seduces and abandons Patty and her aged parents die destitute. The stories are thus brought together through the agency of Glanville. In the last act, desperate for drink Vernon, by now a hopeless wreck, meets

Copsewood delivering wine and spirits, and the two break open the
bottles and become roaring drunk. They break into Franklin's house
to seek for more money, and in the resulting fracas Vernon stabs his
wife and is shot by his false friend, Glanville. Copsewood is taken
prisoner. In both cases Jerrold has established a pattern of loss of
wealth and human dignity, loss of the family unit and the suffering
experienced by those whom drink has deprived of a figure of authority.[11] As a social documentary, however, the play is weakened by the
ubiquitous Glanville whose villainy brings about the two men's destruction. In this respect the play maintains a melodramatic pattern
of villainy, seduction, and despair by one person's single-minded attempts to subvert goodness. Jerrold nevertheless is uncompromising,
and in the unhappy ending there is no easy solution. His concern was
to dramatize a problem, and though the machinery of the plot may
be reduced to the machinations of personal vindictiveness, the play
remains a courageous prototype of the "thesis play."

At the end of 1828, Jerrold left Davidge and went to Elliston at
the Surrey. He produced first of all a melodramatic adaption of
W. T. Moncrieff's *Bamfyde Moore Carew; or, The Gypsy of the Glen*
which Elliston had used during his management of the Olympic in
1816.[12] Jerrold filled it with elements he had explored in his earlier
romantic plays: gypsies, outlaws, and long-lost sons. It was a success
that he followed with a much more adventurous play, *John Overy, the
Miser,* which opened on 20 April at the beginning of the Surrey's
summer season. Jerrold had already suggested an interest in money
and its corrosive effects in a comic interlude, *The Smoked Miser,* which
he had written for Sadler's Wells in 1823. This was much more developed. The play is held together by a strong central character, a
miser who combines the psychopathic qualities of Molière's Miser and
some of the tragic implications of Shylock. The play was strong stuff
assisted by authenticity of setting and local South Bank relevance.[13]
It remained in the Surrey programme until it was replaced by Jerrold's farce *Law and Lions!* on 21 May. This is a clever play that looks
forward to later comedies like *Bubbles of the Day,* full of disguises,
masquerades, cross-purposes, and exuberant verbal sparring. But already Elliston was negotiating with T. P. Cooke to appear for a short
season at the Surrey starting on 8 June, and referring to Jerrold as
"the most rising Dramatist that we have."[14] He was referring specifically to a play that he proposed to mount as an afterpiece during
Cooke's engagement, *Black Eyed Susan.*

Black Eyed Susan; or, All in the Downs. Jerrold's play was not the first to concern itself with the sea. J. C. Cross's *The Purse; or, The Benevolent Tar* had appeared at the Haymarket as early as 1793, and Moncrieff had written *The Shipwreck of the Medusa; or, The Fatal Raft* for the Coburg in 1820, but Jerrold's was the first to coalesce the nautical with the domestic. It was this combination that attracted the critics, particularly when audiences at both the Surrey and Covent Garden responded identically.[15] But its effectiveness stemmed equally from the play's authenticity of experience: Jerrold's contact with poverty, his observation of the hardship experienced by the families of sailors left behind in a town like Sheerness, and his own "two years before the mast."

The title of the play derives from a ballad by John Gay. The ballad was immensely popular, and thus the characters of William and Susan had already been enshrined as popular archetypes of the sailor and the faithful wife he leaves behind. The play is set in and around Deal, a sea port on the southeast coast of England. Its inhabitants live off the sea, legally as sailors or illegally as smugglers. It is an uncertain life governed by the irregular movements of the fleet. To the wives and sweethearts the absence of the fleet brings on the depredations of those who feed on loneliness and poverty brought about by the paltry naval pay. Act 1 shows the sharks circling round their defenseless prey. Doggrass is a property owner who will not allow sentiment to interfere with his collection of rent arrears, even if one of his tenants is his niece Susan. He supplements his income from a trading relationship with Hatchet, a professional smuggler. Susan has been left alone for three years on William's latest tour of duty and has not heard from him for twelve months. She has few allies other than Gnatbrain, a jack of all trades, and Dolly Mayflower, his inamorata, a skittish young girl who makes eyes at the sailors and spins to earn a little money. They are quick witted and loyal but essentially powerless. They also provide the low comedy elements as they leap out of cupboards and physically attack their comic butt, Jacob Twig, a bailiff in the employ of Doggrass, or bicker about their forthcoming marriage. At the end of act 1 we are given our first glimpse of sailors as the scene changes to a smuggler's cave with Hatchet, his mate Raker, and their crew. The smugglers are apprehended by marines who have hidden themselves behind casks of wine and spirits. There is a short exciting fight and the act ends with the first setback to the villains of the piece.

The act is deceptively simple. It opens with Gnatbrain and Dog-grass in the middle of a conversation and proceeds with great pace until the end of the act as Susan is whirled about by the efforts of her enemies to subdue her, and her friends to interpose themselves between her and apparently insuperable waves of circumstance. The second act plunges the audience immediately into the consequences of act 1. Raker and Hatchet have escaped the marines but they now have to face William who enters full of exuberance and exaggerated salty dialogue. The act also introduces the last villain of the play in William's captain, Crosstree, who has eyes for Susan without knowing that she is William's wife. But like Jacob Twig and even Raker, Hatchet's mate, who have doubts about the morality of their actions, Crosstree is aware that his lust for Susan is wrong. He is also the only upper-class character in the play that relates to the lower-class setting. William arrives in time to protect Susan from Hatchet's advances and defeats him in a duel with cutlasses. Hatchet is apprehended by the marines and Doggrass realizes that he must look after himself, since Hatchet is bound to trade his name for some kind of personal immunity. It is William and Susan's moment of triumph. The play's tempo changes as the characters are allowed a brief respite. The sailors sit around exchanging stories, drinking, and singing the song *All in the Downs* that epitomizes the transience of the sailor's home life. As if to reinforce this, William and his messmates are ordered on board. He, however, has already put in for a discharge and Susan hopes that with his prize money they will be able to buy a shop in Deal selling marine stores. Crosstree stumbles drunkenly on Susan waiting for the return of William and clutches at her. The act ends abruptly as William returns, instinctually strikes his wife's attacker, and, too late, realizes that he has committed a capital offense.

Both acts 1 and 2 end with a tableau reinforcing the climactic moments. The stage freezes in a picture that allows the audience to assess its implications. Just at the point when William had overcome his enemies on land and when it seemed as if his seafaring days were to be exchanged for secure domesticity on land, inadvertance and instinctual reaction have combined to bring about his doom. To the audiences of the Surrey, acquainted with the harshness of naval discipline, the play now assumes an awful inevitability.

Though Crosstree was aware of his misdeed and act 3 begins with the news that he is recovering from William's attack, the whole tempo of the play changes again. There is no possibility of a reprieve for William despite the circumstances and lack of premeditation. Each scene now has the tempo of a recessional as characters discard their past ways, like Jacob Twig whom the events have shocked into honesty, or who are discarded themselves, like Doggrass, who is accidently and fittingly drowned. The courtmartial in scene 2 takes place with full naval panoply before an admiral, six captains, marines, and midshipmen. Despite the evidence of character witnesses and William's own plea that a man's duty to his wife is both instinctual and universal, he is condemned to hang. The navy is equally prepared to discard an aberrant member in the interests of "upholding a necessary discipline" (*EPNC*, 191).

The fourth scene is the most moving and best written scene in the play. It takes place in the gun room of the ship. William's feet are chained. He solemnly discards his cherished mementoes, the remnants of his naval experiences, by bestowing them on his shipmates. The scene culminates with William brokenly singing a snatch of *Black Eyed Susan* as his wife rushes in for their farewell. The last scene, as it appears in the text, is only one page long and contains ten lines of dialogue. The tempo, however, is one of the slowly culminating ritual of a public execution. Even if the trappings are naval, members of the theater audience would have equated these with their own experiences of the public hanging of criminals. Jerrold evokes as much tension from the last scene as possible. Crosstree storms onto the stage waving William's discharge papers as William is about to have the noose placed round his neck. In the last line he is freed on the technicality that he was no longer a sailor when he struck his captain. Both the principle of naval discipline is upheld and natural justice is seen to be done.

It is not difficult to understand the play's success, not only on its own terms but also in the light of the need to discover a nationalist mythology just at the time when popular unrest was building toward its first climax in the Reform Bill of 1832. It is also not difficult to understand Jerrold's confidence that prompted him to attempt a serious play which might be judged by the highest literary standards.

Thomas à Becket. Between the opening of *Black Eyed Susan* and the opening of *Thomas à Becket* on 30 November 1829, Jerrold wrote two potboilers at Elliston's request. *The Flying Dutchman; or, The Spectral Ship* was written to accommodate Cooke's performance as Vanderdecken with which he had been successful at the Adelphi Theatre. Unfortunately Cooke had appeared in a version of the story by Fitzball and had further promised not to appear in the role elsewhere. Jerrold's version was designed to circumvent these contractual difficulties. The second was an exotically placed burletta, *The Lonely Man of Shiraz,* which opened on 3 November.

Jerrold's choice of a historical English subject anticipates Taylor's *Ann Boleyn* (1876) and Jones's *The Tempter* (1893). It demonstrates clearly a determination on the part of the popular dramatists to be taken seriously by the literary world. But in 1829 Jerrold's decision had other implications as well. Not only was a minor theater establishing the right to produce the most serious of legitimate drama but was also suggesting that its patrons were as discriminating as those of Covent Garden or Drury Lane. The choice of an English subject as opposed to a French or German one, emphasized the importance Jerrold placed in the cultivation of a native drama. Though the play had only a short run at the Surrey, it was received seriously by both critics and audience. Jerrold chose to write the five-act play in prose rather than verse but to color it with a nineteenth-century version of Elizabethan language that even contemporaries found unnecessarily cumbersome. The subject itself was of personal interest to Jerrold. He shared the anti-Catholic sentiment that was aired at the passing of the Catholic Emancipation Act in 1829. His attitude, however, arose from radical anticlericalism and from his dislike of aristocracy, not from religious principles.

Act 1 concentrates not on Becket but on a human interest story that will ultimately bring about Becket's downfall. Philip de Brois is a priest whose advances to his pupil Lucia are repulsed. She marries her lover Breakspeare and Philip vows to be revenged. It is only in Act 2 that Becket appears to face not only the problem of King Henry's refusal to hand back lands confiscated from the church during the Norman Conquest but Philip's false denunciation of Lucia as a nun who has violated her vows. Act 3 brings the moment of confrontation between Becket and Henry. Both are immovable forces. Henry refuses to admit that the ecclesiastical courts have jurisdiction over the case of Philip and Lucia. When Becket refuses to hand over the case to the secular courts, Henry threatens Becket and his attendant clergy with armed conflict and bloodshed and Becket is compelled to capitulate. His only recourse when he is accused of misappropriating money held during his tenure as chancellor of England is to leave the country and appeal directly to the pope. But little is made of the consequences of this action. In act 5 Becket is at last brought face to face with Lucia in whose innocence he believes. After a scene of careful cross-examination, he sees clearly that not only has he been abandoned by his clergy but he has also turned a perjured case into a matter of principle. The last scene is one of resignation and quiet defiance. When he first meets his assassins in the cloisters of Canterbury Cathedral, their initial attempt to kill him is postponed by the chanting of monks: "The service is begun, gentlemen, I am needed at the altar."[16] And it is at the altar that he is killed and the curtain falls.

Within the context of early nineteenth-century dramaturgy Becket as a subject is an awkward one. As a martyr, Becket himself can only be sympathetic in spite of antipapist feeling or popular opposition to autocratic unaccountability. Nor can his antagonist, King Henry, representing the secular, and therefore by inference, popular interests, be turned into a melodramatic villain. For this reason Jerrold invents the Philip de Brois story. It tends to trivialize the story. Ultimately, however, the playgoer would have been unable to comprehend either Becket's or Henry's standpoint. We may be more interested today in the mortal struggle between two arms of totalitarianism; the nineteenth-century playgoer would have identified with the little people scurrying between the legs of the megaliths, safeguarding their own interests. For this reason Jerrold devoted as much time to the servants in the play—Swart, Moldwarp, Bacon, and Snipe—as he did to the protagonists.

The popular success of *Black Eyed Susan* and the respectability of Jerrold's attempt at tragedy seem to suggest that it was time to invade the world of the patent theaters. He had served his apprenticeship and had demonstrated that he was familiar with burletta, melodrama, and farce, the three main forms of popular drama. He therefore offered a costumed melodrama, *The Witch Finder,* set in the time of the Restoration, to Drury Lane. It opened on 19 December 1829 and closed the same night. This came as a bitter blow to Jerrold and he lashed out at the theater's audiences and critics. He would not, however, have another play produced at the major theaters for two years. Meanwhile, he returned to the minor theaters in order to consolidate his reputation as the dramatist who had done most to justify the claim of the minor theaters to legitimacy.

Social Criticism and
the Development of Comedy to 1838

Jerrold's socially critical plays came at the period of greatest political and economic unrest in England in the first half of the nineteenth century. Jerrold, however, was not alone in reflecting a theatrical concern with social problems. R. B. Peake wrote *The Climbing Boy* for the Olympic in 1832 about the horrors experienced by youthful chimney sweeps, the same year that Jerrold wrote *The Factory Girl* for Covent Garden. Though attempts were being made in Parliament to alleviate the conditions of child labor through the Factory Act of 1832 and the act of 1834 prohibiting the apprenticeship of children under ten to chimney sweeps, industrial unrest gathered momentum particularly with Chartism as a forum for action on economic grievances after 1836. Unrest continued to be reflected in the theater with John Walker's *The Factory Lad* at the Surrey in 1832 and G. F. Taylor's *The Factory Strike* at the Victoria (formerly the Coburg) in 1836.[17] After 1832, however, Jerrold's output of serious plays about social injustice declined to be replaced by an increasing absorption in radical journalism and satirically colored comedies.

Jerrold returned to the Surrey and contributed two plays to the last years of Elliston's management, both of which were provided as vehicles for T. P. Cooke's portrayals of sailors. *Sally in Our Alley* was produced at the Surrey on 11 January 1830 and *The Press-Gang; or, Archibald of the Wreck* on 5 July. Both were melodramas, the first was again based on a popular tune and included conniving lawyers, poverty-stricken and bitter old curmudgeons, thwarted lovers, and a potential rival in Captain Harpoon, played by Cooke, whose presence dramatically is completely unnecessary. In the second, Cooke played Arthur Bryght, who is press-ganged into the navy just after his marriage. He escapes, is recaptured, and sentenced to flogging through the fleet. This barbarous sentence is averted at the last moment by the intervention of Archibald, a recluse who reveals that Arthur is in fact a peer of the realm. The irony of the ending was not lost on the reviewers. It showed only too clearly the double standards affecting the common man and the aristocrat.[18]

The Mutiny at the Nore; or, British Sailors in 1797. When *The Press-Gang* opened, Jerrold had already mounted a far more savage attack on naval injustices in *The Mutiny at the Nore*, which opened at the Royal Pavilion Theatre on 7 June. Its popularity was immediate and before the end of the year it was playing at the Coburg (9 August) and the Tottenham Street theaters (4 October). It is Jerrold's only instance in which he dramatized actual events within the memories of many of his audience. He must also have remembered stories of the mutiny when he was a midshipman. The actual story line, however, was indebted to Frederick Marryat's novel *The King's Own* published earlier in 1830.[19] The play gave Jerrold the opportunity to attack directly the arbitrary nature of acts by officers, the poor pay and living conditions in the navy, and the savagery of its discipline.

The play's focus is split between two contrasting men, both sailors, and both leaders of sections of the naval mutiny. In act 1 it is Jack Adams who is the ringleader. The mutineers have set up a Council of Delegates and he acts as go-between with the Admiralty. It is he at the end of the act, as sailors and marines face one another, who brings the news just in time that the Admiralty has agreed to the sailors' demands. Jack is shown to be loyal and above all brave. His support of his mates is based on the recognition of their bravery rather than on the justice of their demands. He feels that if the mutineers succeed it will be due to the Admiralty's tardy recognition of how much Britain owes her sailors. The officers, on the other hand, are shown to be blindly confident of their authority. Though the play is concerned primarily with the navy, the civilians are represented by Timothy Bubbles and Dicky Chicken who combined the traits of Doggrass and Jacob Twig. They are quite prepared to milk the sailors of their money and their sweethearts, and equally prepared to act as informers when necessary.

In the second act, the action shifts from Portsmouth to Bubbles's farm house near Sheerness. In Bubbles's absence, his housekeeper, Dame Grouse, has given shelter to the wife of Richard Parker. He is the leader of the mutineers but, unlike Adams, Parker is a driven man, victimized by a sadistic Captain Arlington, who has tried to seduce Parker's wife Mary in the past. Arlington has had Parker savagely flogged for a crime he did not commit and Parker uses his personal animus to fire his sense of general injustice. He is a brutalized man, like John Overy, and there is little that his wife or child can do to dissuade him from his course of action. Parker is joined by Adams who has been sent by the Admiralty to serve on board ships at the Nore and to act as a calming influence. The last scene of the act brings the two men together on board the *Sandwich* commanded by Arlington. When Arlington refuses to release sailors who have been clapped in irons on suspicion of mutinous intent, the battle lines are drawn. Adams, however, only steps in when Parker trains the forecastle guns on the captain and marines, not to interpose himself between the two forces as a matter of principle, but to rescue Parker's child who has fallen asleep across the mouth of one of the guns. When the sailors fall back, Arlington is quick to trade on the display of sentimentality. He seizes the child and threatens to have the marines shoot unless the sailors give up. This display of gratuitous cruelty is too much even for the marines, who refuse to obey their orders.

When Bubbles returns in act 3, he is dismayed to discover that his servants have turned his farm house into a sailor's refuge. He is, however, delighted that it houses Parker, now a refugee from the law. The Admiralty has promised to honor the sailors' demands if Parker is given up to the authorities. Adams tries to spirit Parker away but he is too late. Arlington enters to apprehend Parker and in the struggle Parker shoots him dead. The irony is now that he is arrested and condemned to be hanged not as a mutineer but as the murderer of an officer. Scene 4 between Parker and his wife is not dissimilar to the scene of parting between William and Susan but made even more pathetic by the presence of their young son. Jerrold thus shifts the emphasis of the scene from the parting to its effects upon those who remain behind. Adams undertakes to care for Mary and her child, and the last scene in which Parker is hanged is as short as that at the end of *Black Eyed Susan*. This time it is far more perfunctory with little attention to detail of the earlier play. The curtain drops as the noose is placed round Parker's neck.

"D.-G.," the author of the remarks that preface the published play, was in two minds about the play. That it was powerful was undeniable, and the last scene with its "paraphernalia of death" was horrifying. He found, however, that Jerrold's fictional elements—the personal vindictiveness of Arlington and Parker's ample personal motivation for revenge—disturbing: "these mitigating circumstances, when put forth in connection with history, . . . are likely to produce a wrong impression—to inspire horror at the sword of justice, when justice is mercy" (C, 8). These elements tended to whitewash Parker and to justify the mutiny by making Arlington a typical representative of upper-class officers.

After *The Press-Gang*, Jerrold wrote no more plays for the Surrey until 1845. Instead, his next play was presented at the Adelphi. The melodrama, *The Devil's Ducat; or, The Gift of Mammon,* opened on 16 December 1830, though Jerrold had written the play a year earlier. It was a technical experiment written just after *Thomas à Becket,* a serious play in verse about money and its corrupting power. Stylistically, the play is a mixture of *Don Giovanni, Faust,* the Gothic demons of *One O'Clock! or, The Knight and the Wood Daemon* by Monk Lewis, and a nineteenth-century morality play. Though the verse is undistinguished, it is an interesting play that uses supernatural elements both as separate characters like the Tempter in Jones's play of the same name, and as externalizations of a sense of guilt as Leopold Lewis was to use them in *The Bells* in 1871.

Jerrold followed this play with another of at least implicit social criticism, *Martha Willis, the Servant Maid; or, Service in London.* It opened at the Royal Pavilion on 4 April 1831. The play explored an enduring Victorian theme, that of the young country girl exposed to the moral dangers of urban life.[20] But the play's potential is never realized. The play was a success at a theater particularly identified with dramatizations of crime, but tells us little about Jerrold's attitude toward the problems of the great numbers of female domestic servants in London. Far more significant were the two plays performed at Drury Lane in 1832.

The Rent Day and The Factory Girl. Sir David Wilkie had painted his popular genre paintings about rural life and its hardships, *The Rent Day* and *Distraining for Rent,* in 1807 and 1815 respectively. Jerrold may have felt that a play about the harsh consequences of poor crops, high prices, and absentee landlords presented at Drury Lane, particularly after the laborers' revolt in the winter of 1830–31, was asking for trouble. Perhaps he needed Wilkie's hugely popular genre paintings as visual justification for his play. What ever the reason, both paintings appear "realized" at the beginning and end of act 1. Jerrold himself certainly felt at one with Wilkie in his lifelong concern with a vernacular art and was gratified by the painter's approval of his theatrical realization.[21]

Unlike *Martha Willis,* the play has a village rather than urban setting. The two worlds are those of Grantley Hall, the home of the squire, and Heywood's farm, which is under threat of confiscation. The play opens on an exact visualization of Wilkie's first painting, a frozen tableau that dissolves into action. Grantley's steward, Crumbs, is collecting the due rents. For those who can, it is a regular settling day; for those who cannot, like Martin Heywood, it is a day of reckoning. Heywood's farm has proved unprofitable with dying cattle and blight-stricken crops. His brother, Toby, an usher at the local school, has come to beg for time on Martin's behalf. It is to no avail, however, as Crumbs prepared to notify his bailiffs to start their process of distraint. Martin Heywood is another of Jerrold's men embittered by circumstance. He is also a self-dramatizer. His rhetoric is that of John Overy and Richard Parker and his position is certainly serious. But when his self-pity becomes too indulgent, even his wife, Rachel, and brother Toby are moved to comment: "I tell you what, brother; you are one of those people who are so very fond of ill-luck, that they run halfway to meet it."[22] Jerrold also introduces another qualification to Heywood's picture of destitution and the Poor House. He has been offered a post on an estate in the West Indies, should all else fail. It is Rachel who provides the stumbling block. She refuses to leave her village, her vision of Eden, for foreign parts. It gives her, rather than her husband, the motivation to stay, and therefore the dramatic motivation to involve herself directly in the play's subsequent action. The fourth scene of the act shows Crumbs's unwelcome past acquaintances who have recognized him as a former highwayman and who intend to blackmail him, making themselves at home in Grantley Hall. Crumbs is forced to explain them away to a friend of his master's as "the richest of the Squire's tenants—devout religious men" (L, 144), which they patently are not. The first act ends with the bailiff, Bullfrog, and Crumbs entering the Heywood farmhouse to begin an inventory and as Martin "buries his face in his hands. . . . The other Characters so arrange themselves as to represent Wilkie's Picture of 'Distraining for Rent' " (L, 150).

Act 2 is the more dramatically interesting of the two. Rachel overhears Crumbs's associates planning to rob Grantley's friend at the Hall. She determines to warn him. Martin is also on his way to the Hall to make a last approach to Crumbs. He has promised to respond that day to the offer of employment in the West Indies. When Rachel is discovered at the Hall, Martin immediately assumes that she has been unfaithful to him and with the same overindulgent rhetoric banishes her from his life. But the villains are already in disarray. In the last scene of the play, the characters converge on Heywood's farm. The mysterious guest is revealed to be the absent squire on a tour of inspection who explains the situation to Martin. The villains are all caught and Crumbs is revealed to be another man twisted by a compulsive need for revenge. Grantley's father had seduced his wife and he determined to extract as much from the estate as possible, thereby blackening the Grantley name. He is forgiven by his master, who generously as a token of thanks to Rachel Heywood makes over the freehold of the farm to Heywood. But fortune has already smiled on Martin. In a struggle over his grandfather's chair, the back falls off to reveal three hundred guineas and a will guaranteeing Martin's and Toby's entitlement. The Heywood future at any rate is secure.

What social criticism there is in the play is confined to act 1, and to lines like those of Toby when he speaks of "money wrung like blood from the wretched" (*L,* 133). The major source of criticism is that implied by the realization of the paintings, and it is used to stimulate the emotional resonances that the audience brought to them in 1832. Furthermore, Jerrold's dramatic interest lies with the enterprising Rachel, the comic villain Bullfrog, and, to a lesser extent, the rapacious Crumbs. Martin emerges as an undeveloped and rather unlikable character who is easily persuaded to be a victim of circumstance.

The Rent Day was a great success at Drury Lane and the radical sentiments were hardly noticed. *The Factory Girl* was a different story. It opened at the same theater on 6 October 1832 and closed within two nights. Though the radically inclined journal *Figaro in London* found that Jerrold's desire "to plead, through the medium of the stage, the cause of the poor and oppressed classes of society" was a commendable one, the *Times* reviewer, by contrast, was hard put to understand why Jerrold should have selected such a "ticklish subject," and went on to describe the antagonism of the first night audience.[23] The reasons suggested for the play's failure are interesting. On the one hand, the *Times* and the *Age* suggested that the dress circle rose in disapprobation and that the management of Drury Lane should be justly condemned for mounting a play redolent of "republican principles."[24] On the other hand, *Figaro in London* blamed the half-price audience but criticized the play on structural grounds as well: "the comfortable arrangement for a happy ending" was inconsistent with the aims of the play.

We have seen that domestic melodrama was a relatively new phenomenon, but many audience members would have traveled to the Surrey to see Jerrold's *Black Eyed Susan.* Nevertheless, its presence in Drury Lane may well have disconcerted those in its audience who were particularly sensitive to the violence happening throughout the country. To the more theatrically discriminating, the ending, which

resolves the plight of Catherine Skelton, the factory girl, in melodrama's personal terms of unforeseen inheritances and good-hearted
factory owners who dismiss their villainous foremen, may have suggested a loss of integrity. Certainly when compared with Walker's
The Factory Lad, the play appears genteel in its insistence that good
must eventually prevail.[25] Though the play was a failure, it offers an
interesting example of the limits of popular tolerance. Even in 1863,
when Taylor's *The Ticket of Leave Man* was performed at the Olympic,
audiences were surprised at the appearance of the seamier side of life
in a theater north of the Thames.

This play marked the end of Jerrold's serious preoccupation with
social injustice on stage. For the rest of his career he was to devote
himself to comedy with three exceptions: *The Hazard of the Die* set at
the time of the French Revolution and produced at Drury Lane on 17
February 1835; *The Painter of Ghent,* a one-act play written for the
opening of his own management of the Strand, and presented there
on 25 April 1836; and finally, *The Mother,* written for the French actress Madame Celeste, which appeared at the Haymarket on 31 May
1838. They were all respectfully received but reveal little new about
Jerrold's abilities. Nor do gambling and motherhood suggest any thematic enlargement of the parameters of popular dramatic writing.[26]

Comic Plays of the 1830s

After the failure at Drury Lane of *The Witch Finder,* Jerrold did not
try to approach the patent theaters until 1831. In 1831, however, he
submitted the first of his comedies, *The Bride of Ludgate,* which
opened at Drury Lane on 8 December. Set in the Restoration period
it is the first in Jerrold's series purporting to be historical. In this
King Charles and Sir Charles Sedley appear incognito to make the acquaintance of Melissa who is to marry Andrew Shekel, a wealthy
moneylender. She is in love with Mapleton, a supporter of the Com-
monwealth and therefore a traitor. The play is merely an account of
the attempts to insure that Melissa marries her true love, despite misunderstandings. The presence of King Charles enables the traitor to
be pardoned and the jilted moneylender to be recompensed by a
knighthood. The play is slight and romantic, relying on plot and a
pseudo-Restoration dialogue.

The Golden Calf.   In 1832, at the height of his portrayals of
social injustice, Jerrold returned to the theme of money and its wor-

shippers. Up to this point he had treated it melodramatically. He now approached it satirically. He must have felt insecure about offering it to the patent theaters, and it was produced at the Strand on 30 June. Like the Vavasours of Taylor's *New Men and Old Acres,* the Mountneys are desperately in need of money and must sell their estate. They are contrasted with the Pinchbecks who are coarse vulgarians, again like Taylor's Bunters. Lord Tares, on the other hand, who hopes to borrow money from the Mountneys, is the first in a long line of Victorian aristocrats seeking to establish links with men of commerce from the Eagleclyffes of Robertson's *Birth* to the Umfravilles of Jones's *The Middleman.* In the midst of this society appears John Chrystal, who wishes to buy Mountney's house and castigates the society for its superficiality. He is a raisonneur, like Robertson's Jack Randall, and shares the same austere attitude toward money and its outer show as Alfred Evelyn in Bulwer Lytton's *Money.* He is also the agent of retribution and deus ex machina who leads the money-hungry by the nose in order to expose their inadequacies and to humiliate them. He reveals that his mission is to show Mountney the error of his ways as a means of repaying a kindness shown to him by Mountney's father in the past. In act 2 he organizes Mountney to invite Lord Tares and the Pinchbecks to a party on the promise that he will send Mountney a parcel containing the means to regain his wealth. The party is Jerrold's tour de force as the guests vie with each other in pretentiousness of dress. In the midst of this the parcel is opened to reveal an apron, a day-book, and a ledger. "What were the means," asks Chrystal rhetorically, "which gave your father the wealth and honourable station of an English merchant?" (*C,* 9:48). The sentiments are those of Carlyle and Samuel Smiles.

By act 3 the Mountneys are forced to reassess themselves but not before a final act of desperation by Mountney himself who gambles away the remainder of his money. He is saved from suicide by Chrystal and shown the error of his ways. The play ends with Chrystal's call for a return to the austere philosophy of Diogenes and the Cynics. The play's humor is Jonsonian and its characters are types, rigid in their absorption with acquiring wealth. Its lack of sentimentality distances the play from the mainstream of popular writing, and it was consequently less successful than Jerrold's later, more romantic plays. He was to write only one more satirical play in this period, the one-act *Swamp Hall; or, the Friend of the Family,* which lasted two performances at the Haymarket in 1833. It too is concerned with wealth and the willingness to sacrifice self-respect in the course of its acquisition. In the light of Jerrold's future career these plays can be seen as precursors of his writing for *Punch*, helping us to understand the savagery of the magazine's early numbers. The reception of the plays also explains why Jerrold abandoned the stage as a platform for change. The novelist, short story writer, or satirical journalist could achieve more in this period with the individuals who made up the theater audience in the privacy of their own homes.

Nell Gwynne; or, The Prologue.   At the beginning of 1833, Jerrold saw his second "Restoration" play produced at Covent Garden on 9 January. The play is of interest in its depiction of the theatrical world, anticipating Taylor and Reade's *Masks and Faces* (1852) and Robertson's *David Garrick* (1864). As with these other plays, however, the world of the theater is there for its coloring. The play is about a good-hearted orange girl's relationship with an equally good-hearted King Charles, of whose identity she is unaware until the end. Jerrold was at pains to base his play on fact and used both Pepys and Downes as his sources. Thus we see historical identities like Betterton, Mohun, Hart, and Haynes. Jerrold was also conscious of the need to interpret history and chose to ignore the tradition of licentiousness and to emphasize the kindness and generosity of Nell Gwynne in the same way that Taylor's Peg Woffington acts in *Masks and Faces* from a selfless desire to assist others in distress. Charles becomes in the play the hero, rescuing Nell from the clutches of an old lawyer, Crowsfoot, by pretending to be her husband. She eludes him and when he sees her at Drury Lane as an orange seller, he makes it known to the management that her attractions would be welcome on the stage itself. Her debut is arranged as the prologue to Dryden's *Conquest of Granada*. This infuriates her rival Orange Moll and again Charles is forced to rescue her and take her to the Mitre Tavern.

In act 2, Charles discovers Nell's true worth at the Mitre Tavern. Her dream is not so much the stage but the fulfillment of her aim to found the Chelsea Hospital for war pensioners. She is even able to come to Charles's aid when he discovers that he is unable to pay the Tavern's bill. For the rest, there are farcical elements as actors enter to rescue Nell, and succeed in abducting the lawyer Crowsfoot who has tried to disguise himself as a woman. Nell then goes to the theater for her debut and forgets her lines when she recognizes Charles in the king's box. The play itself was regarded as a delight. Not only was history made palatable but the play was a celebration of theater itself.

Between 1833 and 1835 Jerrold had four major successes and three failures. Of the latter he felt worst about *Beau Nash, the King of Bath* which he had written with the sophisticated audience of the Haymarket in mind. Jerrold, however, would have felt little for the elegance of Nash's world, and this obviously communicated itself to the audience who found little to interest itself in the play. Nevertheless, he had a string of successes starting with *The Housekeeper; or, The White Rose*. This opened at the Haymarket on 17 July 1833 and was set among Jacobite attempts to dethrone William of Orange. But this is not central to the theme, which concentrates on the attempts of Felicia to win the love of her cousin, Sidney Maynard. His second success was *The Wedding Gown*. It was the first play of Jerrold's to be put on at Drury Lane since the disastrous performance of *The Factory Girl*. Apart from *The Hazard of the Die* in 1835, he would only have one other play performed at Drury Lane in his lifetime. *The Wedding Gown* opened on 2 January 1834. The title refers to the gown that Augusta, a young Polish exile, makes for her employer. The play is a neat, romantic game of musical chairs colored by the presence of Polish émigrés forced to flee to England after the Kocziusko rebellion of 1794.

Far more dramatically interesting is *The Schoolfellows*, which opened at the Queen's a month later on 16 February. Jerrold had submitted the play to the patent theaters and was disappointed by its rejection. In the dedicatory epistle to Thomas Searle that prefaces Duncombe's edition of 1835, Jerrold hit out at the tyranny of the two theaters which prevented serious writers from competing with the equine drama and foreign spectaculars that he saw as their staple fare. To a modern reader its interest lies in Jerrold's conception of a group of classmates who return for a reunion at the old school eighteen years later. It is a leisurely play with little action as old friends recount the events of eighteen years. It forms an interesting experiment in reversing the traditional emphasis on situation in favor of dialogue. Jerrold, however, was not a writer of character and the lines, rather than illuminating idiosyncrasies, reflect the mind of a skilled after-dinner conversationalist.

Doves in a Cage. Jerrold's last major success in this period was *Doves in a Cage* in 1835. It opened at the Adelphi on 18 December and was to be revived again during the Jerrold management of the Strand in 1837. It came as a welcome relief after the failure of two burlettas that he had written for the Vestris management at the Olympic earlier in 1835.[27] Although the play is once again set in the

period of the "Restoration," Jerrold abandons any attempt at historic-
ity. The action centers on Prosper and Mabellah, both in the Fleet
prison for debt, who play elaborate charades in order to convince one
another that their presence in a debtor's jail is the product of a chari-
table visit to comfort friends. Prosper, who has been a shiftless fortune hunter, turns into a hero when he agrees to give Mabellah up to
an aging but wealthy rival, Sables, on the grounds that it is her only
way out of prison and debt. Matters are resolved when Mabellah's uncle, Bezant, whom everybody thought penniless, reveals that he has
ordered the events in order to test the determination of the two lovers. When they come through with flying colors, he enables them to
be married and promises them his wealth in due course. The aging
rival is given a dressing down for harboring intentions unsuited to his
age. The interest of the play lies in the relationship between Prosper
and Mabellah that develops in a prison setting. The uncle is a combination of John Chrystal and fairy godfather embodying in his character the ideal elements of nineteenth-century dramaturgy, instruction,
and pleasure.

Jerrold's last exercises in comedy during the 1830s were written as
occasional pieces during his Strand management: three burlettas, *The
Bill Sticker; or, An Old House in the City* (21 July 1836), *The Perils of
Pippins; or, The Man who "Couldn't Help It"* (8 September 1836), and
A Gallantee Showman; or, Mr. Peppercorn at Home (27 March 1837),
and one farce, *The Man for the Ladies* (9 May 1836).

By the end of the 1830s Jerrold had established himself as a writer
of consequence. His plays could be seen at both the major and minor
theaters. Up to 1832 there were critics who mistrusted his radicalism
and audiences who may have felt threatened by his uncompromising
stand on social injustice. By the end of the period, however, even his
worst efforts were received sympathetically. Some of this support undoubtedly can be attributed to the fact that he remained a working
journalist. Jerrold had enlarged the parameters of melodrama in particular by suggesting that serious subjects could be raised within a
popular and broadly based dramatic form. At times this needed to be
reconciled with melodrama's insistence upon what Eric Bentley calls
"the naturalism of the dream world": the juxtaposition of the authentic and the specific with wish fulfillment and a highly colored and
stylistically compressed experience. The comedies, however, reveal
less of Jerrold's structural freedom, though again, up to 1832, his
social concerns make the plays much blacker and angrier than his later

work. The change in emphasis starts with *The Bride of Ludgate*. He saw that the ingredients of success as far as the major theaters were concerned lay in a romantic setting using history to prettify the picture. The characters should mingle some who were historically verifiable with some who were fictional. The former would gratify the audience's desire for authenticity, while the latter would be identifiable on the level of common, human experience. In Jerrold's nonhistorical comedies, the situations become almost a formula of conflicting love interests, temporary disinheritances, and deracinated individuals trying to discover their roots. With these as dramatic *données,* Jerrold weaves arabesques of conversational wit around situations that are often static rather than dynamic. It is as though he wanted to concentrate on an intricately worked episode rather than to relate that episode to an organically structured plot line. It is this feature—which we will notice recurring in his mature comedies—that insured their life only as long as Jerrold's wit held currency.

The Mature Plays to 1854

Between 1837 and Jerrold's return to the stage in 1841, the plays of Bulwer Lytton had demonstrated not only the fruits of close collaboration between an actor, Macready, and an author, but also the importance to melodrama of French structural principles. French themes and stories had been a ready source of material for English authors since the turn of the century, but dramatic structure had never been an English strong point. Lytton's *The Lady of Lyons* in 1838 and *Richelieu; or, The Conspiracy* in 1839 demonstrated the value of a tightly organized "well made" narrative. His play *Money* in 1840 provided the nineteenth-century theater with one of its most enduring comedies, lampooning society's quest for wealth in a manner not dissimilar to Restoration comedy and Jerrold's *The Golden Calf*. Unlike Jerrold's play, however, the raisonneur and the hero are made into one person. It is far more structurally satisfying to an audience and personally gratifying to an actor/manager. As a critique of society the play looks forward to the comedies of T. W. Robertson. In March 1841 Jerrold attended the premiere of Dion Boucicault's *London Assurance* at Covent Garden. It was at once a tribute to the comedy of Goldsmith and Sheridan with its artificialities and conventions and an embodiment of contemporary nineteenth-century values. The play also took cognizance of a new development in acting technique by providing Charles Mathews, who was making his name with a relaxed and casual performance style, with the character of Dazzle. With both these developments Jerrold thoroughly approved, though he was already seeing the beginnings of his own demise as a playwright.[28]

Bubbles of the Day. Jerrold was unfortunate to have the play open at Covent Garden a month before *London Assurance.* The play is a five-act comedy of manners about the fads of contemporary society. Its characters are upper-middle-class stereotypes, easily recognizable and capable of eliciting easy laughs. The first act is the most glittering, as Jerrold brings onto the stage the representatives of the follies he wishes to satirize. The action takes place in the mansion of Lord Skindeep, a foolish old politician whose presence in Parliament is ridiculed by the press. Even his servant Cork writes scathing attacks on his master under the pseudonym "Brutus the Elder." He is followed by the Browns, father and son. Chatham Brown is an unwilling member of Parliament, placed there at his father's insistence. He is more interested in pursuing young ladies than attending parliamentary sittings, much to the disgust of his father who sees "but one path to substantial greatness—the path of statesmanship."[29] But Brown Senior's idea of statesmanship is political sophistry: "The great art of life is to pass off our ignorance with such a confident grace, that people shall take the counterfeit for the true thing" (*W,* 7:5). Sir Phenix Clearcake, on the other hand, is a grandiloquent fool, a lineal descendant of a Restoration Sparkish but turned into a London alderman.

The characters' odor of sanctity and respectability is somewhat dispelled by the appearance of Captain Smoke, whose speculative ventures include leasing Mount Vesuvius to make matches, a company to mount a trip round the world, and one to float a Grand Junction Temperance Cemetery. All the gullible older men have become directors in one or other of his companies. Chatham Brown, however, manages to avoid Smoke's quick sales talk and enthusiasm by the fortuitous arrival of Mrs. Quarto, an indefatigable traveler and writer, like the historical Fanny Trollope. She is indeed a redoubtable lady too busy with her writings to spare Sir Phenix more than an hour at his fete even though he is the intended of her niece, Florentia. She is also aware of Chatham's pursuit of one of his fair constituents and dangles her present whereabouts in front of him, quite prepared to make time for a little scandal.

Act 2 introduces the second young lover, Melon, a poor lawyer, beset by rapacious liquor merchants and the father of a woman for whom he feels nothing but distaste. Spreadweasel is a widower, who had contracted to have his daughter, Pamela, marry Melon from birth so that their two estates might be guaranteed. He is flattered by titles and impressed by property and money. Each of the characters enters in pursuit of one another: Smoke looking for his friend Malmsey Shark, Skindeep and Brown Senior looking for Mrs. Quarto. The more disreputable characters are passed off to Spreadweasel as people of substance while Skindeep and Brown find in Spreadweasel a man whose connections will help to quell a growing popular dissatisfaction on the part of the constituents of Muffborough with their elected representatives. Pamela, who has come with her father, is revealed to be the mysterious girl whom Chatham has been pursuing. Skindeep finds himself attracted to Pamela and her fortune, and invites the whole company to dine at his mansion.

In act 3 the "bubble of the day" is love. Pamela and Florentia are old school friends, quite capable of manipulating the men who suppose themselves to be in love. Love itself is shown to be an illusion engineered by commercial considerations or provoked by superficial appearances. Pamela and Melon find nothing in one another despite their contractual obligations. Skindeep wishes to marry her for her canvassing abilities and her father's twenty thousand pounds. Sir Phenix's civic respectability is suspect when it is revealed that he had an affair with a sixteen-year-old servant girl, now in Florentia's employment. Mrs. Quarto believes she can regain her youth by marrying Melon.

Once the extent of the old men's rigidity is established, the fourth act shows them being duped by the young lovers. The function of the last act is to show the reality behind the facade of respectability and self-righteousness maintained by Skindeep and Spreadweasel, and thereby to facilitate the marriages of the true young lovers. Skindeep is shown to have had a liaison with a Katherine Waller and to have had a son, who turns out to be Captain Smoke. Spreadweasel's real name is exposed as Waller when his younger brother arrives, thus making Skindeep and Spreadweasel de facto brothers-in-law. Sir Phenix's claim to Florentia is dismissed on the grounds that his servant girl is still alive, while Brown Senior's ambitions for his son are finally shattered when Chatham advises him that he will be giving up his seat.

It is an energetic play full of scintillating throw away lines, but its energy is inward looking. The characters and their complications are set up in the first two acts. The remaining three are devoted to a process of untangling these rather than to the development of a narrative line. Nor does the satire have any implications other than for the characters themselves because they are only seen within the context of two closed environments, Skindeep's mansion and Melon's chambers. It would, therefore, be easy for an audience to recognize the characters' attitudes but to dismiss their foibles as peculiar to themselves alone and socially irrelevant. There is a sense of triviality which the dialogue cannot mask.

The Prisoner of War. Though *Bubbles of the Day* was overshadowed by the resounding success of *London Assurance,* Jerrold must have been gratified to see two of his plays being performed simultaneously at the two patent theaters. *The Prisoner of War* opened at Drury Lane on 8 February 1842 with Phelps playing Captain Channel and the Keeleys, who were to be so influential in advancing Taylor's career, playing the quintessential English couple abroad, Polly Pallmall and her overprotective brother, Peter.

Once again Jerrold used his naval experience of ferrying troops from Ostend during the Napoleonic Wars to flesh out his story. It is set in Verdun in 1803. The English prisoners of war lead a reasonably pleasurable existence in the town provided that they keep to the terms of their parole. The French women find them irresistible. The prisoners have been joined by other English who have been trapped by the resumption of hostilities, like Captain Channel, a distinguished old sea dog, and his daughter Clarina, and the Pallmalls. The latter have been apprehended because of Peter's misplaced patriotism: "He quarrelled with some French dragoons, because he would insist, that the best cocoa-nuts grew on Primrose-hill, and that birds of paradise flew about St. James's" (*W,* 7:21). To lie for one's country, Pallmall suggests, is the civilian's duty. The hero is Firebrace who has been married to Clarina for the past two years without informing her father. He finds himself unexpectedly confronted by her, and, to make matters worse, a rival suitor.

In the second act matters come to a head when Channel discovers Firebrace in his daughter's room and challenges him to a duel. For this both of them are arrested by the French authorities, to be joined by Pallmall who has assaulted yet another Frenchman in the cause of England. As they are about to be marched off to solitary confinement after an abortive attempt to escape, word arrives that they are to be exchanged. Daughter and father are reconciled and Firebrace is accepted as a son-in-law. The play ends, however, on a curiously wistful note as Channel reminds those who are to be exchanged, including the Pallmalls, that not everyone is to be set free: "Though the list's a long one, many stay behind. Therefore, let not those set free fail in their best wishes for—THE PRISONER OF WAR" (*W,* 7:244).

Despite the presence of Pallmall, the play is no piece of strident nationalism nor is there any evidence of xenophobia. The villain of the piece is an English merchant, Beaver, and the comic butt is Pallmall, the ludicrous English tourist. Jerrold keeps the sentimentality to a minimum by having the sentimental couple already married and Polly's relationship with a midshipman, Heyday, constantly interrupted by her brother's interference. The final ingredient is Channel, who combines aging heroism and kindness with a crusty exterior. The success of the play can thus be attributed to the mix of characters in an unusual setting. It offers an opportunity for deeds of heroism and a situation that brings out the best and worst in the people involved. It is, after all, the formula for the post–World War 2 prisoner of war films. In its day Charles Kean revived the play in 1851 before Queen Victoria and it was admired by the discriminating G. H. Lewes.[30]

The success of *Prisoner of War* prompted Jerrold to repeat the formula in *Gertrude's Cherries; or, Waterloo in 1835* at Covent Garden on 30 August. Apart from two eccentric low comedy roles, the play refused to work. Jerrold reintroduced the formula of his earlier comic writing—disinherited son, crusty old father, pretty cherry (instead of orange) seller, lovers, and a contrived ending—and tried to make it work literally on foreign soil, the environs of Waterloo. It was less than well received.[31] The play seemed like an occasional piece written for Covent Garden to capitalize on its rival's success with the earlier play. Jerrold, moreover, was heavily involved in his journalism and would write no more for the stage until 1845.

Time Works Wonders. Jerrold thought this his best play.[32] It was given a long run at the Haymarket after its opening 26 April 1845, not the least because the play was being performed by the best comic cast Jerrold had ever obtained. William Farren played Goldthumb, Charles Mathews, his son Felix, Buckstone played Bantam, Madame Vestris, Bessy Tulip, with Mrs. Glover as Miss Tucker.

The play is written in five acts and covers a five-year period. The first act takes place at a country inn. Felix Goldthumb, the young son of a trunk maker, tries to help Clarence Norman abduct Florentine from her school. She is accompanied by her friend, Bessy Tulip, and both are trying to escape from the clutches of their headmistress, Miss Tucker. When Felix recognizes Florentine as "the girl next door," he agrees to help Clarence on condition that he is satisfied that Clarence's intentions are honorable. Their plan is foiled by the arrival of Miss Tucker and Felix's father who take the tearful girls back to school. The second act reveals the same characters five years later. Miss Tucker's reputation has been ruined by the scandalous elopement and she lives now as a dependent of Florentine, who occupies a cottage near the estate of Sir Gilbert Norman, Clarence's aristocratic uncle. Clarence has been sent abroad to cleanse his system of love and Felix to Batavia to learn merchandising. Felix's father through an inheritance has become a wealthy man and also lives near the mansion. Bessy has returned to India and nothing has been heard of her. When Clarence returns to England cured, he finds that his uncle is in love with the girl who paints in the neighborhood, and who turns out to be Florentine.

In act 3 Felix returns with Bessy as his wife, but till they find out his father's probable reactions to them they resolve to keep the marriage a secret. Clarence finds Florentine less than genial to him. She is determined to revenge herself for her humiliation at the abortive elopement and decides to respond to the advances of Sir Gilbert. In the last act, however, she cannot bring herself to marry him. Clarence in turn, after Felix has asked him to justify the trust he had in Clarence in act 1, informs his uncle that Florentine is to be his wife. Felix makes himself known to his father who forgives him any past misunderstandings. Even Miss Tucker rediscovers love in the form of Professor Truffles, an old flame from her teaching days.

Jerrold's scope in the play is ambitious. It is an exploration of the processes of time and change as they affect people. Rigid attitudes and preconceptions are softened and immature impulses are replaced by considered reasoning. It is also a play about education of the young. Jerrold's female characters are themselves interesting. Miss Tucker is a genuine comic creation combining disciplinarian arrogance with whining humility as she moves from being a headmistress to being a kept companion. In Bessy and Florentine he presents two contrasting heroines, the one down to earth and mischievous, and the other romantic and prone to let out her frustrations in hysteria. Jerrold, however, gives Florentine a splendid scene of sustained emotion in act 5 when she begs Gilbert Norman to release her from the marriage agreement. So successful is her plea that when she kneels before him all he can do is raise her up: "Rise, madam, you are free. I sought a wife, and not a victim" (*W*, 7:140). He leaves slowly, in silence. In that exit Jerrold transforms one of his silly, immature, old men into a genuinely pathetic figure, and he remains as such until the end of the play. If there is an awkwardness in the play, it lies not with the characters but with its cumbersome five act structure and the dependence of four acts upon the premise of act 1.

Apart from a farce, *The Honeymoon Scruple*, which Jerrold quickly knocked off for the Surrey in May 1845, and which was neither reviewed nor published, there was yet again a hiatus in Jerrold's dramatic writing until 1850. Although Nicoll lists a production of *The Spendthrift* in 1850, the play was probably not performed in Jerrold's lifetime. He ended his dramatic career, however, with a flourish. His last four plays were all successful. The first two, *The Catspaw* and *Retired from Business*, were performed in the last years of Webster's management of the Haymarket Theatre; the last two, *St. Cupid; or, Dorothy's Fortune* and *A Heart of Gold*, in the early years of Charles Kean's management of the Princess's.

The Catspaw and Retired from Business.   These were Jerrold's last overtly satirical plays. They are set in the present day and were both performed by virtually the same company. The first opened on 9 May 1850 with many of the cast who had appeared in *Time Works Wonders*. The Keeleys played Snowball and Rosemary, Buckstone played Appleface, with Webster himself playing Coolcard. Jerrold reintroduces some of his favorite targets: the professional fraud, not this time educational, but medical in Dr. Petgoose; the confidence trickster, not a share speculator, but a scavenger of money and food in Coolcard. The action centers on the relationship between Snowball and Mrs. Peachdown. She has been left the estate of Lord Wintercough, and Snowball, his great-nephew, proposes to contest the will. But Snowball is a gullible man and a social hypochondriac. His imagined illnesses are magnified by Petgoose and Snowball uses these to distance himself from situations he cannot handle. Mrs. Peachdown is a shrewd manipulator of men's emotions, and dangles herself and her fortune in front of Snowball and her lover Burgonet. If Snowball is like Argan in Molière's *The Imaginary Invalid*, then Rosemary is like Toinette, the pert maid who sees through Petgoose's quackery and is at the same time engineering the means to keep her lover Appleface from being discovered as an army deserter. The house is fur-

ther invaded by Coolcard, disguised first as Busby Knox, an itinerant
scholar who manufactures verse for the recently bereaved, and then as
Chevalier Podovy, who wishes to interest Snowball in a patent invention. The characters are all either rogues or doubledealers who play
elaborate charades with one another. There is no sentimentality in the
play because there are no idealists and strictly speaking no heroes.
Both men and women are unscrupulous and self-seeking. Because Jerrold refuses to identify himself with any of the characters or their attitudes, the play emerges as a distinct departure from the mainstream
of popular writing; its sardonic quality suggests a continental farce
tradition.

Retired from Business opened on 3 May 1851. In it Jerrold satirizes
not individual eccentricities but a whole class, that of the small businessman who has made money and retired to village life in order to
enjoy the benefits of hard bargaining and thrift. Pumpkinfield is a
village made up of former leather merchants, pawnbrokers, and tai-
lors. The newest immigrants are the Pennyweights, former greengro-
cers. Mrs. Pennyweight, however, has caught the virus of upward
mobility and insists that she and her forthright husband be now
called the Fitzpennyweights and that their house be enhanced by a
coat of arms and a footman. "Why he looks like a caterpillar on a
holiday," responds her disgruntled husband (*W*, 7:249). The neighbors all enter the Pennyweight house to pay their respects. The Puf-
fins bring in their son Paul who refuses to be sociable ("a child of
nature" murmurs his doting mother at every manifestation of rude-
ness) and goes to sleep as soon as he can. The reasons for his dissatisfaction become clear when he comes face to face with the Pennyweight's daughter, Kitty. He had met her in France and thought
never to see her again. Their delight is mutual, as is the consternation
of both sets of parents. Act 1 ends with the amusing spectacle of parents forcibly carrying off their children in opposite directions. Even
if Pumpkinfield is classless, where children are concerned their parents insist on matches if not with royalty, then with the wealthy upper class.

Acts 2 and 3 appear to belong to a different play. The focus
changes to the affairs of two neighbors and friends, the old soldier,
Gunn, and the old sailor, Tackle. The connection with the world of
the Pennyweights is a tenuous one. Though the characters lend a distinctive texture, they are irrelevant in a satirical picture of small-town
snobbery. The play becomes perforce bogged down in the mechanics

of resolving the love interests of Kitty and Paul, while the picture of a helpless old soldier and his orphaned niece slow the comedy's impetus. The play also reveals clearly a kind of schizophrenia in Jerrold's makeup. He is merciless in his picture of middle-class pretension but uncritically sentimental about children. His friends like Wilkie Collins and Charles Dickens attested to Jerrold's love of children in private life and his memorialist, James Hannay, referred to him as both "inveterately satirical" and "spoonily tender."[33] The play bears this out.

St. Cupid; or, Dorothy's Fortune and *A Heart of Gold.* Both plays are examples of Jerrold's "historical" writing and were perhaps influenced by Charles Kean's production of Boucicault's *The Corsican Brothers* in 1852 which ushered in a vogue for French influenced melodramas requiring a restrained acting style. Actors like Kean and Walter Lacy were able to achieve this, and it much impressed Jerrold even though he disliked Kean's acting and production of the classics, especially Shakespeare, during his tenure of the Princess's Theatre between 1850 and 1859.

St. Cupid was performed as a preview before Queen Victoria on 21 January 1853 and opened at the Princess's the following night. It was praised particularly for its "quaint" conception and the apposite characterization. Historically the play is set in 1715 but this merely adds to the play's fairy-story atmosphere. Sir Valentine May is the nephew of Under Secretary Zero who is in charge of unearthing Jacobite plots. Valentine comes across an innocent letter that has been intercepted by Zero's agents from Dorothy Budd, the daughter of Dr. Budd who runs a private school for boys. She is a superstitious young girl much given to gypsy fortune telling. Valentine decides to go to the school and fulfill her desire for a Prince Charming. When he arrives he discovers that the school is advertising for an usher. Dorothy's beauty persuades him to stay, and despite his lack of background Dr. Budd employs him. In the course of the play Valentine discovers that Dorothy's cousin, Ensign Bellefleur, is a Jacobite spy but contrives with the help of a gypsy fortune teller, Queen Bee, to spirit him away for Dorothy's sake, just before Valentine's uncle and soldiers arrive to arrest him.

The plot itself is of little consequence or even dramatic importance. The play works through charm: the charm of a secluded setting, the charm of a Sleeping Beauty waiting to be woken, the charm of wish fulfillment. Robertson was to use the setting of a secluded country school for a Cinderella story in his play *School* in 1869. The play is also unusual in that there are few funny lines. The comedy is confined to the lovable Dr. Budd and his earnest attempts to attract boys to his school. He even believes that one of Zero's agents is a prospective father and cannot make up his mind whether Valentine has arrived as a pupil or an usher.

The strain in the relationship between Jerrold and Kean started with this production and became a contest between the rights of a dramatic author and those of an actor/manager. Jerrold was at the height of his powers and Kean was enjoying the envy of the theater profession at his royal patronage. Matters were further complicated by the active dislike felt toward Kean by Jerrold's friends—Dickens, Forster and Lewes. Kean, on the other hand, had bought *A Heart of Gold* outright from Jerrold and was determined to put it on. But he was going to teach Jerrold a lesson. The play opened on 9 October 1854 with no attention paid to either appropriate setting or casting. The reviewers came to Jerrold's aid and it was praised far beyond its real merits.[34]

The action supposedly takes place in the mid-eighteenth century but nothing is made of this. The subject is once again the effects of wealth upon people. John Dymond is dying and gives his chest of gold to a young clerk, Pierce Thanet, who promptly makes overtures to the girl, Maude, with whom Dymond was in love. Unfortunately, Dymond does not die and returns to demand back his gold. Thanet refuses to surrender it and his callousness only succeeds in antagonizing Maude who agrees to marry Dymond out of a sense of justice. This, together with his remorse, drives Thanet to return the gold and a wiser Dymond is forced to agree that honesty and truth are worth as much as gold. The play is in fact rather pedestrian, and Jerrold may well have realized this. He had written it in 1849 about the same time as his unpublished play "The Spendthrift." In part, therefore, his protests at its performance may have been prompted by his realization that the play no longer represented his current dramatic outlook. In its own terms, the play's language and seriousness of tone look backward toward his melodramatic plays like *The Devil's Ducat* or *John Overy*.

Jerrold is one of the most interesting of the Victorian popular dramatists not only in the variety of his dramatic output but also in his determination to reflect the concerns of his society at all levels, and to comment on them. In this he shares something of the passion of

Henry Arthur Jones but without Jones's sometimes sanctimonious adherence to received social dictates. The citizens of Pumpkinfield, however, and those of Steepleford in Jones's *Saints and Sinners* are drawn with the same exactness of detail and with the same savage distaste of meanmindedness and hypocrisy. Jerrold also shared with Jones a lifelong dedication to extracting his raw material from the lives of his English audiences. This gave his work immediacy and relevance but, to feed the mouth of an ever-hungry popular art form, the writer needed to tread carefully a path between its traditional forms and values, and a personal need to investigate and report on social inequities. Jerrold trod this path uneasily throughout his life. Tom Taylor, on the other hand, negotiated it with consummate ease.

Chapter Three
Tom Taylor

Tom Taylor's works perhaps embody the best and clearest representations of mid-Victorian attitudes seen on the stage. He himself was not only a dramatist but a spokesman on matters of aesthetics, public health, politics, and literary values. All his writings demonstrated remarkable consistency. In the preface to his edition of *Autobiographical Recollections by the Late Charles Robert Leslie,* published in 1860, Taylor commented approvingly on Leslie's paintings: "Stamped in every line with good taste . . . [and] . . . graceful sentiment," they embodied the kind of art that helped "to counteract the ignobler refinements of industrial occupation by their inborn refinement, their liberal element of loveliness, their sweet sentiment of nature, their literary associations, and their genial humor."[1] We can hear the authentic tone of a paternalistic, well-meaning, urbane mid-Victorian. When Taylor died in 1880, Thomas Hughes, his lifelong friend, remembered him as being "at his desk early every morning, often at five o'clock, for three hours work before breakfast, after swallowing a cup of milk. . . . Then, at play hours, if the company were at all sympathetic, he would turn himself loose, and give the rein to those glorious and most genial high spirits, which thawed all reserves, timidities and conventionalities, and transformed all present for the time being into a group of rollicking children at play. . . ."[2] We thus have a corroborative reminiscence of Taylor at home, industrious, paternal, and kindly but with a ruthless ability to discipline himself, and, by inference, a tendency to discipline others.

Tom Taylor was a consistently successful polymath. His career spanned journalism, art criticism, poetry, law, university teaching, the public service, and, above all, the theater. Though he was to give up the law and teaching, he would remain involved in writing comic poetry for *Punch,* art criticism for the *Times* and *Graphic,* and plays for the major London theaters from the age of twenty-seven until his death. As if this were insufficient, he was also to become heavily involved in the public service, writing influential articles on public sanitation. As a playwright, he finished eighty plays in thirty-six years, the majority of which were performed and revived both in England and the United States. Had Taylor lived twenty years later to enjoy the benefits of copyright and percentage agreements, he would have died the wealthiest playwright in the English-speaking world. What differentiates Taylor from the other dramatists we are considering is his critical objectivity which distances his writing from the narrowing effects of engaged satire, reforming zeal, or moral fervor. While other dramatists rose or fell according to their audience's willingness to accept these predilections, Taylor was generally able to judge in advance the limits of his audience's tolerance. This facility goes a long way to explaining his unchallenged success in the period 1845 to 1870. But when critical sights and audience expectations were raised after 1870, it is this very dispassionate lack of engagement that helps to explain Taylor's speedy posthumous eclipse.

The Life and Career of Tom Taylor

Taylor was born on 19 October 1817 in the North of England and he was to retain an affection for his home town Sunderland and Northerners for the rest of his life. He was the son of a wealthy, self-made man who had risen from laborer to brewer and alderman in the city of Durham, the very type satirized by Robertson and Jones as uncultured and money-oriented. Tom, however, was given considerable leeway to develop intellectually and artistically. At an early age he and his sister involved themselves in puppetry and toy theaters, an interest that he retained during his school days.[3] The attention devoted to his intellectual development resulted in a distinguished academic record both at the University of Glasgow to which he matriculated in 1832, and at Trinity College, Cambridge, where he graduated in 1840 with first-class honours in mathematics and the classical tripos. Between 1842 and 1844, Taylor stayed at Cambridge as a Fellow of Trinity College, gaining particular distinction as a linguist, and coaching undergraduates when his father died in 1843 and the allowance awarded to Taylor went toward the education of his younger brothers. His reputation at Cambridge was of a benevolent and accessible tutor with wide interests,[4] and while there he collaborated in establishing "The Old Stagers," the forerunner of the Cambridge Amateur Dramatic Club which was to be the seedbed of so

many English actors and directors down to the present-day Dudley
Moore and John Barton.

In 1844 Taylor left Cambridge for London, and began his association with journalism and the theater that would remain for the rest
of his life. He met the Keeleys and Alfred Wigan at the Lyceum Theatre and immediately began to write burlesques for them together
with the entrepreneur/performer Albert Smith. At the same time he
began preparations for admission to the bar as a lawyer and to write
for the newly established satirical journal *Punch*. His first contribution
appeared in October 1844. By 1847 he was contributing fifty columns a year and this strong connection with the journal would cumi-
nate in 1874 when he would become its editor. Taylor was admitted
to the bar in 1846, but not before being appointed as professor of
English language and literature at the University of London in 1845.
He held this position for two years before resigning to practice law in
the north of England and to renew his former connections. Although
the writing of burlesque was a product of his days as a university wit,
his aptitude for languages was to prove more enduring and, ultimately, useful. A familiarity with the writings of Scribe and the principles of the "well made play" resulted in a one act farce, *To Parents
and Guardians,* performed at the Lyceum in September 1846. As
Charles Kent notes in his account of Taylor's life, it was "the first
piece of Taylor's that signally attracted the public. . . ."[5]

Between 1846 and 1850 he continued with his law, writing for
newspapers and journals, and providing short plays for the Keeley
management. In 1850 he was appointed assistant secretary to the
newly created Board of Health and gave up law permanently. It is
hardly surprising that he should have an interest in public welfare,
and public health was a convenient channel for him. He rose to be
secretary in 1854 and he remained in this position until 1871 on a
salary of 1,000 pounds a year. When the position was abolished and
Taylor was made redundant, he was given the opportunity of retiring
on an annuity of 650 pounds which he retained until his death in
1880.

The early period from 1850 also demonstrated his flair for adaptation and collaboration with other writers and with actors. For the vet-
eran comedian William Farren at the Strand Theatre he adapted *The
Vicar of Wakefield,* which ran for a month in 1850, and he followed
this up with an adaptation of the Sir Roger de Coverley essays for
the same management in 1851. That year he met his first prominent

collaborator, the novelist Charles Reade, and began a professional relationship that was to last the next six years and a personal friendship that lasted for the remainder of his life.[6] Reade had already been trying his hand at the adaptation of French novels and plays for the English stage with little success. Their collaboration resulted in *Masks and Faces* produced at the Haymarket Theatre in 1852. It introduced Taylor to the Haymarket company, which from 1853, when Buckstone took over its management, would become recognized as the best eccentric comedy company in England. Taylor would return to them many times and through their association establish his own reputation as a writer of comedy. The play proved immensely successful and was to remain firmly established in both the English and American repertoires for the next thirty years. In fact, revised by Laurence Irving, it would still be performed in 1908.

The year 1853 was an important one for Taylor. First, he began his association with the world of fine art by writing art criticism for the *Times* and *Graphic* newspapers and editing the autobiography of Benjamin Haydon, the romantic painter who had committed suicide in 1846. Nothing could have been more disparate than the characters of the two men: Haydon, tortured, poverty stricken, and unaccepted by the Establishment, and Taylor, tolerant, untroubled by financial worries, with "an infinite capacity for taking pains."[7] In the same year, Taylor's friend Wigan took over the management of the Olympic Theatre hoping to establish a reputation for sophisticated French adaptations and classic comedy. It was a strong company with Wigan himself, a suave and restrained actor, Frederick Robson, dwarflike and brilliantly expressive, and Mrs. Stirling, who had acted with Macready in Shakespeare and could play everything from Cordelia to Lady Teazle in Sheridan's *School for Scandal.* Taylor provided them with a romantic spy drama, *Plot and Passion* in 1853, and two farces, *To Oblige Benson* and *A Blighted Being,* both adapted from the French, in 1854. In March 1854 he also began an association with the Adelphi Theatre, the home of strong melodrama, with a play called *Two Loves and a Life.*

In 1855 Taylor married Laura Barker, the daughter of an Anglican minister in Yorkshire. She was a talented musician and had been associated with both Paganini and Mendelssohn. She was to help Taylor with incidental music for his play *Jeanne D'Arc* in 1871 and would outlive him by twenty-five years. Between his marriage and 1859, Taylor wrote principally for the Olympic and Haymarket theaters with two excursions to the Adelphi: *Helping Hands* in 1855 and *The House or the Home?* in 1859. He was also to have a notable success with the distinguished Phelps company at Sadler's Wells in a poetic drama freely adapted from Victor Hugo, *The Fool's Revenge,* also in 1859. He was by now recognized as the house dramatist of the Olympic, and from 1857 he provided the Haymarket as well with a string of successful comedies culminating in *The Overland Route* in February 1860.

Winton Tolles put 1860 as the turning point in Taylor's career.[8] He was by this time the most prolific and popular playwright writing in English. This popularity extended to both sides of the Atlantic. His plays were performed in America within months of their first performance in London, and were popular vehicles for actors like Jefferson, Wallack, and Edwin Booth. He was the undisputed master of skillful adaptation. Critics and audiences were looking for comedies that depended on plot construction rather than verbal pyrotechnics, and melodramas that incorporated strong, coherent domestic situations and richness of realistic detail. Taylor's academic training had given him a clear sense of form and structure. He was shrewd enough to take as his model French dramatic organization as exemplified by Scribe, and skillful enough to mold this into a play that was seamlessly English. If weaknesses were to appear, they would become evident in the areas where Taylor would have to be at his most inventive, those of dialogue and characterization. Both, however, could be obscured by the strong collaboration of a Charles Reade or a rich original like the novels of Charles Dickens, as in *Tale of Two Cities,* which Taylor adapted for the Lyceum Theatre in January 1860. More often than not, a deficiency in dialogue or chracterization could also be obscured by excellence in performance. The Olympic company had a nucleus of actors who specialized in restraint, and in the negotiation of the hazardous path between comedy and pathos. The Haymarket company were remarkable for highly individualized performers of eccentric comedy. Both needed a writer who would supply them with clearly delineated outlines that they could fill in by their playing strengths. In a sense Taylor's lines were immaterial as long as his situation showed the actors up to advantage. And this he was able to do. The trouble would come when companies broke up or when a writer appeared who would demonstrate a dexterity in dialogue quite independent of his interpreters.

The new theater season began in September 1860, and Taylor was asked to write three plays for three different managements. The result was a moderate success with *Babes in the Woods* in November at the Haymarket, and two failures, *The Brigand and his Banker,* based on *Le Roi des Montagnes* by Edmond About at the Lyceum, and *Up in the Hills* at the St. James's in October of the same year. The last was probably Taylor's biggest disappointment since it was written for his friend Wigan who had high hopes for a success to open his management of a new theater. The play was set in India and involved the kind of domestic intrigue that would characterize Henry Arthur Jones's *Carnac Sahib* in 1899. Nevertheless, the overlay of exotic locations if anything threw the mechanics of contrivance into even sharper relief. Failure must have been a bitter pill for Taylor after a period of continued success. For the next three years he wrote nothing new, although his name remained prominently in the minds of playgoers. In November 1861 E. A. Sothern arrived at the Haymarket Theatre after a highly successful run of Taylor's *Our American Cousin* at Laura Keene's theater in New York. It was a play that Taylor had written in the aftermath of the Great Exhibition of 1851 with its attraction of vast numbers of American tourists. He had sent the play to the Wallacks in New York who, in turn, had shown it to Laura Keene. With the Buckstone company and Sothern repeating his role as Lord Dundreary, it became, after a hesitant start, the most discussed and fashionable comedy in London for over 400 performances.

In 1863, Taylor returned to the theater with a new play, one by which he is still best remembered. Again adapted from the French, *The Ticket of Leave Man* is a compendium of mid-Victorian popular dramatic tastes and arguably one of the best examples of melodramatic form in the nineteenth-century. It opened at the Olympic in May and was playing in New York by November of the same year. By 1864 it was playing in three theaters simultaneously in New York. For this Taylor was paid the standard fifty pounds per act. Twenty years later Henry Arthur Jones's *The Silver King,* with many of the same ingredients, would begin to earn its author 18,500 pounds in royalties.

The following year Taylor began to devote his attentions to advancing the careers of the Terry family. He had known them from the early 1850s. This association would now influence his writing and the careers of Kate and her younger sister Ellen. To Ellen he was to become a surrogate father who advised her on her career and interfered in her private life. But for Kate Terry he wrote a series of plays, and her appearance in them guaranteed their success: *The Hidden Hand* in 1864 and *The Settling Day, The Serf,* and *Henry Dunbar,* all in 1865.[9] Kate Terry, however, left the stage in 1867 and Taylor had no further stage successes until *Mary Warner,* a domestic drama colored by the world of finance and speculation, which he wrote in 1869 for Kate Bateman, the daughter of the American entrepreneur "Colonel" Bateman. Though the period from 1860 was increasingly dominated by serious plays, Taylor wrote his last, and possibly best, comedy for the Haymarket Theatre in *New Men and Old Acres* in which he collaborated with Augustus Dubourg. Ever conscious of popular taste, it owed much by way of indirect homage to Robertson, who himself, in 1869, had come to the end of his comic career.

Already, however, by the end of the 1860s, there were some ominous notes being sounded in critical appraisals of Taylor's work. Critics like Dutton Cook were starting to question the validity of ostentatious physical realism as a framework for artificial and unquestionably "theatrical" characters and situations. Taylor had based his reputation on the appeal of Scribean formulae to the English playgoer. He was therefore unprepared for an undercurrent that was already gathering force and identifying French influence with the superficiality of the boulevard. Nor were critics as tolerant of casual, if expert, adaptation. In 1869 William Gilbert, the father of the playwright, sued Taylor on the grounds of plagiarism over the source of his play *Mary Warner,*[10] and in 1871 Thomas Purnell in *Dramatists of Today* accused Taylor of calculated failure to acknowledge his sources.

In the final decade of his life Taylor joined W. G. Wills and Tennyson in trying to initiate conscious literary awareness of English playwriting through the revival of verse drama. Perhaps it was his attempt to claim somewhat belatedly a seriousness of purpose. Taylor had already evinced an interest in poetic drama with *The Fool's Revenge* in 1859. In 1870 and 1871 he wrote *Twixt Axe and Crown* and *Jeanne D'Arc* for Clara Rousby, a spectacularly beautiful actress of seventeen, whose career like that of Ellen Terry he might have molded had she not died an equally spectacular alcoholic death in Wiesbaden in 1879. He only tried once more to write verse drama with *Ann Boleyn* in 1876. It was his "only complete failure."[11] Nevertheless, he was still able to write effective historical pieces. In 1873 he wrote *Arkwright's*

Wife, a prose drama on the ambitious subject of Luddite rioting and the takeover of men by machinery. It was produced at the Globe Theatre in October. Tolles persuasively suggests that the play was the model for Henry Arthur Jones's *The Middleman* in 1889.[12] Taylor's last major success came in 1874 with another prose drama, *Lady Clancarty,* set amid attempts by Jacobites to overthrow William of Orange. First performed in March at the Olympic, the theater with which Taylor had been so long identified, it ran for six months and enjoyed popular revivals for the next twenty years. Again to demonstrate his dramatic credentials, Taylor collected his historical dramas and had them published in 1877. But in this he was before his time. Fifteen years were to elapse before a reading public divorced from the theatrical business were to respond to a play's publication and a copyright convention was to make it worth a publisher's while.

Taylor was by now the full-time editor of *Punch.* His last two plays, *Such is the Law* and *Love or Life,* were written with Paul Merritt in 1878. Taylor had already written over eighty plays, but the actors on whom he had depended were already disappearing. Alfred Wigan died in December 1878 and Buckstone in October 1879. Taylor himself was still active and gregarious, and insisting "that it was possible for everyone to have a good time,"[13] when he died suddenly from a stroke on 12 July 1880. "He was," said Thomas Hughes, "very able in many ways, as a scholar, poet, critic, dramatist. . . . But where shall we turn for the man who will prove such a spring of pure, healthy, buoyant, and kindly fun for the next, as he has been to us for the last thirty years?"[14]

Taylor's Comic Writing

When Taylor arrived in London in 1844, comic writing was dominated by Planché and Charles Dance in burlesques and extravaganzas, Boucicault and Jerrold in comedies, and John Maddison Morton in farce. Through a casual acquaintance with Albert Smith, Taylor met the Keeleys, the managers of the Lyceum Theatre. Mrs. Keeley was a versatile actress equally at home as Poll in Jerrold's *The Prisoner of War* and Audrey in *As You Like it.* She was a great friend of Planché and Buckstone, the Haymarket's principal low comedian and in her company were the Wigans who were family friends of Douglas Jerrold. It was, in other words, a tightly knit circle of mutual influence.

We saw in chapter 1 how fluid the lines of demarcation were between burlesque and extravaganza, comedy and farce. Taylor's dramatic apprenticeship between 1844 and 1852 demonstrates this clearly. *Whittington and his Cat* and *Cinderella,* both produced at the Lyceum in 1845, are labeled burlesques though they are closer to pantomime and extravaganza. *To Parents and Guardians* is labeled a comedy but its physicality suggests the basic ingredient of farce. *Diogenes and his Lantern* produced at the Strand Theatre in 1849, with the reduction of myth to its lowest common denominator, suggests an extravaganza like Planché's *Olympic Revels* rather than strict burlesque.

The Farces.   Taylor began his career with *A Trip to Kissengen,* a farce produced at the Lyceum on 14 November 1844, but his first success independent of Albert Smith or Charles Kenney was with the one-act *To Parents and Guardians* produced two years later in the same theater on 14 September 1846. In Dicks Standard Plays edition it is labeled a comedy possibly because the physical business of farce is outweighed by the sentimentally motivated behavior. It enabled Wigan to play the English version of a stage Frenchman in the character of Tourbillon, and Mrs. Keeley to play a breeches part in the character of Nettles, the schoolboy protagonist.

The story is a slight one about schoolboy pranks, made familiar by *Tom Brown's School Days,* and the play depends on a ready indulgence toward such pranks, on a popular approval of transvestite roles, and on a sense of superiority over foreigners. The characters of Nettles and his fat "fag" Waddilove are enduring ones and are to be found in the *Boys Own Paper* as well as in twentieth-century manifestations like Richmal Crompton's "William" stories or Frank Richards's adventures of Billy Bunter. The title suggests a humorous plea for indulgence on the grounds of remembered youth.[15]

Our Clerks was again written for the Keeleys and Wigan but this time under the management of Charles Kean at the Princess's Theatre. The play opened on 6 March 1852 on the same bill as Charles Kean's very successful production of Boucicault's *The Corsican Brothers.* The farce's major strength lies in its organization of material and its total lack of sentimentality. The humor emerges from the situations and the ingenuity with which the impoverished lawyer, Hazard, and his clerks extricate themselves from their monetary and amorous predicaments. There is virtually no verbal humor so typical of one act afterpieces on the English stage. Taylor had taken G. H. Lewes's advice to English writers that they needed to construct "a story as the development of some idea—grouping around that the characters which will most clearly set it forth. . . ."[16] In its review of the play and Taylor's contribution to comic writing in this form on 8 March 1852, the *Times* critic was less impressed by the plot construction or "the production of those situations which startle an audience into laughter" than by the "the comic pictures of real life" that this play and *To Parents and Guardians* exhibited. The critic felt that Taylor had brought something entirely new to the comic stage. In this play "it is the atmosphere in which the personages move that gives the piece its distinctive character." This cannot refer to the staging, which must have been relatively simple given the enormous demands of *The Corsican Brothers,* but rather to the illusion of social complexity created by seedy chambers and situations demanding the ingenuity of lower-class clerks and far from exemplary employers. Taylor, concluded the review, was genuinely moving toward the world of Dickens or Thackeray, "without that perpetual striving after wit, which has often shackled the best writers for the English stage."

Our Clerks was never as popular on the English stage as *To Parents and Guardians* or Taylor's "comedietta" *To Oblige Benson,* which he wrote for the opening season of his friend Wigan's management of the Olympic in 1854. The last is a splendid example of Taylor's skill at translation from one social milieu to another, that is, the French to the English, and of dramatic construction in the service of English domestic idealism. Again the play was intended as a vehicle for specific actors with particular qualities: Mrs. Stirling who had played Olivia in Taylor's dramatization of *The Vicar of Wakefield* in 1849 and was the original Peg Woffington in *Masks and Faces* in 1852, and Frederick Robson, whose extraordinary performance in *Plot and Passion* a few months earlier set the stage for a meteoric rise to stardom and the favor of Queen Victoria herself. The term "comedietta' was an attempt to find an English equivalent for the French *coḿedie-vaude-ville.* It was defined somewhat unhelpfully in the *Leader* of 8 April 1865 as "that dwarf species of comedy that is not as broad as farce, nor so light as vaudeville, nor so tragic as melodrama."[17] In this particular case, Taylor adapted an original by Eugène Moreau and Alfred Delacour called *Un Service à Blanchard* that had been performed at the Gymnase in Paris in April 1852. Its popularity was enormous—the French's Minor Drama edition lists six major productions in London,

New York, Philadelphia, and Boston within two years. It became a stock curtain raiser throughout the nineteenth century and Tolles refers to it as still much in demand by amateurs in the 1940s.[18]

The setting is a middle-class drawing room. The characters are husbands and wives devoted to domestic ideals of fidelity and consequent married bliss. Mrs. Benson, however, is much younger than her husband and susceptible to innocent flirtations with dashing young men about town and would-be lawyers like John Meredith. Her husband, to offset his constant absences at his practice and in the law courts, without consulting her has given Meredith leave to take his wife to the opera and to organize vacations in the country. Meredith predictably has fallen in love with her. Unfortunately, his love letter to Mrs. Benson, slipped into her glove on the previous day's picnic, has been picked up by mistake by Mrs. Trotter Southdown.

Mrs. Southdown is the fashionable wife of Benson's business friend, who spends most of his time on his model farm growing "turnips as big as balloons" and raising "mangoldwurzel upon deal tables."[19] She is furthermore determined to give Mrs. Benson an object lesson in the folly of flirtation.[20] She enlists the help of her husband Trotter. He is to manufacture jealousy at the thought that she is conducting a relationship with an unknown lover, all "to oblige Benson." He does this very badly as he "begins to fling furniture about in pretended rage, but putting it gently down again" (F, 13). Benson, however, tries to reason with his friend and obviously believes Mrs. Southdown's story. Southdown now moves from pretended jealousy to real jealousy with the rapidity of transition which Robson made famous. In the ensuing scenes, the more his wife compliments him on his performance, the angrier Southdown becomes. When she realizes that matters have gone beyond a joke, her attempts at explaining the truth simply make her appear to be trying desperately to save her own reputation. In the midst of it all, Meredith becomes hopelessly confused, decides to return a compromising letter of Mrs. Benson's, and attempts to wash his hands of the entire business.

Benson now sees it as his duty to save the reputation of his friend's wife. He employs his own wife to pretend to be the compromised woman so that he can make a show of forgiveness and understanding. In the end after a farcical attempt to prevent the letter being read by either of the two men, Benson magnanimously throws it in the fire as proof of his tolerant nature. There is enough left of it, however, for Southdown to recognize Mrs. Benson's handwriting and to realize his own mistake. They are thus all prepared to say no more about it "to oblige Benson."

It is a clever little play driven by the mechanism of misplaced letters and a middle-class terror of exposure to scandal. The letters themselves are relatively harmless but their significance is blown out by the accepted moral code. The tissue of lies and pretense is played out as an elaborate dance with the Bensons and the Southdowns changing places and allegiances with a rapidity which leaves the lover, Meredith, completely bamboozled. Tolles points out the softening process which the play has undergone in translation from the French setting.[21] In the original there is little doubt that the relationship is more than platonic. In this play it is an innocent flirtation. Benson is not a wayward, preoccupied husband; he merely wants to circumvent his wife's domestic thriftiness. In the end, the husbands triumph and wives echo the sentiments of the wife in J. P. Wooler's *A Model Husband,* produced in 1853: "No more jaunts without my husband—no more amusement but *with* my husband—no more care but *for* my husband."[22]

Burlesques.   Before leaving Taylor's developmental period and examining his full-length comedies we need to consider briefly an example of his burlesque writing.[23] We have seen how popular was the tradition of burlesque throughout the nineteenth century. One of its principal sources of inspiration was classical mythology where the debunking of classical subjects was a useful framework for contemporary satire. We can trace this perennial usefulness through the opera bouffe of Offenbach in examples like *Orpheus in the Underworld* to modern instances like Giraudoux's *Amphitryon 38.*

Taylor wrote *Diogenes and his Lantern, or, A Hue and Cry after Honesty* for the Strand company. It was to become in the period 1858 to 1870 the principal burlesque theater in London and would remain so until supplanted by the Gaiety under John Hollingshead. The structure of the burlesque does not depend on narrative but on a loose juxtaposition of extravagant pseudoclassical costuming with modern attitudes and the presentation of modern situations clothed in the artifice of fourth-century Greece. The story is based on the anecdote of Diogenes's search for an honest man. It enables Taylor to tilt at imposters and commercial frauds, at self-seeking politicians and corrupt share brokers, and to have fun with Greek mythological figures. It is not, however, an extraordinarily funny play. There are a few amusing parodies of well-known tunes from Rossini and Mozart and the verbal jokes are rather tame. The choice of subject also tends to be too literary with no indications of that lively mixture of dramatic forms that insured its perpetual appeal. It perhaps shows where Taylor was weakest. It was written without the discipline of collaboration or strong narrative form. Burlesque was nothing if it was not witty in conception, and Taylor had neither the wit of a Burnand or Blanchard nor the extravagance of his mentor Planché. Just as important, burlesque is iconoclastic, and even in his short farces Taylor shows himself to be an enemy of chaos and unprepared to be pessimistic.

The Comedies

Though Taylor wrote a further farce for Robson, *A Blighted Being,* in 1854, he was to be identified as a comic writer with the Haymarket Theatre rather than the Olympic. This connection he owed to the popularity of *Masks and Faces* in which he collaborated with Charles Reade. This was produced in 1852, though his string of comedies for the Haymarket did not begin until 1857 with *Victims.* Because of Taylor's close identification with the Haymarket, his comic abilities are best represented by his major successes: *Masks and Faces, The Overland Route, Our American Cousin,* and *New Men and Old Acres.*

Masks and Faces. *Masks and Faces* is part of a tradition of plays about quaint, irresponsible but lovable theater folk that in the Victorian period is best represented by this play, followed by Robertson's *David Garrick* and Pinero's *Trelawney of the "Wells." Masks and Faces* was the result of a meeting between Taylor and Charles Reade that Mrs. Stirling had engineered during her season at the Olympic in 1851. The first performance took place on 20 November 1852, the last year of Benjamin Webster's management of the Haymarket. It then remained in the repertoire to be produced by the Bancrofts at the Prince of Wales in 1875, and again during their five-year management of the Haymarket from 1880.

The title suggests that the play is to revolve round the age-old theme of illusion and reality. The central character is the historical actress Peg Woffington (1714–60) renowned for her performance in breeches parts. But this is where historical verisimilitude stops and the characters bear no further resemblance to their historical counterparts.[24] Instead they form the gilt edging to a sentimental picture of contrasting domestic situations. The play is thus a nineteenth-century combination of comedy and pathos set self-consciously within an eighteenth-century context. The play still has considerable elements of eccentric comedy but its blend of comedy and pathos looks forward to the dominant mode of late nineteenth-century comedy.

Peg Woffington is the flame to which men are inescapably drawn. In act 1 she is being wooed by Charles Pomander, an arrogant aristocrat who has callously offered her wealth as a consideration for becoming his mistress, and Vane, a country squire from Huntingdonshire, who has become infatuated with her and wishes to rescue her from her detractors. Her most engaging admirer, however, is Triplet (played by Benjamin Webster), an impoverished playwright, painter, and sometime actor. He looks to her as the entry to fame and fortune at Covent Garden and arrives in the Green Room of the theater clutching a painting of Peg. He hopes his three tragedies will be accepted by the management: "Master of three arts, painting, writing and acting, by each of which men grow fat, how was it possible I should go on perpetually starving?"[25] His hopes, however, are dashed, until Peg takes the plays and undertakes to present them personally to Rich, the manager. She has recognized Triplet from the time that she was an orange girl at Goodman's Fields Theatre seven years before. As "a judge of painted faces" she promises to let him finish off her portrait and commissions him to write some occasional verse for her. When she turns to Pomander, her attitude is entirely different. With Triplet, Peg is the genuinely kind woman who remembers her past poverty and can differentiate between his apparently carefree attitude and his real financial desperation. Pomander cannot believe it when she refuses his offer. He, however, is not to be rebuffed so easily. When he discovers that Vane is in fact married and that his wife of a year is arriving in London, he resolves to have his revenge at the party that Vane is to give in honor of Peg Woffington.

The second scene at Vane's house introduces Mabel full of enthusiasm at the prospect of seeing her husband. When the guests arrive Mabel, after depositing her bags, makes a surprise appearance to the great discomfiture of Vane. When Triplet enters with his prepared verses, Mabel mistakenly believes his presence is part of a surprise prepared for her by Vane. Pomander, however, is determined on his revenge and he enlightens Mabel about her husband's real motives. Though she refuses to accept his word, she cannot resist hiding behind a chair to overhear Vane declare passionately to Peg that he is prepared to renounce everything including Mabel for her. The act ends with Vane catching a fainting Mabel in his arms.

Critical attention was drawn particularly to act 2. The scene changes to Triplet's garret where, surrounded by a sick wife and hungry children, he is desperately trying to write a comedy. In comes Peg bearing food and wine, and quite prepared to stitch Triplet's coat while she slips a ten-pound note into the pocket. She has invited her entourage to view Triplet's painting of her, but before they enter, Triplet slashes the inadequate painting with a knife. As Cibber, Mrs. Clive, and Quin enter, Peg cuts a hole in the canvas and inserts her own face. It leads to an amusing scene in which the arbiters of elegance and artistic ability criticize Peg's face because Triplet has "the chiaroscuro . . . all wrong" (R, 158). The scene is at once a witty parody of a viewing at the Royal Academy, and a succinct statement about the nature of artistic illusion. It is Triplet's moment of glory as he throws out the discomfited "critics." It is only when he compares Peg with "the sweet lady" he met at Vane's house, that Peg's assurance collapses.

When Mabel enters to get away from a pursuing Pomander, the two women confront one another. Mabel extracts from Peg an undertaking to force Vane to give her up. Part of the plan will involve Peg impersonating Mabel to an unsuspecting Pomander and to bring Vane to Triplet's house. The men appear and are about to come to blows, when a masked Mrs. Vane appears as though to confirm Vane's suspicions. Only when Vane admits "how bitterly I repented the infatuation that brought me to the feet of another" (R, 169) does she throw off her disguise to reveal Peg Woffington. The rest of the company return filled with apologies to Triplet, who has had one of his tragedies accepted by the manager of Covent Garden.

Henry Morley rather stuffily liked the play because it embodied a nice balance between showing the degraded life of an actress and her determined efforts to rise above it.[26] G. H. Lewes was more taken by the abilities of the actors: Webster's juxtaposition of seediness and personal vanity as Triplet, Leigh Murray's "unscrupulous coxcomb" Pomander, "whose quiet self-mastery and steady intellect imply that he is capable of playing a part in the world," and Mrs. Stirling's Peg who made Vane's infatuation understandable but his fascination with conjugal love for Mabel totally incomprehensible.[27] All critics, however, were fascinated by the play's use of dramatic irony that complemented the title. Triplet oscillates between "mask" and "face" as a half-deliberate device to elicit sympathy from the other characters. Peg allows her onstage mask to slip three times: once with Vane and then briefly with Triplet and Mabel. It is through the asides that the audience is made constantly aware of the conflict between mask and face and the effort required to keep the two apart.[28]

Our American Cousin. Though *The Overland Route* appeared on the London stage the year before *Our American Cousin,* the latter was written much earlier and performed in New York in 1858. It gained a subsequent notoriety as the play Lincoln saw the night of his assassination at Ford's Theater. In *Masks and Faces* actors were given the opportunity of exploring the disparity between illusion and reality. *Our American Cousin* is a vehicle for eccentric comedy based on physical mannerisms, comic speech patterns, and outlandish costume. Nevertheless, when Taylor wrote the play, its focus was rather different. He had written it for an American actor Josiah Silsby who was contracted to the Adelphi Theatre under Benjamin Webster's management. By the end of 1851, when interest in the American tourists to the Great Exhibition had waned, Webster did not proceed with the production.[29] Taylor subsequently showed the play to the Wallacks and, through them, to Laura Keene. The Keene company's reactions were less than enthusiastic. The play was after all written by an Englishman, lampooning American idiosyncrasies through the character of Asa Trenchard, the Vermont backwoodsman who inherits an English fortune.

E. A. Sothern was at this stage a rather less than successful English actor in the Keene company. On being given the part of Lord Dundreary with some forty-seven lines of dialogue, he agreed to perform it on condition that he could build up the part. Laura Keene must have been somewhat relieved. An asinine English lord was a perfect humorous butt and it would allow Joseph Jefferson to play the part of Asa sympathetically, with "simplicity and truthfulness."[30] The play opened to a cautious reception, but Sothern's "Dundrearyisms" in the course of the season turned it into a personal triumph for him. He played it over eight hundred times before opening it at the Haymarket on 16 November 1861. As in New York, London audiences were slow to accept the play. But eccentric comedy with an anti-aristocratic bias had always been successful in the British popular theater. In Sothern's hands it was a monstrously self-indulgent "turn" that could be excused and even applauded on the grounds that there was no narrative tension in the play anyway, and that the character of Asa relied on exotic turns of phrase rather than on intrinsic idiocy. As well, 1861 saw the beginning of the American Civil War, and En-

glish sympathies tended to lie with the Confederacy rather than with
the Yankees with whom Asa might have been identified.

The play itself chronicles the effect of Asa upon his impoverished
relatives and their guests at Trenchard Manor. He is loud, aggressive,
and full of life. When he first sees Dundreary, he reels back in aston-
ishment at the huge check trousers, monocle, mutton chop whiskers,
and lisp: "Concentrated essence of baboons, what on earth is that?"[31]
He is immediately suspicious of the unctuous butler Binney, refuses
to allow him to unpack his clothes, and when he needs help he pulls
a cord in his bedchamber and empties the shower on himself. But Asa
is also resourceful, and it is he who thwarts the ambitions of Coyle,
the family's agent, to dispossess the Trenchards of their estates, and
exposes his mismanagement. He also falls in love with Mary Meredith
whose claim to the estates and personal wealth of the American
branch of the Trenchard family he has preempted. Her rustic charm
and farming abilities, however, promise to make her a perfect Vermont farmer's wife. He thus emerges as an amalgam of Twain's Connecticut Yankee and Anna Mowatt's Farmer Trueman in *Fashion*.
There is little in the plot to suggest Dundreary's centrality and why
all action stopped to allow Sothern to perform what amounted to a
self-contained music hall turn. Sothern, however, played Dundreary
with a combination of childlike literalness and disarming stupidity
and used the text merely as a springboard for idiosyncratic digres-
sions.[32] These had no textual validity and would have been unbearable
had there been a real dramatic tension in the play that needed resolution.

The Overland Route.   More characteristic of comedy at the
Haymarket was the play that had opened over a year before, on 23
February 1860. While *Our American Cousin* was a star vehicle, *The
Overland Route* was intended to show off the company's talents. It has
strongly farcical characteristics of symmetrical relationships, confus-
ing numbers of identical doors, elusive false teeth, and elaborate disguise. At the same time there are strongly sentimental and romantic
elements in the young, heroic doctor who brings together the erring
wives and husbands, and a desert island location in the last act. Again
the strengths of the play do not lie in its narrative but in the opportunities it gives to individual actors to explore the humor of separate
and tenuously connected situations. The three old men, all colonial
civil servants and merchants, were played by the theater's leading low
comedians, Chippendale, Compton, and Buckstone, while the heroic

doctor was played by Charles Matthews who had made his reputation in light comedy roles.

The story concerns the fortunes of a motley group of passengers on board the P. and O. ship *Simoon* bound for England from Singapore, Calcutta, and Aden. It features shipboard romance, mistaken identity, and a calculated exploration on Taylor's part of farcical coincidence. Even the *Times* found that the play had "ostentatiously shown a disregard for the artifices which belong to a well constructed play."[33] We can argue that the structure of the play is a response to the popular audience's desire to see its favorite comic actors go through their paces, that the scenes are dramatic arias to be appreciated for their own sake with little connection to a dramatic "through-line." But Taylor himself seems to have been a little uneasy. The first two acts are structurally identical. The first halves are devoted to marital intrigues and their consequences with a concerted effort devoted to giving Dexter, the doctor/hero, a central role. The second halves bring in old Lovibond and his farcical efforts to deceive his oppressive wife. The result is the construction of two parallel and quite discrete story lines.

As a character Dexter is far less interesting than Lovibond. His heroism and managerial abilities are much spoken of, but dramatically hardly revealed. Everything seems to happen offstage, and since everything is made to depend on him, he becomes an unbelievable hero. On stage he manages a rather gauche love scene with the heroine, Mary, and manifests an oppressive desire to keep the married women chaste for the sake of their absent husbands. Charles Mathews, who played the role, had considerable status in the Haymarket company. Taylor's role suggests an actor of authority, charm, and quietly expressed amusement. It may have satisfied Mathews (and Bancroft in 1882), but the role is dramatically weak. The real energy in the play comes from the older men and Mrs. Lovibond, the older woman. They rush about losing teeth, clothing, and self-esteem with little sentimentality, but they gain the audience's sympathy. Nevertheless, Taylor was by nature essentially sentimental: at the end of the play fathers are proved to care for their daughters, estranged husbands and wives for each other, doctors for their patients, and heroes for helpless females. These sentimental elements in the play are jarring. Taylor's failure to resolve the conflicts between the dictates of farcical form and his own temperament perhaps explains why he turned away from comedy and the Haymarket Theatre. After *The Overland Route,* Taylor wrote three more comedies for the Haymarket company: *Babes in the Woods* (1860), *A Duke in Difficulties* (1861), and *Lesson for Life* (1866), all of which lacked the success of his earlier association.

New Men and Old Acres.   On 25 October 1869 the Haymarket saw the opening of Taylor's last comedy, *New Men and Old Acres*. Between 1860 and 1869 comic style had changed perceptibly. There was still scope and demand for eccentric comedy, but the plays of Robertson were already suggesting the new style that became its dominant comic mode from the mid-1870s. The focus of his comedies was a much narrower one (see chapter 4), concentrating on the minutiae of domestic realism with eccentric characterization subordinated to the depiction of precisely defined characters. It is hardly surprizing, therefore, that *New Men and Old Acres* should suggest distinctly Robertsonian resonances. It owes much in its tone, as well as some structural aspects like contrasting love scenes, to *Society* and *Caste,* while its theme bears a considerable resemblance to that in *Progress.* Nevertheless, Michael Booth regards *New Men and Old Acres* as far superior to any but the best comedies of Robertson.[34]

Act 1 opens in Cleve Abbey, a gracious estate owned by the feckless Vavasours. They have squandered their money, and the property, complete with ruins, is to be sold to the mortgagee about whom nobody knows anything other than that he is "in trade." Their only hope is that young Lilian, a modern tomboy, with a liking for modern jargon, will marry into wealth in time. She is quite willing to sacrifice herself: "In our class fortune is the main, nay, indispensable condition of happiness" (*EPNC*, 3:257), but not to the young nobleman Bertie Fitz-Urse. He, however, is attracted to Fanny Bunter, daughter of the self-made man of industry, Benjamin Bunter. Though Lilian's mother professes aristocratic scruples, she is prepared to sacrifice these when money is around. When Samuel Brown is revealed not only to be the man who holds the Vavasour mortagage but also to be Lilian's partner at the previous night's dance, she no longer urges Lilian to keep such canaille at a distance but piously describes her daughter's find as "one of England's merchant princes—one of the class which has made of this tiny island an empire on which the sun never sets!" (*EPNC*, 3:260). Brown, unlike Bunter, is no admirer of aristocracy, "old acres," or even the acquisition of purposeless wealth. In this he is an admirable foil for the sensible Lilian. Fanny Bunter, on the other hand, is besotted with Ruskin, Wordsworth, and romance and makes a suitable partner for the happy-go-lucky aristocrat, Bertie.

Act 2 is set on croquet lawns among the ruins of the Abbey with ivy and dilapidated arches. But before the romantic coming together of the two couples Taylor reintroduces the suspicious Blasenbalg, a half-comic German associate of Bunter who has been snooping around the estate. Far from indulging in a little fishing, Brown discovers that Blasenbalg has in fact been taking rock samples from about the estate. Brown secretes a piece for future analysis. Lady Matilda Vavasour can hardly conceal her pleasure when Brown requests Lilian's hand in marriage since it means the end of financial uncertainty for her. There follow two contrasting Robertsonian love scenes as Lilian agrees to marry Brown and Fanny agrees to marry Bertie. But their happiness and Lady Matilda's relief are short lived. Brown's stockbroking firm has been caught by a downturn in the market and he desperately needs 40,000 pounds. This the sententiously hypocritical Bunter is prepared to lend him on the security of a transfer of the Cleve Abbey mortgage. Bunter is also aware through his agent, Blasenbalg, that the results of the mineral assay point to a high presence of iron ore in the estate which makes it of inestimable value. Brown is now a ruined man and Lilian's mother sees that a marriage is out of the question. Lilian is caught on the horns of a dilemma: she is an eighteen-year-old girl asked to decide between the man she loves and the mother, of whose hopes she is the repository.

Act 3 moves to Beaumanor Park, the Bunter's estate. In contrast to Cleve Abbey's old-fashioned and subdued decor, it is flashy and modern, as seen in its bright chintzes and "modern pictures, in costly frames" (*EPNC,* 3:297). The structure of the act is built around a series of scenes showing, on the one hand, the Bunters determination to be more impressive than the Vavasours, and, on the other, the gradual thwarting of Benjamin Bunter's ambitions. When Brown returns and makes it known that he too is aware of Cleve Abbey's real value, Bunter at first dismisses any interest and then on the advice of Blasenbalg offers to give Brown a share if he says nothing to the Vavasours. But they have indeed been informed and arrive to discharge the mortgage. When it is revealed by Secker, the Vavasour lawyer, that Brown secretly passed on the information to him, Brown is immediately welcomed into the bosom of the Vavasour family. Bunter cannot extricate himself from his promise to allow Fanny to marry

Bertie, whom he mistakenly believed would inherit a peerage. The play ends with a tableau celebrating the two engagements and Brown's selfless generosity in helping the Vavasour family.

It is a skillfully constructed play about prejudice, wealth, and birth. The Vavasours are pretentious, irresponsible, but, ultimately, good-hearted. Their survival and that of the landed gentry, Taylor suggests, depends on their union with responsible men of business. To show what responsibility means he presents us with two differing examples of the New Men. Though the Vavasours' financial escape is engineered by chance and coincidence, Brown's diffidence at exposing his contribution to their salvation is illogical. It is simply present to show his good breeding and tact. He does not wish the Vavasours to feel under an obligation to him and is prepared to go to Australia to seek his fortune. Thus his conduct is a barely disguised form of knightly chivalry, translated into the behavior of "an English Gentleman." Brown is the Victorian model of innate courtesy combined with innate resilience and independence. The humor of the play comes out in Lilian's boisterously expressed attitudes constrasted with Fanny's self-indulgent romantic posturing, in the Bunters' transparent attempts to appear socially acceptable, and in Lady Matilda's instant ability to accommodate aristocratic principles to monetary gain. There are also some very funny lines. But there is a serious edge in Lilian's inability to resolve the conflict between love and duty—a basic thematic consideration of melodrama. It is also potential in the prospect of Brown's financial ruin. But it is Brown's gentlemanly behavior and Secker's equally gentlemanly confession of Brown's implication that insure that natural justice and comic comeuppance become one and the same thing at the end.

Domestic Melodramas

We have seen that it is a fine line which divides comedy from melodrama throughout the nineteenth century. In plays like *New Men and Old Acres* there is no pathos but a considerable injection of seriousness. Conversely, in melodramas like *The Ticket of Leave Man*, humorous characters and situations offset the sentimental ones. It is a mixture that seems to have suited Taylor's temperament. "His temper was of fire," wrote John Coleman, who had acted and managed some of Taylor's plays, "but his heart was of gold." He was gentle and generous "despite his petulance, his intolerance of contradiction, his *brusquerie*. . . ."[35] The comments suggest a man of melodramatic seriousness and overcompensating sentimentality.

Still Waters Run Deep. It was Fanny Kemble who suggested to Taylor the idea of adapting Charles Bernard's novel *Le Gendre* for the English stage. Alfred Wigan was looking for plays that would enhance the reputation of the Olympic Theatre as the home of sophisticated French adaptation. In *Still Waters Run Deep* Taylor provided him with an exemplary domestic melodrama which, together with the later *Ticket of Leave Man,* forms a compendium of mid-nineteenth-century ideas about plot construction as well as domestic relationships and roles. It opened on 14 May 1855 with Wigan as Mildmay and George Vining as Captain Hawksley. The play's subsequent production history illustrates its enormously enduring popularity. Within four months it was being presented in two rival productions in New York, at Barnum's Museum and Burton's Theater with C. W. Clarke and William Burton playing Mildmay respectively. In less than a year it was being performed in Boston, Philadelphia, Cincinnati, St. Louis, Charleston, and Providence before returning to Wallack's and Laura Keene's theaters in January 1856, with Wallack and Laura Keene appearing in their own productions. In 1867 Wigan repeated his performance to the Mrs. Mildmay of Ellen Terry and the Hawksley of Charles Wyndham. The Kendals performed it in 1880 at the St. James's Theatre with John Hare and William Terriss in the cast. By 1889, however, its popularity had waned and the failure of Wyndham's revival at the Criterion was attributed critically to the play's old-fashioned, creaky construction.[36]

It is tempting to conjecture that Taylor's interest in marital domesticity coincided with his marriage in the same year. The play is about a husband's hidden depths, the temptations that beset a young wife, sexual affairs, and the concept of "home" as "castle." Its tone is paternal and in keeping with its title, quietly authoritative. John Mildmay is a man under siege in his own home. He is bullied by his aunt-in-law, Mrs. Sternhold, and misunderstood by his wife of one year, Emily. He is of honest, Lancashire stock more comfortable in his garden than among the social gatherings that his wife craves. She is indulging in a flirtation with Captain Hawksley, a predatory adventurer, who has persuaded her aunt to invest Emily's settlement in a

spurious company. But Emily has found herself in deep emotional
water and when Hawksley proposes a midnight assignation in her
bedroom, she protests mildly at his proposal. Mildmay appears to be
unconcerned about Hawksley's success with his wife and in fact has
been called away on business to Manchester, thereby giving Hawksley
his opportunity. Mildmay's business trip, however, is canceled and he
overhears Mrs. Sternhold confront Hawksley and reveal that she is one
of his discarded lovers. Her concern for her niece's reputation is thus
motivated as much by jealousy as anything else. But Hawksley has
retained some letters and he uses this to threaten her with social disgrace.

Act 2 is divided into two scenes. In the Mildmay breakfast room,
Mildmay retains his role as an unimaginative cipher and refuses to
help Mrs. Sternhold in her predicament. He does, however, offer to
buy back the Galvanic Navigation Company shares from Hawksley.
In the second scene the two men confront one another in Hawksley's
sumptuous apartment. Mildmay reveals that he has placed a private
detective on Hawksley's tail, and now knows that he is a forger and
swindler. Mildmay's hidden depths are further uncovered by the revelation that he used to work in a stockbroker's office. He has now in
his possession a forged bill that he uses to force Hawksley to hand
over Mrs. Sternhold's indiscreet letters and to return Emily's money.
The infuriated Hawksley threatens to kill Mildmay.

Act 3 returns to Mildmay's villa in Brompton. Mildmay hands
over the letters and money. He now has his "in-laws" at his mercy.
He refuses to endure Mrs. Sternhold's influence over his wife any
longer: "You thought proper to ridicule and despise me, and she followed your lead."[37] With his wife he is no less stern: "Trust to me,
henceforth, to make you what a wife should be . . . ," to which she
replies, "I will honor and obey you as a wife should" (F, 50). Hawksley then arrives to challenge Mildmay to a duel in the middle of a
dinner party. Mildmay dictates his own terms and hides two pistols
under a tablecloth, only one of which is loaded. He challenges Hawksley to take his chances but Hawksley turns out to be a posturing
coward and is arrested by the detective Gimlet on a charge of forgery.
In the best villainous tradition, Hawksley is dragged out grinding his
teeth and threatening Mildmay with revenge. The company file in to
their interrupted dinner secure in their knowledge that "all is not
gold that glitters" and "still waters run deep" (F, 58).

Allardyce Nicoll regards this play as "perhaps Taylor's greatest contribution to the theatre of his time."[38] Certainly the character of Mildmay, outside the parameters of comedy, is an unusual one: the apparently bumbling and amenable husband who turns out to be imaginative and even brave. The play would have been more powerful had Taylor retained his French original's mother and daughter relationship, but this would have given their rivalry over Hawksley an incestuous overtone that audiences would not have tolerated. Even as it is, there are enough sexual nuances in Mrs. Sternhold's jealousy and in Emily's terrified but acquiescent attempts to put off her assignation with Hawksley. The play works as long as the audience accepts devices like Mildmay's eavesdropping, which gives him an unexpected emotional leverage, accepts structural weaknesses like Mildmay's prior knowledge of Hawksley's character, and accepts the women's change from discontented viragos to pliant femininity as a reversion to the natural order of marriage. The suddenness of this reversal is again close to comedy. Nevertheless, though the style and some structural and character deficiencies may detract from the play, it is a recognizably modern play. In Taylor's selection and treatment of his dramatic material he looks forward to the mature dramas of Henry Arthur Jones and Pinero.[39]

The Ticket of Leave Man. This is the only play of Taylor's that can still be found in the English-speaking repertoire (the last professional production seems to have taken place in England in the mid-1970s). It was revived repeatedly in the nineteenth century (1873, 1875, 1879, 1888), yet the ingredients show melodrama in its most traditional form: a sentimental hero and heroine, a comic juvenile, a pair of lovable theater folk, a gang of resourceful villains, a relentless detective, and the structure of a journey from despair to temporary happiness, from disastrous reversal to final vindication and triumph. Hawkshaw is the first instance on stage of a fully fleshed out representative of the British police force; Gimlet in *New Men and Old Acres* and Moleskin in *The Overland Route* are plot functionaries rather than developed characters.

Between 1855 and 1863, Taylor had concentrated on the writing of comedy. Nevertheless, *The Ticket of Leave Man* caused a sensation and had a run equal to that of *Our American Cousin*. In its review of 29 May 1863, the *Times* attributed this sensation to the uncompromising depiction of low life. Taylor, it suggested, had transplanted a type of play from its usual venues of the Victoria or Surrey theaters, to the Olympic, the seat of fashionable audiences. In the genteel comedies with which the Olympic had been identified, the urban poor had been treated as picturesque adjuncts to the main story. Taylor had included the seamier side of life as an integral part of the plot, and audiences were liking this integration. "The tone of thorough reality" together with the strong domestic interest in the play might be "likely to cause an important change in the class of entertainment . . . [at] . . . the more fashionable theatres," was the review's conclusion.[40] The play thus coincides with the heightened awareness of poverty stimulated in the middle-class consciousness that manifested itself in commissions of inquiry, statistical reports, and detailed accounts of personal investigation such as we find in *Household Words* or Mayhew's *London Labor and London Poor*.

The play was adapted from Edouard Brisebarre and Eugène Nus's *Léonard* that had first appeared on the Paris stage in 1862, but as in all of Taylor's adaptations there is no evidence of French influence. Bob Brierly, the Lancashire lad exposed to the temptations of London, was played by Henry Neville, and Hawkshaw, the detective, by Horace Wigan, Alfred Wigan's brother, also known for his quiet, realistic acting. He had been with the Olympic company since 1854 and had played in Taylor's comedies *Nine Points of the Law* (1859) and *A Christmas Dinner* (1860).

The play opens at the Bellevue Tea Gardens, a popular meeting place on a summer evening, with a tavern and concert rooms attached. Milling around are a crowd that comprise "carriage company"—"heavy swells on the lark, white ties and pink bonnets" (*EPNC*, 2:93), villains like Dalton and Moss, and the detective Hawkshaw looking to arrest Dalton for armed robbery and murder. The villains are looking to pass off counterfeit banknotes and settle on young Bob Brierly, a Lancashire lad, out of his depth in a big city and squandering his money on cheap champagne. He is the epitome of country innocence corrupted by urban sophistication. But there is also urban innocence in the figure of May Edwards, an orphan who wanders about trying to earn a living playing her guitar and singing. It is inevitable that these two should seek one another out. It is to her that Bob gives two sovereigns from the change he has obtained for a forged twenty pound note. It is in her company that he is arrested, at the end of the act, after a furious struggle with the police in which the real villains, Dalton and Moss, escape. In the middle of this the comic relief is provided by Green Jones and his fiancée Emily. He is a young, good-hearted theatrical hopeful and she is in a theater ballet line.

The *Times* review found the first act weak, as it did the first act of *Still Waters Run Deep*. This is not the case to a modern reader or viewer. The act forms a complex social mosaic that depends on color, movement, scraps of half-heard conversations, and only momentary pauses to bring people together or to advance their relationships. There is little conventional plotting or sense of forward narrative, which forms the basis of the critical comment. Taylor carefully identifies each group by characteristic slang that aids the sense of truth, and it is this texture that would have appealed to the audience. Tiger Dalton and Melter Moss are two contrasted underworld figures, the prototypes of Skinner and Coombe in Henry Arthur Jones's *The Silver King*. May and Bob are the innocents abroad clinging to one another for mutual protection and quite unequipped to deal with criminal entrapment or callous pleasure seekers. Hawkshaw is the implacable but kind-hearted policeman, who, though he tries to get Bob out of Dalton's clutches, is quite prepared to arrest him when the occasion demands.

Act 2 takes place three years later in May's room that she rents from Mrs. Willoughby. Green and Emily are now married and trying to sell themselves to theatrical managements as a comic double act, but without success. In fact, one of the structural devices of the play is the see-sawing career of the Joneses: in act 1 they had money, in act 2 they are destitute. Bob has been writing assiduously and is about to come out of prison. Using melodrama's structural principle of time compression, Bob instantly appears at May's lodgings. May has been earning a little money as a seamstress and the punctiliousness with which she has paid the rent has earned her the respect of her garrulous landlady, Mrs. Willoughby. May's reputation for good work has been helped by the recommendation of the Gibsons who have taken a kindly interest in her. It is Mr. Gibson who offers Bob a position in his bill broking office, thinking that he is her brother returned from military service. At the end of the act it appears that Bob and May's future is a rosy one. The drama of the act is lightened by the comic elements of the Joneses, and by Mrs. Willoughby, ever anxious about her exuberant fifteen-year-old grandson Sam, who leaps over chairs to frighten her and smokes a clay pipe with jaunty bravado.

Act 3 is set in Gibson's office where Bob is now employed as a

messenger. Bob and May are about to be married and Mr. Gibson
has forgiven their little deception. When Hawkshaw enters to consult
Gibson on a forged bill, he recognizes Bob but does not give him
away. On the other hand, it is Melter Moss, pretending to be a repu-
table business man, who betrays him to Gibson. The marriage is put
off when Bob is dismissed. No ticket of leave man can be employed
in an office, the symbol of mid-Victorian commercial respectability.
It is an act dominated by the theme of the genuine and the counterfeit. The dramatic business concerns the difference between genuine
and forged bills. It is Hawkshaw and Gibson who can tell the difference, yet Hawkshaw is taken in by Dalton's disguise as an elderly
business man and Gibson refuses to trust in his own experience of
Bob's honesty when there is the slightest possibility that respectable
people may doubt it.

The first scene of act 4 is set in the Bridgewater Arms. It is a
lower-class version of the Bellevue Tea Gardens populated this time
with laborers drinking beer and Dalton and Moss planning to rob
Gibson's office. They intend to force Bob to help them. He has been
successfully hounded out of every job by the stigma of "jailbird" and
is at his wits' end. Hawkshaw, however, is still on the trail of Dalton
and is disguised as the foreman of his work gang. His disguise is im-
penetrable to the villains, to Bob, and this time, to the audience. It
is only at the end of the scene, after Bob has pretended to succumb
to Dalton and Moss's offer and writes a note of warning to be taken
to Gibson, that Hawkshaw reveals himself. Once again the Joneses
are down on their luck: Emily is reduced to singing the popular sensation song *The Maniac's Tear* for a few coins, and Green to selling
pig's trotters. Bob, however, is utterly consistent. He weans the
cocky young Sam away from gambling with the likes of Moss by exposing Moss's card sharping and sends Sam back to his grandmother.
He is mortified to discover that May, to whom he is now married,
must take up piece work at the Sailor's Ready Made Clothing Warehouse to keep the wolf from the door. Even when the workers reject
him on the grounds of his past, he remains determined to be honest.

The second scene is a "carpenter's scene"—a transition scene intended to allow the stage to be set up for a detailed set piece. It is a
street scene showing Hawkshaw dogging Dalton to the churchyard of
St. Nicholas, where the tools for breaking and entering are hidden.
With Dalton is Bob who is playing along with the gang. They are
hotly pursued by May, who believes that Bob has abandoned his hon-

est ways. The scene then becomes the churchyard that is next to Gibson's office. After the robbery has been committed Bob confronts Dalton. But it requires the joint efforts of Hawkshaw and the exuberant Sam to subdue him. Bob has been struck down by Dalton but is conscious enough to hear Hawkshaw give him the credit for Dalton's apprehension, and Gibson promise to repay him. The play ends on this moment of triumph.

What then are the ingredients of the play's enduring success? Structurally the play is based on a series of clearly contrasting situations portrayed in primary colors. Bob and May's fortunes are exactly paralleled by those of Green and Emily in each act. The sentiment is counterpointed by humor. Public scenes of great activity are juxtaposed by private scenes of great activity. Taylor has gone to great lengths in the first three acts to set the environment exactly in order to be convincing. The Bellevue Tea Gardens, May's room with its birdcage, work table, American clock, chiffonier, and flowers, and Gibson's office to which Emily responds: "I did so want to see an office—a real one, you know. I've seen 'em set on the stage often, but they ain't a bit like the real thing" (*EPNC*, 2:122). Finally, the Bridgewater Arms, in act 4 with colored hogsheads, piano, cellar doors, itinerant food sellers, and sweaty workers, gives a sense of clearly defined but interconnecting worlds. The dialogue is carefully modulated to accord with the way in which audiences expect the denizens of the particular environment to speak. The plot, in keeping with the structural contrasts, is developed as a series of obstacles. To hurdle these the hero must show courage and stamina. Natural justice at the end rewards Bob for his successful negotiation of these hazards and for his incorruptibility. The wider problems of discharged prisoners in society are ignored and little reason advanced to explain why Gibson should sacrifice his social principles at the end of the play. But this is not the province of melodrama, which does not seek to reform but to realize the possibilities of wish fulfillment. Nor should we expect a reformer of Taylor, who was concerned with giving the audiences what they wanted to see and only cautiously prepared to extend the parameters of their taste. Nevertheless, the characters and story are melodramatic archetypes just as prevalent in the stories of television series today like *Magnum* or *Macmillan and Wife*.

The Settling Day. Between *The Ticket of Leave Man* and this play, Taylor wrote only one melodrama, *The Hidden Hand,* for the Olympic, an adaptation of *L'Aieule* by Adolphe Dennery and Charles

Edmond. We have seen that both in his comedies and the domestic melodramas, a recurring motif has been the relationship between financial security and marital happiness. In this play it becomes a central issue. It is therefore a play in which everybody is concerned with money and derive their living from its manipulation. The two central characters are Markland and Meiklam, partners in a private bank. Markland lives in a palatial villa and is at the end of his honeymoon with his young bride. His association with the bank makes him sought after as a member of Parliament and his reputation is one of scrupulous honesty. Meiklam, on the other hand, is a speculator, and a rash one at that. Markland's wife is young, ingenuous, and eager to learn about the exciting life of the City of London. She and her sister, Miss Hargreave, are both independently wealthy and are impressed by their friend Mrs. Vernon's financial perspicacity. The two poles of bank investment and speculation in the share market are brought together in the character of Harrington who intends to invest 40,000 pounds in Markland's bank but who has lost heavily on the stock market. Between them all is Rocket, "a companies" promoter. He is a fast talking speculator in specious companies through whom we learn that, far from being financially stable, Markland's bank has been involved in some unwise investments through the agency of Meiklam.

Act 2 is set in the stock broking offices of Fermor and Laxton with as much attention to physical detail as Taylor had lavished on Gibson's office in *The Ticket of Leave Man*. To this office come Frank Meiklam, the elder Meiklam's nephew, to whom horse racing and share speculation are identical, Harrington and his elderly guardian Moleworth in order to pay off his account, Mrs. Markland and Mrs. Vernon, and finally Markland himself, to discover that his partner Meiklam has indebted their bank for the sum of 39,780 pounds. Disgrace and dishonor stare him in the face.

In contrast to the gaudy offices and feverish activity of clients in act 2, the bank setting for act 3 is somber and the tone is hushed and discreet. But all is not as it appears. Meiklam has concealed the bank's ledgers and is only too prepared to misappropriate Harrington and Molesworth's 40,000 pounds. Furthermore, he has been a trustee of Mrs. Markland's personal fortune and refuses to release her money to help her husband, on the grounds of banking propriety. Thus women's financial independence, as demonstrated by Mrs. Vernon, is shown to be ultimately spurious.

Act 4 starts interestingly in the middle of a birthday fete for Mrs. Markland. As the couples dance, Frank Meiklam urges Markland to try to persuade his wife's sister to marry him. He reveals that he knows of Markland's financial difficulties and threatens to expose the bank's misappropriations. Harrington proposes to Miss Hargreaves but gets more than he bargained for. Though she loves him, she plainly states her belief in female financial equality and independence in the management of money. Harrington is full of stuffy Victorian prejudices about women who bother to think about money at all, but she is not to be dissuaded and tells him that she has personally invested her fortune in a matter of her own choosing. When Frank Meiklam carries out his threat, and denounces Markland, his wife seeks his assurance that he is not the guilty party but he refuses to disclaim responsibility.

The last act is one of timely reversals. Markland is about to throw himself into the river when he is rescued by his wife's selfless love. Miss Hargreaves has undertaken to marry Frank Meiklam when the news arrives with a breathless Molesworth accompanied by the ubiquitous Rocket, that the Harrington securities have been saved from the stockbroker's hands. Harrington discovers that Miss Hargreaves's "investment" was the payment of the Markland debt. Frank Meiklam and his uncle are advised to emigrate hurriedly, and they leave cheekily with a total lack of acrimony.

The play has some fascinating elements and is a particular insight into Victorian attitudes to money and its management. Despite the acute independent views of Miss Hargreaves (whom as a character the *Times* found to be an encumbrance,)[41] there is nothing to suggest an alternative to accepted attitudes about the male dominance of financial matters. Mrs. Vernon is revealed to be largely self-seeking and brittle, the result, suggests Taylor, of meddling in unfeminine matters. Miss Hargreaves's views are revealed to be merely a ruse to conceal her act of generosity. Nevertheless, the views remain and are not discredited. Markland and his wife, played in the original production by Henry Neville (who had played Bob Brierly) and Kate Terry, are the least interesting of the characters because they are recipients of the action rather than instigators. Meiklam and his reprobate nephew emerge as likable rogues rather than villains, since their actions, though potentially disastrous, cause only temporary inconvenience. Their actions combine jauntiness and an outrageous flouting of ac-

cepted financial and social principles, and as characters they lack the
malevolence of a Hawksley in *Still Waters Run Deep*. Though the
world of speculation and the "fast buck" that they inhabit has a gloss-
iness and an excitement that Taylor himself obviously feels, there is
no doubt that his ultimate sympathies lie with the solidity of the
bank, whose respectable facade must be preserved in spite of the
shady dealings of its managers, and with the verity that it is love not
money that brings happiness.

   Mary Warner.   Though Kate Terry seems to have acted as an
inspiration for Taylor, she retired early from the stage. He had written five plays for her in two years and it seems to have exhausted him.
It was not until 1869 that he would return with two outstanding successes, both at the Haymarket Theatre: *New Men and Old Acres* and
Mary Warner, which anticipated the former by four months. He
wrote the play this time as a vehicle for Kate Bateman, an American-
born actress who had been living in England since 1851. She had
returned to England in 1868 after an American tour, and Taylor provided her with what the *Times* critic regarded as his best play since
The Ticket of Leave Man and the epitome of mid-Victorian domestic
drama.[42]

   Like Isobel in *East Lynne,* the character of Mary is central to the
story of the play and, as in the previous plays we have considered,
money is the emotional and narrative trigger. The story is of a wife's
selfless devotion to her husband who is falsely accused of stealing his
employer's money. She is prepared to go to prison for him and to endure his unmerited suspicion that she is a thief. After five years of
prison, she once again takes responsibility for a poor girl friend's lapse
in honesty. In the end, Mary and her husband George are reconciled
through the confession of the real thief, Levitt, who can no longer
tolerate his own guilty conscience. It is an interesting play, though
the *Times* tempered its praise by finding the characters "too uniformly
plebeian."

   The play is a case history of unquestioning devotion of the kind
advocated by Markham in *The Settling Day.* Mary, however, is unsentimental and even has an unforgiving pride when she thinks that
George is thankless. If she lacks anything, it is a sense of humor. She
feels that it is her duty to shoulder the burdens of others, and this
makes her unrelievedly serious and narrow-visioned. It is to this that
the *Times* review perhaps alludes. But the serious tone of the play sug-

gests that Taylor wished to insure that no frivolity would detract from his exemplary portrait of an idealized Victorian woman.

Historical and Verse Dramas

Between 1870 and his death Taylor devoted himself almost exclusively to writing verse plays, and plays illustrating a historical subject. He had, however, been interested in historical subjects since *Masks and Faces* in 1852, and had tried his hand successfully with verse (other than comic verse) in *The Fool's Revenge* in 1859. In his last period his verse plays, with the exception of *Twixt Axe and Crown,* were unsuccessful. Their historicism was dramatically clogging and their verse was pretentiously heavy. But with historical subjects that allowed a measure of freedom, Taylor was able to continue writing effective costumed melodrama.

Plot and Passion. Taylor had already demonstrated considerable flair for using quasi-historical settings as early as 1852. In *Masks and Faces,* however, the comic elements outweighed the melodramatic; in *Plot and Passion,* produced at the Olympic one year later, Taylor wrote about the world of spying and political intrigue set in Napoleonic France. It was the first of his French-inspired dramas for Wigan's new management, and the play became a personal triumph for Robson, who played the part of Desmarets. Although there was some later controversy about the play's originality, the story and plotting were Taylor's even if the original idea may have been suggested by John Lang, a minor novelist who wrote a novel on the same theme, *Secret Police,* in 1859. Nevertheless, the French setting and Taylor's attention to physical detail and the intricacies of plot immediately suggested what the *Times* called the play's "literary taste." It also drew attention to the play's dramatic shape that was an improvement on the "carelessness" of much contemporary writing. If there was a fault to be found, said the reviewer, it was in Taylor's tendency to make characters reflect, rather than demonstrate.[43]

As a dramatic piece its effectiveness rests on an audience's fascination with the clandestine world of spying and its trappings. Thus we have Fouché, Napoleon's spymaster, who operates a network of spies in order to keep ahead of any Bourbon plot to overthrow Napoleon. His agent is Desmarets, a sinister little man whose loyalty depends on the balance of power. Like any modern agent, he has taken care to secrete evidence of his master's deviousness for his own protection. With this world even we are familiar through the dramatizations of the novels of Ian Fleming and John Le Carré. We are also familiar with the characters who inhabit this world: heroines kept in subservience by their personal addictions to money, sex, or drugs, heroes who try to pit their wits against the malign forces, and the expendable dupes manipulated by their "controllers."

The Fool's Revenge.   Between 1853 and 1859, historical subjects continued to provide Taylor with a series of successful plays: *Two Loves and a Life* at the Adelphi Theatre in 1854, *The King's Rival* at the St. James's in the same year, *A Sheep in Wolf's Clothing* and *Payable on Demand,* both for the Olympic, in 1857 and 1859 respectively. Taylor's choice of subject for *The Fool's Revenge* was suggested to him by Robson who had seen a production of *Rigoletto* and felt that the character of the ridiculed jester would suit his mercurial ability to oscillate between wit and passion, that he had demonstrated as Desmarets. Taylor, however, decided to return to the original source in Victor Hugo's *Le roi s'amuse* and to adjust the sprawling romantic tragedy to the form of romantic melodrama. In particular he wanted to rectify what he took to be his original's lack of dramatic coherence and prepared climaxes. He further decided to change the location of the play to the world of the Italian Renaissance, a concession to its popular operatic adaptation.[44]

Robson rejected the play probably because he felt insecure with Taylor's chosen form of verse rather than prose. Taylor then offered it to Phelps at Sadler's Wells Theatre where it was produced with Phelps's scrupulous theatrical consistency on 18 October 1859. Critics were unanimously impressed by Taylor's adaptation, especially its marriage of the elements of Hugo and Verdi and the ingenuity of plotting that turned a "nightmare story" into "a wholesome English-natured plot."[45] By this they meant the adjustment of the character of Bertuccio, the jester, the engineering of a pure love interest for his daughter, Fiordelisa, and an exciting third-act climax that saves Bertuccio's daughter in the nick of time and purges him of his relentless desire for revenge.

Bertuccio maintains a double life. He is employed as a jester at the court of Count Manfredi where he has used his inviolable position to antagonize the servile courtiers who surround the Count. His bitterness stems from the fact that when he was a young notary his wife was abducted by Count Malatesta, seduced, and subsequently died.

This has resulted in a hatred of all aristocracy. In act 1 he is provided with an unexpected opportunity when the now aging Malatesta visits Manfredi accompanied by his young wife Ginevra. Bertuccio urges his immoral master Manfredi to abduct Ginevra but the enmity of the courtiers subverts this plan. They have heard that Bertuccio has a young mistress whom he is sedulously keeping away from the court, and they resolve to abduct her instead. Little does Bertuccio know that his moment of triumph against the "fair, false, big, brainless, outside shows of men" (*H,* 21) is a hollow one.

In act 2 the other side of Bertuccio's double life is revealed. He has told his pure young daughter Fiordelisa nothing of his employment and enters not dressed as a court jester but in the sober dress of a former notary. He has in fact kept her in complete ignorance of his background and even his real name. He also keeps her isolated from the world of the town in an effort to preserve her from the corrupting influences of courtly sophistication. But he is already caught in circumstances he can no longer control. His daughter has met a young poet Serafino dell'Aquila on one of her regular visits to church, and Manfredi and his friends have bribed their way into his house. They overhear Bertuccio's story to his daughter about his plan for revenge and, realizing that she is not his mistress, resolve to teach him a lesson. It has now become a struggle between aristocratic villains and a maltreated commoner. Before they can act, however, Aquila enters over the balcony to warn Fiordelisa that a plan to abduct her that evening is afoot, and, unknown to her father, she flees for the sanctuary of the Countess Malatesta who has befriended her. The scene is now set for the final irony. Bertuccio capers around the conspirators urging them on with their abduction outside the Malatesta palace. They themselves can hardly restrain their own mirth as they scale the walls, abduct a struggling figure, and leave a triumphant Bertuccio convinced that he has had his moment of triumph over Malatesta.

The third act forms a series of mounting climaxes which, said the *Times,* "ruthlessly screws the audience to the highest pitch of anxiety." It is a carefully planned series of reversals as Bertuccio's corrosive revenge is shown to be itself destructive. The momentum starts with a distraught Fiordelisa pursued by a relentless Manfredi. As she tries to get away, he calmly and remorselessly guides her to his private chambers. When Manfredi's wife arrives unexpectedly, whose jealousy has been fed by rumors of his numerous infidelities, Bertuccio loses no time in telling her of her husband's latest conquest. She resolves to kill her husband by poison and sends it in to Manfredi's chambers with the wine which is to be part of his seduction plan. At this point Malatesta enters together with his wife Ginevra and Bertuccio for the first time sees that his plan has gone awry. When Aquila enters with the news of Fiordelisa's abduction, the jester is devastated to realize that he has brought about his own daughter's destruction. He becomes frantic as laughter is heard from inside Mandredi's chambers but is prevented from entering. Only when there is a scream from inside are the doors thrown open to reveal Manfredi dead and Fiordelisa at his feet. She, however, is alive: "She never drank! Thou hast her pure as when / she kissed thy lips last night!" (*H*, 56). The shock drains Bertuccio of further thoughts of revenge while a grim faced Countess Manfredi challenges her husband's courtiers to apprehend her, as her father and his soldiers stand at the gates of the palace.

The last act is a most successful exercise in sustained tension. Throughout the play Taylor manages to evoke a sense of baroque corruption which marries with a Victorian depiction of filial and paternal love. He uses many of the favorite melodramatic devices of eavesdropping and secret passageways but integrates them naturally into the depiction of a Renaissance society governed by a passion for the clandestine and the devious. Though the character of d'Aquila is a sketchy one, introduced so that Fiordelisa should not be deprived of a hero nor of a domestic future, he is structurally important. It is his ingenuous act that brings about Bertuccio's downfall and final liberating catharsis.

Arkwright's Wife.   This was not one of Taylor's most successful plays but it is an interesting one. It brings together some of the elements he had explored in *Mary Warner,* especially the mutual dependence of husband and wife, and sets the exploitation of labor within a historical context—the Luddite riots of the mid-eighteenth century. In some ways the play is a curious anticipation of Hauptmann's *The Weavers,* especially in its depiction of a society caught between new, time-saving inventions and their threat to established modes of work and employment. The plot itself was suggested to Taylor by a historical story of John Saunders called *Joan Merryweather,* and the play was first toured before opening at the Globe in London on 6 October 1873.

Peter Hayes is a single-minded inventor obsessed with trying to perfect a new spinning machine. He and his daughter Margaret are rescued from their grinding poverty by Arkwright, a bluff, smooth talking Northerner from Bolton who is adept at seizing any proferred opportunities and developing any original ideas. Margaret and Arkwright are married and the whole family moves to Bolton. But Hayes is deeply suspicious of Arkwright and himself invites machine wreckers to enter Arkwright's house to smash the spinning jenny that Arkwright has been developing. That it should be based on Hayes's original idea is the key to the older man's intense jealousy.

The first two acts of the play gain their strength from the picture of demeaning poverty, the obsession with the new technology, and the toll that it exacts in human terms. Margaret is a central figure coping with her father's irrationality, her domestic insecurity with Arkwright who has absorbed some of her father's obsessiveness, and finally with bailiffs and determined, equally obsessed wreckers. The third act, however, set eight years later, is a disappointment given the framework of an exciting confrontation between technology and the terror of human redundancy. Taylor, like Robertson and Jones, was unprepared to allow events to triumph. Arkwright has now become a wealthy man. Margaret and her father whom he disowned in act 2 wander the countryside living off the allowance Arkwright has given them. In a setting of a picturesque ravine with a stream, a new mill, and cottages, Margaret almost single-handedly thwarts yet more machine wreckers from destroying Arkwright's property. After the mob backs off, Arkwright is reconciled with Margaret and even with Hayes to whom he promises a royalty for his share in the development of his invention. It is an unconvincing attempt to prettify the new world of technological progress. The reconciliation at the end is equally unsatisfying. It ignores Hayes's deep-seated hatred of Arkwright and unquestioningly accepts Margaret's eight-year-long devotion to Arkwright. Arkwright's motives and methods of self-advancement can also appear to us as suspect, but Taylor regards his enterprise and ingenuity as justifiable and even meritorious. What makes the play interesting, however, is its investigation of industrial unrest and Taylor's genuine feel for North Country manners and dialect. It is his only instance in which he relates to his own background.

Lady Clancarty. A few months after the opening of *Arkwright's Wife,* Taylor returned to the late seventeenth century for the subject matter of *Lady Clancarty,* which opened at the Olympic on 9 May 1874. He had first shown interest in this period and the Jacobites in

A Sheep in Wolf's Clothing. This time he set the play around the Assassination Plot of 1696 and conflated two historical incidents that he had read in Macaulay: the clandestine return to England of Clancarty, a proscribed follower of James II, his subsequent arrest, and final pardon through his wife's intercession, and the Plot itself with its eventual betrayal. It was to be Taylor's last play for the Olympic and his last popular success, with enough potential in the roles of Clancarty and his wife to attract the Kendal-Hare management of the St. James's Theatre as late as 1887. The play was written in prose, though Taylor continued to be attracted by verse and two years later would attempt his last verse drama with *Ann Boleyn.* It is also a play of character aided by plot rather than subservient to it, although the Clancartys' relationship depends on the narrative twist that they have not seen one another since childhood. The historical context gives the play little more than pseudo-authenticity and courtly glamor. The *Times,* in its review on 11 March found historical reality to be if anything an intrusion: "a number of persons . . . appear on the stage simply by virtue of their historical names and are not only ineffective in themselves but counteract the interest . . . carried on by the principal personages alone." Though history might provide the context and even the plot, it was the engagement of the characters with one another which provided the dramatic engine. This may appear to us as self-evident, but in the 1870s the shift from plot to characterization was a significant development in popular dramatic taste.

Taylor could provide some strong characters as we have seen but generally they only emerge as strong in relation to the events that confront them. Their inner strength is usually their unquestioning reliance upon social dictates or codes of behavior. Where there is some evidence of doubt, as in *New Men and Old Acres,* it is excused on the ground of temporary role playing or uninformed aberration. In his last plays Taylor continued his writing of considerable women's roles that he had begun in the early 1860s for actresses like Kate Terry. Despite the prominence of their roles, however, Taylor was unprepared to have them question their position in society or to grant them true independence. This reflected his own deep conservatism as well as his adherence to Victorian middle-class values, which by the time of his death in 1880 were already being questioned.

Chapter Four

Thomas William Robertson

"Poor Tom Robertson—it is, even today, the universal phrase of sorrow and affection that is used in speaking of him; of affection, because they who love the stage easily allow good fellowship to become a legend; of sorrow, because fate seemed always to have a blow prepared for Robertson while he lived. . . ." So wrote the dramatic critic of the *Times* to mark the centenary on 9 January 1929 of Robertson's birth. The occasion was further marked by a revival of his most enduring success, *Caste,* which had been originally produced in 1867. That Robertson should have been remembered so clearly is itself somewhat extraordinary, when successful contemporaries like Tom Taylor and H. J. Byron had long been forgotten. It suggested that critics and perhaps even audiences regarded him as something more than a man of his time. In fact, rightly or wrongly, Robertson was acknowledged by writers as disparate as W. S. Gilbert, Shaw, and Jacob Grein as the father of modern theater practice in England. Furthermore, that he should have died at the early age of forty-two gave romantic credence to the notion that "those whom the gods love, die young."

Robertson's Life and Career

His life and career were unexceptional for a would-be playwright in the nineteenth century. He was born into a theatrical family the year that Douglas Jerrold's *Black Eyed Susan* became a universal success. His family managed the provincial Lincoln circuit, but, in common with other stock companies, they were faring badly. Robertson's formal education ceased when he was twelve and he joined his family's company as a general handyman, managing the box office, performing juvenile roles, and acting as prompter. No doubt at his father's insistence he learned French in order to familiarize himself with the principal source of quick theatrical adaptations. It was armed with this, and little more, that he left the company for London in 1849.

From 1849 to 1860 his life was to be an endless series of professional setbacks and disappointments. He was employed by the publisher T. H. Lacy as a casual translator of French plays, while he tried his hand at writing original material. He supplemented his meager income by prompting for the Vestris management at the Lyceum Theatre in 1854 and by performing secondary roles at various minor theaters around London. He was later to call these his "starving engagements." In 1856 he married Elizabeth Burton, herself an actress. For the next two years they performed together throughout the provinces of England and also in Ireland, eking out a hand to mouth existence. About 1858 Robertson decided to devote himself wholly to writing. While his wife continued to act, he wrote feverishly: articles for magazines like the *Illustrated Times* and *Fun,* comic songs on commission, and plays, many of which were destined never to be performed.

In 1861, a short farce, *The Cantab,* had a reasonably successful run at the Strand Theatre. It brought him to the attention of the literary Bohemians of the London club world, in particular those of the Arundel and Savage Clubs. Robertson's journal contributions had already introduced him to the world of the working journalist which appreciated his ready wit and supply of anecdote. It was this association too that brought him into touch with E. A. Sothern. Sothern was a comedian. As we have seen his enormous popularity rested on his portrayal of the minor role of Lord Dundreary in Tom Taylor's *Our American Cousin.* Outrageous clothing and bizarre affectations on stage insured him a cult following for his London performances. Because he became so identified with this role, he depended on a supply of parts that would suit his eccentric style of acting. In 1863 he was looking for a suitable vehicle. Robertson had adapted a French original into a novel developing a fictitious incident in the life of David Garrick. Translated into stage terms, its appeal was obvious. Sothern, personally erratic and insecure, needed constant professional reassurance. The opportunity to play England's greatest eighteenth-century actor, adept at both comedy and tragedy, was too attractive to ignore. *David Garrick* opened first in Birmingham—Sothern wanted to test the water out before committing himself to a London season. It then transferred for a successful run in London at the Haymarket Theatre in 1864.

Robertson felt that he owed much to Sothern. He was also quick to realize that theatrical success meant tailoring his dramatic cloth to the abilities of a particular actor. He started work, therefore, on a new play that would again offer scope for Sothern's talents and those of the rest of the Haymarket company. The result was *Society,* which he gave to Sothern in early 1865. Though Sothern liked it he felt uncertain, in view of the fact that Buckstone, the Haymarket manager, had condemned it out of hand. Robertson then proceeded along the dispiriting path of hawking his manuscript around the theaters, but without success. It was eventually given a provincial premiere in Liverpool on May 1865. But Robertson was unsatisfied and to add to his setbacks, his wife, who had supported him through his years of disappointment, died at the age of twenty-nine.

In order to help his friend, H. J. Byron, himself a successful writer, journalist, and fellow club member, approached Marie Wilton who was managing the Prince of Wales Theatre in London. She had Robertson read it to her and it was produced at her theater in November 1865. So began the intimate relationship between playwright and theater that was to bring fame to both. *Society* was followed in 1866 by *Ours* and in 1867 by *Caste,* which formed the third consecutive success with the same company.

By 1867, Robertson was an established, popular playwright. A touring company was formed to play Robertson's major successes and, with *Caste* as the centerpiece, it traveled extensively for the next seventeen years. Robertson now had his first opportunity since he arrived in London in 1849 to rest on his laurels. He took a holiday in Germany where he married Rosetta Feist and wrote his next play for the Prince of Wales company. This was *Play,* which opened in 1868. When he returned to England, he resumed his habit of writing feverishly. He was, as a consequence, able to offer four plays to different theaters in the following year. At one point he had three plays being performed in London simultaneously: *Home,* at the Haymarket, *School* at the Prince of Wales, and *Dreams* at the Gaiety. *School* was to prove to be the last of Robertson's popular successes. Despite this, however, his output remained phenomenal and this exhausted him both physically and artistically. By the end of 1869, bronchial problems, exacerbated by a highly nervous temperament, started to become acute. He had little over a year to live. Perhaps conscious of the need to guarantee his family some measure of financial security, he wrote as much as he could for as many managers as possible. *Progress, Birth,* and *M.P.* were variations on themes implied in the titles of *Society* and *Caste. Dreams, The Nightingale,* and *War* were departures into a more serious style but were uniformly unsuccessful. The last was his only attempt at a seriously conceived thesis play that he wanted to be a plea for mutual understanding amid the hatreds generated by the Franco-Prussian War. It embodied Robertson's own need to reconcile his emotional and artistic allegiances to France and Germany. But by this stage, January 1871, it was too late. He had neither the artistic energy to be persuasive nor the ability to take a new dramatic direction. He died on 3 February 1871.[1]

Tentative Beginnings

Robertson's first produced play was a melodrama called *A Night's Adventure*, a disaster in 1851. Even *The Cantab* of 1861 brought him little satisfaction or notice. It was *David Garrick* that was to form a turning point in his career. Significantly, just as Douglas Jerrold's success had been inextricably tied to the career of a successful performer, T. P Cooke, so Robertson's attractiveness to the playgoers was tied to that of another popular star, E. A. Sothern.

David Garrick.   What was it about the play that appealed to both critic and playgoer? At first, they came to the Haymarket to see a popular star run through his repertoire of familiar tricks. They stayed, however, because the play extracted dimensions till then unrecognized in Sothern. Moreover, it had a refreshingly different approach to an enduring theme of popular theater: respectability outraged by the lovable antics of disreputable actors. If we compare the play with Robertson's later successes, we are likely to find only the barest sketch of his developed techniques. The play is a costumed melodrama with considerable injections of comedy. It provides an actor with a central bravura performance combining dashing histrionics with sentimental moralizing. It does, however, introduce us to a preoccupation of Robertson, the contradictions between superficial semblance and reality that he would later turn into a dramatic principle.

The play is set not in an aristocratic milieu but in the home of a middle-class merchant, Simon Ingot. His daughter, Ada, has fallen in love at the theater with the Romeo and Hamlet of Garrick. This infatuation threatens to ruin Ingot's plan to have her marry her apparently respectable cousin, Squire Chivy. Resourceful and wealthy, Ingot makes Garrick a financial offer to leave the stage and emigrate. Garrick, however, offers to disenchant Ada over a dinner party and pledges his word. "As a gentleman?" asks Ingot. "As an actor. Precisely the same thing," Garrick retorts (*PDW*, 158). The dinner party is attended by business friends of Ingot from the City of London who are vulgar, inept, and unrefined. Garrick is devastated to discover that Ada is the very girl who attracted his attention at the theater and whose enthusiasm acted as an inspiration for him some nights previously. The act ends with the company retiring for dinner.

What must have surprized Sothern in this act is the lack of opportunity for eccentric characterization. If anything, Garrick emerges as the "straight man" to the eccentricity of Ingot's friends, whose middle-class affectations Robertson ridicules. They fall asleep, fidget in agonies of social embarrassment, yet have the gall to comment unfavorably on Garrick's arrival by coach as above his station. It is their behavior that demonstrates Robertson's familiarity with the business of the "low comedian" which he had absorbed from his years with the Lincoln circuit. On the other hand, the character of Ada has an unexpected depth. She has the sentimentality of the Victorian heroine but she also has a mind of her own. Her rejection of Chivy, who assesses women in terms of racing fillies, shows considerable liveliness and a determination to tackle men on their own ground without coyness. Her father is a self-made man and a widower, yet his commercialism is offset by genuine concern for his daughter. He is determined that she will not suffer as he did when a poor employee of the East India Company.

But it must have been act 2 that convinced Sothern of the play's suitability. Robertson counterpoints shrieks of outraged propriety from the dinner guests with the roars of an outrageously drunk Garrick. In order to keep to his word Garrick convinces everybody but a complacent Ingot that he is the rogue and vagabond that everyone suspected. The act is carefully constructed to allow Garrick to play the drunken guest convincingly, as measured by the reactions of the other characters, and, as well, to reveal his own inner turmoil at the need to convince Ada. At the end, he storms out wrapped theatrically in a curtain he had torn from the windows, while savaging the assembled company with a line from Shakespeare's *Coriolanus*, "You common cry of curs, whose breath I hate" (*PDW*, 173). It has a seriousness undercut by the knowingly complacent Ingot and the apoplectic guests. A genuinely drunk Chivy then arrives. He has met Garrick on the road, and Ingot's plans are revealed. A jubilant Ada is ordered from the room by her discomfited father.

Act 3 is the most obviously artificial of the acts as Robertson resolves the problems raised. He changes the location to that of Garrick's lodgings and brings all the characters to them using concealment to expose their real motives. The need to organize a solution does not allow Robertson to do more than utilize dramatic conventions to unravel the plot. Even the characters assume conventional social attitudes. Ada's disconcerting personality, for example, is subordinated by her need to be a dutiful daughter. Garrick is given a treatise on filial duty that rides rather uneasily on the character of the actor so far presented. Ingot assumes the role, albeit briefly, of the stern, unforgiving father of a wayward daughter, rather like a figure in an Augustus Egg painting.

Nevertheless, even if act 3 proved a disappointment, the play was a success. Sothern's playing of the drunk scene insured it as a vehicle for any star actor wishing to combine showy extravagance with underlying sincerity. The play, as a consequence, would remain in the repertoire for actors like Charles Wyndham or John Martin Harvey to play as late as 1928. Enough was revealed of Robertson's potential to indicate that a new dramatic voice had been raised. The structure of act 2 showed a compositional skill that undoubtedly stemmed from his absorption of French models. Actors were pleased with the idiosyncratic vignettes of the minor characters because they were allowed to divest themselves if they wished of the older techniques of broad strokes of characterization. Finally, characters like Ada and her father, strong willed yet possessing a sense of humor and an endearing emotionalism, gave audiences the illusion of depth.

We can see that Robertson's innovations relate to technique rather than to substance. He was perhaps the first Victorian dramatist to realize the importance of ironic counterpoint. In *David Garrick* there is little to suggest innovations in theme, let alone any radical stance. The characters of Ingot's dinner guests do contain strong elements of satire directed against the monied upstarts among the middle classes, but they are muted by the pseudohistoricization of the eighteenth-century context. As we shall see, though Robertson was prepared to lampoon, he would always remain aware of the limits of middle-class tolerance.

Success and the Prince of Wales Company

Because Robertson's success always remained in later years associated with this particular theater, we need to examine why his play *Society* should have been consistently rejected by theater managers before it was taken up by Marie Wilton, and why she responded so favorably to it. Its run was extraordinarily successful and it established both Robertson's and the theater's reputations. In *David Garrick* we can see the uneasy expression of a very particular talent. It was a talent best seen in a grasp of appropriate and unexpected detail and in the ability to juxtapose comic strokes with acute observations of behavior. But the character of David Garrick occupied less of the centrality expected by traditional star actors. Managers might also be forgiven for thinking that the story line had been sacrificed for individually telling situations. On these grounds *Society* appeared even more radical. Though the part of the hero, Sidney Daryl, was intended for Sothern, it offered no bravura potential at all. Moreover, the rest of the characters suggested an unusual degree of unanimity in performance, rather than the collections of eccentric mannerisms with which audiences identified specific actors.

At the same time, Marie Wilton was consciously trying to attract a particular audience to her theater. Her avowed intention was to woo West End playgoers to a small theater off the beaten track and which itself had seen better days.[2] She herself was a popular burlesque actress. She had surrounded herself with actors who believed in her aims and complemented one another's talents. Those who would contribute most to identifying the theater with the works of Robertson were Squire Bancroft, whom she would later marry, and John Hare, who would play the comic roles and later become a distinguished theater manager in his own right. All Marie Wilton needed in 1865 was a playwright who would provide them with a vehicle that would, at the same time, reflect the mores of the audience she hoped to attract: "No mere chance brought them together. Their union at the Prince of Wales's was almost as inevitable as it was timely."[3]

Society. We can see in act 1 glimpses of what would fascinate playgoers and critics alike. In scene 1 the setting is the rather seedy chambers of Sidney Daryl, a poor and hardworking lawyer. They are visited by Tom Stylus, a cynical and disillusioned journalist, and by the Chodd family, father and son. The Chodds are vulgar and energetic materialists who believe that the key to social acceptance lies in having "lots of brass" and a ready checkbook. Sidney is to be persuaded to show Chodd Junior the way to becoming a "real gentleman." Tom's interest, however, lies in the fact that Chodd Senior wishes to invest money in a daily newspaper that will require the services of an experienced journalist as its editor. While Sidney and

Chodd Junior discuss his future, the chambers are invaded by a bailiff, Moses Aaron, demanding immediate payment of a debt, by prize fighters with whom Sidney enjoys warm relations, and finally, by Little Maud, a young child upon whom Sidney inexplicably lavished gifts and affection. Obviously he has considerable emotional as well as sporting commitments. Nevertheless, he rejects Chodd Junior's offer to reward him handsomely for any social introductions: "My friends are my friends; they are not marketable commodities" (*PDW*, 695). It is enough to insure him Chodd's enmity.

There is little of the conventional exposition about this scene. Although the character of Sidney—poor but a man of discrimination—is unexceptional, he is surrounded by a surprizing collection of characters who speak unselfconsciously in the jargon of journalism and prizefighting. It reveals Sidney's catholicity of social taste. He is quite prepared to tolerate his relative poverty since it is the key to his cosmopolitanism and the ready acceptance of him by all social classes. At the same time, there is an uncompromising belief that money cannot buy social credibility. And, however wealthy the Chodds may be, they lack the essential ingredient of social status.

The second scene reveals that Sydney is in love with the niece of Lord and Lady Ptarmigant. She too is called Maud. They disapprove of Sidney's poverty and lack of prospects. Consequently, the two lovers must meet surreptitiously. Robertson changes the scene to the garden of a West End square. He specifies a visual and aural texture that includes a street band in the distance and the reflections of the setting sun in the windows of the surrounding houses. Across the stage stroll nursemaids with children and Life Guardsmen in uniform. There is a strongly realistic texture against which Sidney and Maud try to exchange pledges of their love. It forces the scene to be antiromantic in tone as they combine the affectionate and the furtive. They cram as much as they can into the few minutes they have before nine o'clock strikes and Maud's aunt and uncle arrive. This gives the situation an amusing urgency which culminates in Sidney's exasperated reminiscence of *Dr. Faustus* as the clock strikes: "Why doesn't time stop, and Big Ben refuse to toll the hour?" (*PDW*, 698).

With the entry of the Ptarmigants, the play enters a world of genteel farce. Lady Ptarmigant, "a very grand, acid old lady," is the predecessor of Wilde's Lady Bracknell. In her shadow trails her husband, "a little old gentleman," who promptly falls asleep in any convenient chair and, like Lewis Carroll's Dormouse, only wakes when absolutely necessary. All that Sidney and Maud can do in the face of such authority is to keep silent. The Chodds enter and escort Maud and Lady Ptarmigant out. The act ends with Sidney, while trying to catch a last glimpse of Maud, falling over the sleeping Lord Ptarmigant's legs.

The attractions of act 1 lie in its juxtapositions of old recognizable forms with a new and ironic point of view.[4] It also gives us another clue why more traditional theater managers might have rejected the play. Robertson writes with idiomatic informality. The dialogue is suggestive rather than explicit and no apologies are made for the use of specialized vernacular. At the same time, there are strong sentimental elements cheek by jowl with knockabout farce. There is also perhaps a slightly iconoclastic suggestion that snobbery and a concern with social status are as unattractive in the Ptarmigants as they are in the Chodds.[5]

The second act is divided into two scenes that reflect contrasting milieus. The first concerned Robertson deeply. Set in a room of a public house inhabited by journalists and literary hacks, the characters of the "Owl's Roost" were modeled on existing figures of the Bohemian literary world. Their dialogue and behavior were authentic. Robertson felt as a consequence that his "revelation" of private behavior might be interpreted as a betrayal of confidence. In fact, the scene was received as a tour de force. "Up to this time," wrote Clement Scott, "we had not heard much dialogue like this on the modern English stage. I mean dialogue that contained such humorous banter, such cheerful cynicism."[6]

The second scene is set in the world of aristocratic society—a soirée at the Ptarmigants. With this Robertson is less happy. Instead of characters there are stereotypes of aristocratic eccentricity. Its dramatic function is to contrast a world of genial bonhommie as seen in the "Owls Roost" with the forced gaiety of a world of horse racing, cards, and quadrilles. In the midst of this the well-heeled dandies casually go to Parliament to bring down the government and force an election. Despite an evident lack of personal experience of such a society, Robertson was to remain fascinated by its ways. Throughout the two scenes the conflict between Sidney and the Chodds intensifies as Maud unwillingly allows her engagement to Chodd Junior to be announced, and Sidney gate-crashes the Ptarmigant party to denounce her as faithless and to win handsomely from Chodd Junior at cards. There is no lack of strong situations as act 2 ends with Sidney pushing his way drunkenly through a crowd of dancers.

Act 3 brings together the various elements of society we have seen so far. Sidney challenges Chodd Junior at the polls for his own family seat, aided by Tom Stylus, the denizens of the Owl's Roost, and Sidney's prize-fighting associates. Despite her agreement to marry him, Chodd finds he is more interested in politics than Maud. To his chagrin he is worsted both in love and at the hustings as Sidney wins the seat, becomes a baronet on the convenient death of his elder brother, and smooths away any misunderstandings with Maud. Even Lady Ptarmigant has a change of heart as she discovers that Little Maud is her dead son's child for whom Sidney has been secretly caring.

The development of the act is contained within three interlocking contrapuntal scenes as Robertson brings the differing levels of society together. Again the low life characters on the fringes of polite society have an immediacy that springs from personal observation. The behavior of the Ptarmigants, however, has an arbitrariness that makes us rather impatient, particularly in the light of the vigor and inventiveness of Robertson's other creations.

Successful the play certainly was, assisted by the playing of Marie Wilton and her future husband, Squire Bancroft. It was a happy conjunction. The genteel ambiance of the Prince of Wales Theatre, a sense of freshness about the new venture, and the belief of the middle-class audience that it was on the threshhold of a new social era all contributed to the creation of an ensemble between playwright, actors, and audience.[7] Furthermore, the play does contain some genuinely fresh ideas. It cannot be called a thesis play nor does it aim to analyze the composition of English society, despite its title. What it does suggest is that society can be depicted in a more complex manner than previous writers were prepared to explore. It asks questions about the relative values of wealth and breeding and, rather disconcertingly, suggests that snobbery and hypocrisy are not the preserves of any one social class. As a comedy, its originality lies in Robertson's ironical depictions of human relationships. These are exemplified by the "love scenes" between Sidney and Maud and Chodd Junior and Maud. They come as a surprise. Both scenes exhibit conventional attitudes and sentiments but both are undercut by the situations in which the protagonists find themselves. Sidney and Maud can only snatch a few moments together while Chodd pays less than undivided attention to Maud's reluctant marriage agreement as he listens in act 3 to the progress of the election poll outside. The other strength lies in the accuracy with which Robertson can depict the society with which he is familiar—the cavalier world of the "Owls Roost."

Ours. After the euphoria of the successful season, the Wilton company looked to Robertson for another vehicle. He offered a play that he had written in 1864. *Ours* was even more radical than *Society,* so much so that the Wilton company tried it out in Liverpool before transferring to London. They need not have worried. John Oxenford, the *Times* reviewer, led critics in suggesting that playwright and company had brought a new era to the London stage.[8]

Although *Ours* is labeled "an original comedy," Clement Scott remembered it as "one of the most stirring and dramatic little plays that Robertson ever wrote."[9] In strict terms *Ours* refers to a military regiment, but the play's title also encompasses the whole idea of "belonging." Human relationships are investigated: do the men and women of the play "belong" to the appropriate partners? Do the people with money deserve their possessions? But the position here is much more complex than in *Society.* Wealth is represented by the figure of Hugh Chalcot whose money has come from industry. Unlike the Chodds, however, he is no vulgarian. Like Brown in Taylor's *New Men and Old Acres,* Chalcot possesses a sensitivity that he cloaks with an elaborate mask of misanthropy and cynicism. His is probably the most interesting of Robertson's creations so far. He is not the obvious sentimental hero but a raisonneur who interprets and also deflates intentions and situations. Thus Robertson brings together elements found in Garrick and Tom Stylus within the one character. He is also able to blend comedy (insofar as everything ends happily) with a tale of love and honor.[10] The opening of the play has an almost Chekhovian atmosphere of autumn. There is the sleeping figure of a man. As autumn leaves fall, two figures casually come together, one in uniform, and discuss the time of day. As they wander off, two women enter and talk about their relative stations in life. It is deliberately "untheatrical." The scene has none of the expositional bustle that we might expect; it gives the audience time to evaluate what is being said within a mood of melancholy and warmth. The unconventional opening would have been enough to worry any theater management concerned with immediately entertaining an audience.

The characters that Robertson introduces are themselves interesting. The uniformed Sergeant Jones is a bluff, good-humored subaltern bringing up a large family despite his appalling wages. The two girls, Blanche and Mary, introduce us to what will become a favorite Robertsonian device, that of contrasting two young women whose views oscillate between the idealistic and the down-to-earth. Blanche, as the name suggests, is the sentimental heroine, while Mary is sprightly and realistic. Blanche has wealth, while Mary is the "poor" companion. Blanche is in love with poor Angus McAlister, while Mary is in the throes of indecision about wealthy Hugh Chalcot, who seems determined to irritate and antagonize her unnecessarily.

The sleeping figure of Hugh wakes and immediately puts into practice his reputation for churlish behavior. This is interrupted by the appearance of Lady Shendryn. At once we are reminded of Lady Ptarmigant but now described as "languishing, sentimental and frisky (PDW, 427): in other words, a bundle of neurotic contradictions. She is thus far more developed as a character. She is much younger than Sir Alexander, her husband, but she dominates him by preying on his guilt about an indiscretion that he has committed in the past. Chalcot, however, is shown to be not the easy cynic to whom Mary objects. In a scene between Hugh and the penniless Angus, Hugh reveals something of his inner turmoil. He feels a profound distrust of those around him. He has inherited all his money and earned none of it. Bitter experience has taught him that he is regarded as a convenient prey by prospective wives. The result is that he finds wealth and generosity awkward. When he tries to be generous to Sergeant Jones he is dismally self-conscious about it.

The action has taken place at the Shendryns' with a croquet party in progress. When rain starts to fall guests take shelter, leaving Blanche and Angus isolated under one tree and the Shendryns under another. As the young couple tentatively articulate their feelings toward one another, their conversation is counterpointed by that of the Shendryns constantly bickering, a picture of the soured affections of those who have nothing but their own recriminations to hold them together. It is a clever device, an object moral lesson yet retaining its naturalness as the act closes with the rest of the guests returning with umbrellas and inconsequential banter. There is no curtain scene but the quality of a filmic dissolve.

Despite his many reservations about Robertson, even William Archer, a dedicated Ibsenite, found act 1 impressive. With the value of hindsight, he could see affinities between later realism and the play's illusion of reality through the use of minute, characteristic touches. The conflict in Chalcot, for instance, between instinctual generosity and his gauche inability to give it expression, the disturbing sketch of middle-aged marriage and, in particular, the conclusion of the act. It is indeed unparalleled in Victorian popular theater so far. The umbrellas, the rainfall, and the contrapuntal dialogue between the two couples demonstrated for Archer "the genius of the commonplace" and were enough for him to label Robertson "a pre-Raphaelite of the theatre."[11]

Act 2 brings the matter of "belonging" to a head, set against preparations for Sir Alexander's regiment to leave for the Crimean War. Because departure is imminent, the emotional relationships become desperately immediate. Mary and Lady Shendryn are at their most defensive and they express a view of marriage that sounds positively iconoclastic. Both see it as a continuous battle, at best "a blessing which cannot be avoided" (*PDW*, 447). Blanche is noncommittal but reacts nervously at the mention of Angus. Before Sir Alexander can take his leave, he asks Chalcot to perform a private mission for him which his wife readily interprets as the maintenance of a private life in which she does not share. The scene culminates in her adamant refusal to see him off despite the tearful protests of Blanche and Mary. To offset her attitude, Robertson makes her undertake to care for the large family of Sergeant Jones, part of the social aspect of "belonging."

By contrast, the scene of parting between Blanche and Angus has the tremulous quality of Chekhov. "This scene," say the stage directions (*PDW*, 454), "is to be broken up by frequent pauses." Time is running out as Angus asks her for a token to carry with him, as though he were embarking on a knightly quest. The regimental band is heard in the distance playing "Annie Laurie" as they stand near the door: "Angus goes to the door, embracing Blanche. They form Millais' picture of the "Black Brunswicker' " (*PDW*, 455). The stage direction fixes Robertson's attitude toward soldiers and the panoply of war. To him they form the world of bravery and romance that purges its participants of everyday triviality. This is a view that even someone as boisterous and unconventional as Mary is made to share: "Better be a soldier than anything" (*PDW*, 459). In the background there is the insistent sound of the band playing "The British Grenadiers" and "The Girl I Left Behind Me." The stage directions call for sounds of cheering and the tramp of columns of soldiers. Chalcot is caught

up in the excitement and vows to buy a commission, the women tear-
fully wave handkerchiefs, and the act ends in what Michael Booth has
called "the most rousing and theatrically effective expressions of patriotic feeling on the nineteenth century stage."[12]

What makes the act distinctive is its aural and visual texture. The
piquancy comes from the misapprehensions that cannot be resolved
in time. The moments of contact become fleeting as parting becomes
inevitable. In the midst of this Robertson retains the wryness of the
Mary/Chalcot relationship which, however, is stilled by the departure
of the troops. The deliberate pictorialization of the Blanche/Angus relationship to evoke the resonances of a popular painting shows the
affinity of aim between the stage and nineteenth-century genre painting.[13] The use of music is particularly important. It carefully integrates the very essence of melodrama—its music—into the fabric of
the action rather than leaving it merely on the level of an emotional
guide for the audience.

Act 3 wrenches the action from the world of London society to that
of the Crimean battlefront. Though Robertson had no firsthand
knowledge of the war, he compensates by making his constructed environment as realistically detailed as possible. The hut in which Angus and Chalcot bivouac is grubby and dilapidated. But Chalcot has
changed dramatically. His appearance is "entirely altered, hair rough,
long beard, face red and jolly, his whole manner alert and changed"
(*PDW*, 463). He has obviously found the reason for being that he
lacked in act 1. It appears as though the act will chart the tempering
of the men's characters in the forge of wartime experience. In fact,
the war does make itself felt as soldiers leave for sorties and excursions
throughout the act. But inventiveness and reality once again come
into conflict with dramatic conventions. Robertson suddenly has
Blanche, Mary, and Lady Shendryn appear at the front as though they
were on a charmingly exotic excursion. Despite the fact that society
groups can be documented in the Crimea, dramatically they are out
of place.[14] It leaves Robertson open to the criticism that his dramatic
imagination lacked independence and courage.[15]

Even Robertson must have felt uncomfortable with this situation.
The coincidence of the ladies' arrival prompts Chalcot to say, "If this
were put in a play, people would say it was improbable" (*PDW*,
471). It trivializes the dramatic potential and all too conveniently resolves the important issues in unlikely personal terms: Sir Alexander's

secretive actions that so incensed his wife are proved to be merely his concealment of his brother-in-law's forgeries. Angus becomes a military hero and Chalcot is a man redeemed and self-confident. Once again, however, Robertson's eye for effective juxtaposition is seen in the development of the relationship between Mary and Chalcot. She shows her ability to cope with any kind of difficulty and helps the wounded Chalcot to prepare food using the few available items to make the best out of very little. Their mutual dependence turns to admiration and, finally, Chalcot is able to propose and be accepted. The scene has a vigor and robust humor as they discover culinary uses for the objects found in the hut. But the act is generally a disappointment after the unusual effectiveness of the previous two.

If we tend to see the resolution of the play as the surrender of reality to fairy-tale fantasy, it appeared to audiences of the time as perfectly satisfying. Part of its appeal lay in evoking the same heady patriotism that had responded to the publication of *The Charge of the Light Brigade* in 1854. But the play shows clearly the tensions operating in the work of a popular dramatist. Both *Society* and *Ours* reveal Robertson to be a dramatist with an ironic vision of relationships between people and a flair for effective juxtaposition. At the same time, his repertoire of situations is limited by audience tolerance and by his own reluctance to flout theatrical convention. Had he done so, he might have anticipated Shaw, but he would have failed in the 1860s.

What can be construed as dramatic failure in *David Garrick*—the juxtaposition of the old and the new—now becomes for Robertson a dramatic principle. This is particularly evident in his love scenes, where indirection and external circumstances constantly threaten to undermine the elements of sentimentality. Part of a new, and perhaps limiting, principle becomes evident in *Ours*. Robertson's choice of characters is becoming increasingly formalized: two contrasting heroines, one idealistic and sentimental, the other, resourceful and pert; two contrasting male leads distinguished by money or status; a representative of the upper class and of the working class. In this he was being directly influenced by the personnel of the Prince of Wales company. The burlesque experience of Marie Wilton made her ideal for the pert roles, while Lydia Foote played the soft heroines. Squire Bancroft made the most of his rather narrow histrionic abilities by playing the languid but good-hearted "swells" while John Hare played the gallery of eccentrics. While it made good sense to tailor

his parts to the company's abilities, Robertson was to find this a trap
when he tried to write for other theaters, whose actors lacked the
sense of cohesion upon which his plays increasingly depended.

   Caste.   When he reviewed a revival of *Caste* in 1897, Shaw saw
only too clearly the mechanics of Robertson's playwriting. He was
careful, however, to place Robertson within the context of the 1860s.
He could see, for instance, that Robertson's introduction of everyday
commonplaces in dialogue and setting was the key to his novelty at
the time. Similarly, his characters were eminently recognizable stereotypes enlivened by unexpected qualities.[16] In 1867, however, the mechanics were not as noticeable. Even in 1929, a revival of *Caste* was
able as we have seen to evoke memories of "the good old days" and
Robertson himself. It is also worth recording that the play still remains in the theatrical repertoire of English provincial companies.

   With *Caste,* Robertson was able to score his third consecutive success with the Prince of Wales company. He had written a short story,
entitled "Rates and Taxes and How They were Collected," in 1866
for a Christmas volume. It was a pathetic story contrasting English
domesticity with the background of the Indian Mutiny. When he re-
wrote it for the stage it retained many of its literary resonances.
Clement Scott found it to be the most Thackerayan of Robertson's
plays. It is also his most economical. There is a tightly knit cast of
eight that explores some of the issues already raised in *Society.* The
title suggests at the very least a seriocomic investigation of the class
war. Nothing, however, in Robertson's writing should lead us to expect a thesis writer, and, if we look for any kind of investigative
reporting, we are bound to be disappointed. Nevertheless, from a
dramaturgical point of view, *Caste* represents the high point of Robertson's writing. He was never again able to achieve the same econ-
omy nor the same aptness of detail and structural juxtaposition.
Despite these points, however, *Caste* remained in the nineteenth century less popular than either *Ours* or his later play *School.* In part this
is because both of the latter are "public" plays while *Caste* is "private." In the former Robertson tries to make the resonances and attitudes more overtly social, while in *Caste* the decisions of the
protagonists have relevance only to themselves and the sentiment is
kept strictly within the parameters of the sentimental characters, Esther and George D'Alroy.

   The first act of the play tests out the validity of Tennyson's resounding lines that "True hearts are more than coronets, / And sim-

ple faith than Norman blood."[17] These words are quoted by George D'Alroy, who is determined to marry Esther, a poor, hardworking actress. He is the scion of a wealthy and ancient family; she is merely the daughter of a drunken wastrel. It is a situation constantly explored and varied in melodrama. To balance this view, George's friend, Captain Hawtree, offers a far more cynical and worldly attitude which he vindicates by referring to Esther's father, Eccles. Eccles is Robertson at his best, a character study of a ne'er do well, at once servile and ruthlessly predatory. On the other hand, Esther and her sister Polly are immediately engaging. Esther is responsible and unsentimental about her responsibility. Polly is vivacious and full of unexpected actions and turns of phrase. Her "half burlesque" actions were written specifically with Marie Wilton in mind, and she manipulates the bemused Hawtree like a self-possessed chorus girl. Polly, however, is also eminently sensible and her affections are for Sam Gerridge, the hardworking opposite of Eccles. When Sam enters, Robertson gets the most out of his confrontation with Hawtree. Sam views him with extreme suspicion and has an equally rigid view of social caste.

The act has only one scene, whose function is to precipitate Esther and George into marriage despite the objections of Hawtree, the misgivings of George about his future father-in-law, and Esther's own uncertainties. He formally proposes to her when the postman brings Esther a letter offering employment at a theater in Manchester. But the curtain does not fall on this moment of decision and happiness. The door is flung open and a drunk Eccles reels into the room. Esther is filled with embarrassment and George is left thoughtfully "pulling his moustache" (*PDW*, 97). If this is what marriage into the Eccles family will entail, then the problems have yet to be faced.

Act 2 changes the location from the poor house of the Eccles family in Stangate to George and Esther's new home in Mayfair. This is the physical difference in conditions into which Esther has married. Robertson, however, gives us little time to measure the success of the new marriage. George has been posted to India together with Hawtree. Implausibly the action turns on George's inability to tell Esther about his departure. This comes about with the arrival of his mother, the Marquise de St. Maur. She is closely related as a character to Lady Ptarmigant and Lady Shendryn in the earlier plays. Dramatically, she represents the antithesis to Eccles but lacks his keenly observed character traits. Instead, Robertson has her mouth platitudes from Froissart's *Chronicles* and espouse a dogmatic view of male duty that endears her to nobody and is a calculated insult to Esther. It places George in a quandary which Robertson refuses to resolve. We have noted that Robertson admired the figure of the knight errant. The act ends, therefore, with a half-fainting Esther going through the ritual of buckling on George's sword "to please my mother," as the remainder of the characters stand around apologetically.

It is a less than satisfactory conclusion. We know nothing more about George's marriage, and the location in Mayfair turns all the lively lower-class characters into mere intruders. It thus robs the act of vigor. But we also feel disappointment with the character of the Marquise. William Archer regarded her as "a great blot" on the play's integrity. On the one hand, Robertson's sympathies lie with the heroic, soldierly sentiments that she parades. On the other, she and Eccles are impediments to happiness and are therefore to be rejected in a comedy. In her case, however, Robertson refuses to satirize, and thereby, implicitly, to make up his mind. It is with some relief that the final act returns to the house in Stangate.

As though freed from his uncomfortable burden, Robertson can now write with great conciseness and energy. An initial scene between Polly and Sam, played against a full-length portrait of George draped in black and with a baby's bassinette very much in evidence, succinctly provides the information we need to know. George is dead and the family has come down in the world. They have not been assisted by the spendthrift habits of Eccles. To show this Robertson engineers Eccles to be left alone with Esther's baby. Half-drunk and full of his sly ability to seize the main chance, Eccles decides to take action in the name of financial equality. He steals the baby's coral ornament to pawn for money. It is to Robertson's credit that he is able to make the little scene both amusing and pathetic. Eccles cannot be utterly damned since he is, after all, the heroine's father. He can be, however, an amusing scoundrel. In fact, he does not succeed in his intention because Esther enters in time.

In the two scenes that follow, pitting Esther against her father and then against her mother-in-law, the Marquise, Robertson pulls out all his emotional stops. To a modern reader they may well appear "humorless and emotion burdened," undercutting any "truth to life."[18] But in part this is caused by the unexpected strength of Esther for which we are unprepared. It is difficult to ascribe the vengeful fury that subdues Eccles and throws out the Marquise to a newly developed sense of motherhood. But we are presented with this as the obverse of the coin of demure charm.

Though this is an unparalleled reversal, the relationships between characters remain as they have been presented so far. Just at this point, George, clutching a can of milk, makes his surprise entrance. After the initial shock, George and the audience are informed of Eccles's misuse of money and Hawtree's surreptitious financial assistance to the family, a generosity that causes Sam to reassess Hawtree and to confirm in George's mind that "there is something in caste." Polly pleads that there is good in her father; it is a desperate last ditch attempt to retrieve something of Eccles's standing.

After Esther has been carefully informed that her husband is alive after all, the Marquise enters to make amends. It is an awkward and unmotivated entrance given her previous confrontation with Esther. But by then the action is finished. Eccles and the Marquise represent two social polarities that can only be swept under the carpet in the interests of a happy ending. The focus is on reconciliation and good humor. Though Hawtree and Sam have come to acknowledge each other's good points, few lessons have been learned. George can still end the play saying: "Caste is a good thing if it's not carried too far. It shuts the door on the pretentious and the vulgar: but it should open the door very wide for exceptional merit" (*PDW,* 143). It may sound to us like an unsatisfactory emollient. Robertson's audience, self-aware and jealous of their middle-class status, would have been in total harmony with what might appear to sound like aristocratic exclusiveness.

As Michael Booth suggests in his edition of Robertson's plays, the class war is seen here in essentially comic terms. It is thereby rendered harmless and palatable. Sentiment and heroism are, after all, the elements that are of paramount importance. If the strengths of the play are not to be found in any social evaluation or comment, they lie in the "ingenious contrapuntal structure and the rich, comic vigor of situation and character as well as in the detailed and loving observation of a lower middle class setting. . . ."[19] The success of *Caste* was assured, and Robertson was able to go on his well-deserved holiday to Germany.

Play. Enthused by his stay in Germany and encouraged by his new marriage to Rosetta Feist, he submitted his next play to the Prince of Wales Theatre. Called simply *Play,* it is labeled a comedy. Unfortunately, it has little comic potential in a story line that concerns itself with unscrupulous fraud and the gaming tables. It is, moreover, set in Germany, and its visual setting of landscapes and castle ruins creates a kind of Gothic romanticism antipathetic to comedy. There is little novelty or inventiveness. By this time Robertson was able to write to a formula that the Prince of Wales actors could apply effortlessly. Marie Wilton would play the independent and spirited Rosie, Lydia Foote, after Esther, would play the rejected and unrecognized actress wife Amanda, Squire Bancroft would play yet another upper-class "swell," the Chevalier Browne, and John Hare, after Ptarmigant and Shendryn, would play the silly old guardian, Fanquehere.

The play's predictability is offset by the exotic locations but they merely accentuate the reliance on eccentric or colorful extras: German peasants, foreigners who speak no English, and laughable self-made men of commerce. That the play's formulaic quality was recognized immediately perhaps explains its lack of subsequent success. It remained unrevived by the Bancrofts despite the sensitivity of a love scene between Rose and her lover, Frank Price.

School. With *School,* which opened in January 1869, we come to the last of Robertson's great popular successes. Though we need to take Victorian taste into consideration to explain why this play should have displaced *Caste* in esteem, it is nonetheless true that it was revived more than 800 times under the Bancrofts' managements. On closer examination we will see that the play is a dramatic celebration of those apparently contradictory elements in Robertson's writing, his meticulous search for detailed reality on stage and his propensity for the world of fantasy. Wish fulfillment is a commonplace of Victorian fiction. It is often set amid detailed dissections of human behavior and environment such as we find in the novels of Charles Dickens. The contradictions that result are reconciled by suspending normal logic in favor of intervening coincidence in the interests of natural justice. We are not shown Oliver Twist succumbing to the horrors of abject poverty. He is redeemed and rescued through an act of personal generosity. Thus Esther's poverty in *Caste,* for instance, and her consequent self-reliance, are of no further significance when George miraculously reappears. Browne's conversion from self-centered scoundrel, in *Play,* to appreciative husband is brought about by his abused wife's act of forgiveness. This is the stuff of fairy stories.

The most popular Victorian fairy story was *Cinderella* and it is to

this that Robertson looked as a source of plot. *School* derives its plot
formally from a German original, *Aschenbroedel*, by Roderich Benedix.
It opened on 16 January 1869 at the Prince of Wales Theatre at a
time when other theaters were still running their Christmas pantomimes. The connections are obvious. Not only does the curtain rise
to strains of Rossini's *Cenerentola*, but the setting is "a glade" with a
group of schoolgirls listening to the story of Cinderella. The play
never ventures from this pastoral setting into the real world, giving
it an unrealistic timelessness. The principal characters are, by now,
Robertsonian stereotypes: two contrasted heroines, Naomi and Bella,
the one rich and practical, the other a poor orphan. In charge of the
school, are the Sutcliffes, mismatched oddities like the Shendryns,
forever quarreling. They are out of touch with youth and its aspirations and live on memories and borrowed time. There is Beau Farintosh, an old man desperately hanging onto his youth and dressing, in
act 1, in exaggerated high fashion. If pantomime is close to the sur-
face, then he is the epitome of the Pantomime Dame, shortsighted
and a figure of fun. But he is also the Fairy Godmother in disguise.
He reemerges in act 4 dressed as a distinguished old gentleman to
claim Bella as his lost granddaughter. The antithesis to this figure is
the Ogre, here the school porter Krux. He revels in destructiveness
for its own sake, though Robertson suggests motives of lower-class
envy. Finally, there are the young heroes, Lord Beaufoy and Jack
Poyntz. They are the least satisfactory either in real terms or those of
pantomime. Though Beaufoy is the equivalent of the Prince Charming, his elegantly aristocratic persona is that of a London drawing
room and hence out of place in the sylvan setting of the play. Jack
Poyntz, if he has a pantomime equivalent, is Buttons, a jester living
on his wits. But again, possibly because the role was designed for
Squire Bancroft, Poyntz is given an irrelevant world-weariness. His
lines do little more than turn him into a self-conscious prig.

The audiences of 1869, however, were uncritical. They were
charmed by the settings and the pervasive nostalgia. There is constant
reference to the pleasures of school. The Sutcliffes constantly hark
back to their own lost youth. Farintosh desperately wishes to find the
child of his dead son. In act 3, with cigar smoke rising slowly in the
evening air and the moon throwing long shadows over the Park,
Beaufoy is moved to exclaim "Beautiful simplicity!—how you are ne-
glected in this nineteenth century!" (*PDW,* 657). With this the in-

dustrious, middle class audience would have concurred. Self-awareness brought in its wake a nostalgia for past innocence which could, however, partly be assuaged by cheap excursion fares to the countryside.

The last act resolves everything. Bella, who has been dismissed from her position in the school on the grounds of unseemly behavior, returns as Lady Beaufoy "dressed as a bride." Beaufoy assumes the power as Prince to chastise the doubters and cynics. With costumed footmen, a stray pumpkin, and even a wedding present of a pair of glass slippers, the action becomes unashamedly that of the pantomime story. It ends in a final tableau with Beaufoy kneeling at Bella's feet to put on one of the slippers as the older models of respectability pronounce a blessing that is a catalog of Victorian ideals about true nobility.

School is a play about young people and those to whom youth and its loss is a matter for regret. Its enduring success owed much to this. When the play was revived in 1899 by John Hare, its reception was cool. With England at war in South Africa and the world on the brink of a new century, milk jugs and cigars by moonlight must have seemed irrelevant. Perhaps the *Daily Telegraph*'s critic summons up best the sense of regret: "Everyone ought to see *School* whether they like it or not. It will be something to talk about in after years. If, like other old friends, it has to be put on the shelf, all that can be said is, Farewell, but not goodbye."[20]

Robertson's Last Works and His Declining Popularity

As we have seen, Robertson wrote ceaselessly between 1868 and 1869. He returned to his old friend E. A. Sothern at the Haymarket with *Home*. As the title suggests, it is set within a context of home and hearth. It also was written in order to give Sothern yet another opportunity to play a role in which his real identity was concealed. Into the Dorrison home comes the long lost son, Alfred (played by Sothern), in time to protect his father from the depredations of an adventuress, Mrs. Pinchbeck, and her gambling brother. Alfred in the disguise of a "Colonel White" falls in love with Dora, and together they outmaneuver the unscrupulous Mrs. Pinchbeck.

On the serious side, the play examines the disruptive elements that threaten to break up a home: misunderstanding, and a gullibility that is unable to distinguish between genuine and assumed affection. The unifying element is the unassailable nature of filial love. Robertson is careful, however, not to labor the point too seriously. Though Alfred and Dora are the romantic pair, they are complemented by Lucy and the silly but lovable ass, Bertie. As in the earlier plays, the most enjoyable and distinctive scenes are the love scenes. Robertson has two in the second act, one in which "Colonel White" and Dora fumble their way toward an overt statement of affection, and a second in which "Colonel White" simulates affection for Mrs. Pinchbeck. The stage directions explicitly call for two contrasted playing styles. The first is "to be played with great restraint," the second "with intense sentimentality." The first uses the by now familiar device of two young people stumbling over words, and inappropriate furniture, as their actions and their words part company. The second scene has "Colonel White" and Mrs. Pinchbeck gaze into one another's eyes as they read Tennyson's "Lord of Burleigh," suiting their actions to the highly colored sentiments of the poetry. Their prose picks up the unreal quality of the verse and the act ends with flashes of lightning and the revelation to a gullible father that his rival is none other than his long lost son. But this is where Robertson's inventiveness ceases. The last act merely unravels the dramatic knots in an entirely conventional way as Alfred reveals to his father the extent to Mrs. Pinchbeck's dishonesty and father and son become reconciled.

We have already seen that Robertson's successes were closely tied to the abilities of actors whom he knew. When he wrote independently, his own clichés became more apparent. He relied on situations and characters that had worked previously but that might remain lifeless in the hands of unsympathetic actors. There is little to suggest in the remainder of his output that he had anything new to say.

We can perhaps group the remaining plays of Robertson under the umbrellas of serious and comic. Under the first come *Dreams* in 1869, *The Nightingale* in 1879, and *War* in 1871. Both *Dreams* and *The Nightingale* were labeled "dramas in five acts." A familiar touch even here can be found in his opposition of tone and subject, appearance and reality. In *Dreams,* Robertson stipulates that it is "to be played after the style of comedy and not . . . . of melodrama" (*PDW,* 189), while the villain of *The Nightingale,* Ismail, is to direct "no lag-glances at the pit, and private information at the audience, that he is a villain . . ." (*PDW,* 385). Both plays have music as a central thematic concern. In *Dreams,* the hero, Rudolf Harfhal, is a composer of opera (the title of which is the title of the play); in *The Nightingale,* the heroine, Mary, is a would-be singer. The plots, however, have little in common though characters and attitudes are familiar. Robertson's purpose behind writing them would seem to have been, in the first, to provide the actor Alfred Wigan with the dual role of Rudolf and his father, and, in the second, to provide the Adelphi audience, connoisseurs of strong melodrama, with a mixture of the exotic and the sensational.

In the final analysis neither play was successful. Perhaps in his own mind Robertson linked melodrama with the outmoded vehicles of his stock company youth and resented their shallowness of appeal. We can certainly see that he preferred comedies with melodramatic elements. But we can also see that his titles betray a desire to be taken seriously. His last attempt at overt seriousness, *War,* was produced at the St. James' Theatre in January 1871, as he lay dying in bed. It is potentially a thesis play about the futility of war as seen through the eyes of two families of friends, one French and one German, who are torn apart by the Franco-Prussian War. Entrenched warlike values held by the older generation affect the lives of the younger people and, apparently, blight any future they may have. Though the theme is an interesting one, neither Robertson's techniques nor his temperament were suited to it. Once again there are Tennysonian references and sturdy English raisonneurs and a final scene in which the young hero Oscar, miraculously restored from a battlefield grave, places a wedding ring on the heroine's finger. It takes little to share the Victorian audience's sense of dramatic déjà vu.

The loss of imaginative vigor that the play suggests is hardly surprising given Robertson's physical condition. Nevertheless, it does illustrate an essential dichotomy in his work. That he had serious intentions in reforming the techniques of stage management and even dramatic characterization is undeniable. That he also wanted to be regarded as a serious writer is also beyond question. His problem was that, like most Victorian popular dramatists, financial security depended upon an unending supply of plays carefully attuned to the abilities of specific actors and the tastes of audiences. This involved endless ingenuity and a willingness to make artistic compromises. Robertson felt the pressure to make up for the lost time of his "starving engagements." His background of impoverishing hackwork and stock company failure must have made it all too seductive to retain techniques for too long and to mistake striking pictorialization for dramatic texture.

There remain Robertson's last three comedies, if we exclude his two-act farce *Breach of Promise* performed at the Globe Theatre in April 1869. The titles of *Progress* and *Birth* suggest his continuing fascination with the conflict between the old aristocracy and the world of the new technocrats. In both plays the class antagonisms are far more bitter than in any of his previous plays, but in both the significance of the themes is ultimately ignored. In *Birth,* Robertson created the role of Jack Randall once again for E. A. Sothern. Randall is a would-be playwright whose sardonic sense of humor constantly deflates the high emotionalism demonstrated by the protagonists. As a character he is an amalgam of Tom Stylus and Jack Poyntz, but as a vehicle for Sothern he offered little. Unlike Garrick or even "Colonel White" there is no theatrical make believe or opportunity for an actor to show his range. The play went no further than its provincial Bristol premiere.

His last comedy, *M.P.,* is also the last play he shared with the Prince of Wales company. It is, therefore, somewhat poignant that, produced in April 1870, less than a year before Robertson's death, the play should contain so many reminiscences of *Society,* the partnership's first success. As the title suggests, the play is about elections and electioneering. There is Talbot Piers—a more altruistic Sidney Daryl—who is determined to stand for Parliament. There is the coquettish and resourceful Cecilia—a more sophisticated Polly in *Caste*—played, of course, by Marie Wilton. There is the self-made North Country industrialist Issac Skoome, who, like Chodd Senior, believes that the key to advancement in life is "brass." And there is an eccentric but lovable father Dunscombe Dunscombe on the brink of bankruptcy and his son Chudleigh who wishes to become a burlesque actor, the height of irresponsibility. Given these kinds of characters it is not unexpected that we should learn little about politics or Robertson's attitudes to it. The action of the play hinges on mistaken identity, comic Irish-electioneering agents, and simultaneous love scenes between young couples. Talbot succeeds in winning his seat and discomfiting Skoome in virtually the same manner as Sidney succeeded over the Chodds in *Society.*

It is hard to avoid returning to the tone of the *Time's* "Poor Tom Robertson" when assessing the life and work of a man burned out physically and artistically at the age of forty-two. As a writer, he was a spokesman for a middle-class audience rapidly finding its feet and wishing to see its values reflected on stage. The titles of his plays suggest a strong social awareness. His comedies, especially those written with the Prince of Wales company in mind, are filled with situations and character types which the audience would have immediately recognized. To add piquancy the situations are given a knowing, ironical twist, while the characters are demonstrated in such a way as "to catch the gleanings of personality revealed by gesture, facial expression and intonation."[21] It ascribed to the audience an ability to differentiate the new from the old without losing sight of the familiar models. Thus his plays tacitly congratulate the audience on a newly acquired sophistication in taste.

As we have seen, however, Robertson was no revolutionary. His livelihood and that of the Bancrofts depended on retaining the goodwill of their audience. The Bancrofts lavished attention and money on creating an ambience of utmost decorum, and this was mirrored in the plays they presented. The key lay in a complete sense of harmony between stage and spectator. Thus the reforms in stage management—the use of actual, everyday objects instead of discernibly theatrical props, actual food, actual clothing rather than stage costumes, and everyday modes of behavior—reflect a felt need not to disrupt a harmonious continuum stretching from the auditorium to the stage just as much as a desire to advance the practice of the contemporary theater.

W. S. Gilbert felt he owed much to Robertson's meticulous stage management practices, and Pinero incorporated an affectionate tribute to Robertson in the role of Tom Wrench in *Trelawney of the "Wells,"* but by 1890 the "cup and saucer" school of playwriting identified with Robertson seemed trivial. He was criticized for an inability to tell a dramatic story, and, more understandably, for not having the courage to put forward a committed viewpoint on social issues. Robertson, however, would have argued that social reform and popular drama were discrete areas. His job was to retain the audience's affection for himself and for his theater.

We are constantly reminded in Robertson's writing of how much he owed to his predecessors. Though it was left to writers like Pinero and Henry Arthur Jones to integrate casual domesticity with issues of direct social relevance, their techniques remain recognizably those of Robertson. Thus Robertson as a Victorian popular dramatist looks, Janus-like, two ways. On the one hand, he develops and refines the techniques of his predecessors with the expressed aim of pleasing an increasingly defined middle-class audience. On the other, his indirection (if subtlety is too strong a term) allows for a redistribution of light and shade upon recognizable situations and character types. Gilbert's *Engaged* and Jones's *The Case of Rebellious Susan* would owe much to this. But Victorian tolerance could not allow this kind of "reformation" to be taken too far. When Ibsen added inexorable logic to recognizable social situations and an unexceptionable dramatic form, Clement Scott and most of his fellow critics were outraged. Robertson, we might feel, would have been more tolerant, though he would have found the rejection of audience approval incomprehensible.

Chapter Five
Henry Arthur Jones

It is very easy to dislike Henry Arthur Jones. Perhaps because he lived well into the twentieth century, his attitudes can often be identified with those held by our parents or grandparents. When we look at his volumes of essays and lectures about the state of English theater in the last decades of the nineteenth century, we are confronted by a belligerent idealist; when we read his plays we become aware of an uncomfortable chasm between those ideals and his practice. At best we can accuse Henry Arthur Jones of not living up to his ideals; at worst, we can condemn him for arrant hypocrisy. Today we can point to the continued revivals of his contemporary, Pinero, and Jones's almost complete theatrical eclipse. Yet it was Jones and not Pinero who was the most popular dramatist of the 1890s.[1] It was Jones who contributed most to the recognition of the modern English playwright as worthy of literary consideration. Finally, it is Jones's career that best exemplifies for us the vicissitudes and difficulties that confronted the Victorian popular dramatist.

The Life and Career of Henry Arthur Jones

Henry Arthur Jones was born on 28 September 1851, the year of the Great Exhibition, into a family who were Welsh in origin but had settled in Buckinghamshire. His father, Sylvanus, was a tough tenant farmer who worked sixteen hours a day and expected his family to follow his example. Henry Arthur was sent to a local school but, as the eldest son, was soon expected to contribute to the family's income and pay his own way. At the age of twelve he was apprenticed to his father's brother in a draper's shop in Ramsgate, a tedious existence that drove him to incessant reading. After three and a half years in Ramsgate he moved to another draper's shop in Gravesend, and it is there that he wrote his first play at the age of sixteen. In 1869 he moved to London and worked in a warehouse. After he saw his first play at Haymarket Theatre he decided to devote his efforts to becoming a playwright. Meanwhile he needed to earn money, particularly since he had become engaged to Jane Seeley, the daughter of a manufacturing family. He worked as a commercial traveler, finally becoming the West of England representative of a firm of textile manufacturers. He married in 1875 and settled in Exeter where he had his first play produced at the Theatre Royal, a one-act work entitled *It's Only Round the Corner,* on 11 December 1878. Retitled *Harmony Restored,* it was picked up by Wilson Barrett, a provincial manager who would play a decisive role in shaping Jones's career, for performance at Leeds in August 1879. Its success encouraged Barrett to write directly to Jones to solicit a further vehicle. A few days later Barrett and fellow actor E. S. Willard staged a comedy called *Elopement* in Oxford, and this marks the beginning of an association between the three men that would be erratically maintained for the next twenty years.

When Barrett produced *A Clerical Error* at the Court Theatre, in October 1879, it brought both Barrett and Jones to the attention of London audiences. The production also convinced Jones that he should give up his commercial practice and devote himself entirely to writing. A year later he and his family moved permanently to London. Between this time and November 1882 he wrote a number of curtain raisers and had his first full-length play, *My Wife,* staged at Sadler's Wells Theatre in April 1881. It was a promising start. Even if his financial returns in the years 1881–82 only averaged 520 pounds, it was a respectable amount. But in November 1882 came the turning point in his career. Wilson Barrett staged *The Silver King* at the Princess's and it became "the most famous English melodrama of the nineteenth century."[2] Written in collaboration with Henry Herman, it had an initial run of 289 nights and was to hold the stage for the next forty years throughout the English-speaking world, only rivaling Brandon Thomas's *Charley's Aunt* in popularity. Its financial success can be measured by the fact that Jones's income in the year 1882–83 rose by over 600 percent.[3]

Because the production of this play marks the real beginning of Henry Arthur Jones's career as a dramatist, it may be worthwhile to evaluate his progression to this point. That Jones should have become a playwright in the first place is itself unusual. He came from a rigorous Puritan background whose hostility to the theater was well known. He himself had no direct contact with the theater until he was eighteen, and it was not until 1875, when he had married and settled in Exeter, that he started to take part in amateur theater. He hated the drudgery of his early life in his uncle's draper's shop, and it was undoubtedly this that drove him to read voraciously as a means to eventual self-betterment. It is therefore not surprising that his absorption of English and French literary models, particularly Shakespeare, the Restoration dramatists, Molière, Goldsmith, and Sheridan, should make him aim for a theater that was based on a carefully crafted literary text. Nor is it surprising that when exposed to the practicalities of performance and audience acceptance, his models should have been sensation melodrama, knockabout farce, and the known vehicles of the actor/managers. He quickly realized that he would have to rely on actor/managers who would be willing to use his plays for their own ends. It was in their power to educate their audience, but to have influence they needed to be consistently popular. It was this dilemma in the theater that was to obsess Jones for the remainder of his life.

The Silver King opened on 16 November 1882. It relieved the thirty-one-year-old author of any financial strain and allowed him to devote time to perfecting his grasp of melodrama and to encouraging the development of the literary drama. In March 1883 he was already writing in the influential theater magazine, *Era*, "The truth is that audiences want literature, they want poetry, but they do not want unactable, intractable imitations of Shakespeare's form, without his vitality. They want life, they want reality. . . ." These sentiments he expanded in the same year in his first important analysis of the contemporary theater, "The Theatre and the Mob." This would be later collected together with further articles and addresses in *The Renascence of the English Drama* in 1895.[4] In the article he accused both playwrights and theater managers of dereliction of duty by talking down to audiences and pandering to their lowest common denominator. The article was Jones's first public attempt to differentiate between "theater" and "drama" and to suggest that an easily accessible form like melodrama might be a means toward the elevation of audience taste. At the same time, he was careful not to denigrate audiences per se, but rather to suggest that they themselves were craving for responsible leadership. Although Jones was never to admit more than the peripheral influence of Ibsen upon his work, by 1884 he had certainly seen *Pillars of Society* and *A Doll's House*. Even if Jones was essentially too conservative to tackle subjects without compromise, he would have been impressed by the way in which Ibsen was able to extend the parameters of melodrama. He tried, again with Herman's collaboration, to write a version of *A Doll's House*. With Beerbohm Tree and Kyrle Bellew, *Breaking a Butterfly* was a success, but its happy ending was immediately vilified by the Ibsenites as a travesty, and it remained unrevived.[5]

His next noteworthy play was *Saints and Sinners* in 1884 with Thomas Thorne playing the main role of Jacob Fletcher, the nonconformist minister.[6] It was his first attempt to integrate his own experience of small-town religious bigotry with his inherited form of melodrama. Its reception was stormy. Critics and the first-night audience were offended by the play's religious references. Subsequent audiences, however, were not as severe and it enjoyed a more than respectable run of 182 nights generated by the heat of religious controversy. The play gives us some inkling of Jones's attitude to his family as it pillories Dissenting hypocrisy, particularly in the character of Hoggard, who is modeled on his uncle in Ramsgate. From a historical viewpoint the play is important in that it shows Jones's determination to challenge the restrictive conventions that bound the English playwright. It is also important as the first of his plays to be made accessible to a reading public when it was published in 1891. In 1885 he made his first trip to the United States to assist in its production, a visit that was instrumental in launching his enduring popularity on the American stage.

Between 1884 and 1889 Jones continued to write voluminously about the contemporary stage and to argue the right of the dramatist to portray any facet of life he chose, especially religious life.[7] He was also becoming tired of Wilson Barrett's adherence to the melodramatic form and his lack of interest in dramatic reform. Between 1884 and 1889, however, Jones wrote little that could be seen to follow on the lead of *Saints and Sinners*. Until 1887 he wrote exclusively for Wilson Barrett at the Princess's Theatre: melodramas like "Hoodman Blind" (1885), "The Lord Harry" (1886) and "A Noble Vagabond" (1886), all of which remained unpublished. He then renewed his associations with Tree and Willard at the Haymarket Theatre in *Hard Hit* (1887) and *Wealth* (1889), and resumed his writings on the drama, in particular on the subject of the lack of relationship between Victorian theater and its literature. Jones was becoming increasingly preoccupied with the ephemeral nature of the theatrical occasion, which he saw as exacerbated by the capriciousness and irresponsibility of actor/managers. It was, therefore, up to the dramatist to assume responsibility for the taste of the audience.[8]

In 1887 his mother died. Jones felt this deeply. Her long suffering
patience in the face of her husband's intransigent lack of sensitivity
had profoundly affected her son. From her he had gained an overde-
veloped sense of personal responsibility and a detestation of falsehood.
Most of his plays feature a woman who is the focus of his hero's enemies, and for whom the hero is prepared to sacrifice his most deeply
felt principles. These situations may be tardy attempts on Jones's part
at expiation or vindication in his mother's eyes before she died.[9]

The period to 1891 was an unremarkable one: "Before I knew that
the piece [Saints and Sinners] has settled into an assured success, I had
weakly sold myself to what the Saturday Review justly calls, 'the dull
devil of spectacular melodrama.' And I remained a bondslave for
many years."[10] This dissatisfaction evaporated somewhat in 1889 with
the production of The Middleman in which E. S. Willard played the
part of Cyrus Blenkarn, a role with which he would be closely identified for the remainder of his career. The play was immediately successful both in London and New York and was the first of Jones's
plays to be produced on the Continent.[11] It marks the end of Jones's
period of apprenticeship during which he perfected his grasp of melodramatic structure and conventions. From now on he would try to
subordinate theatrical mechanics to the exploration of social issues. In
this the influence of Ibsen is unmistakable, although Jones maintained to the end of his life, perhaps rather disingenuously, that his
debt to Ibsen was a very small one.

The success of The Middleman encouraged Jones to try out a more
radical stance. In Judah he tackled a theme that has distinctly modern
resonances, the credibility of spiritual "gurus" who claim supernatural powers of healing. It continued his collaboration with Willard
who played the title role and the play was hailed as daring, original
and lyrical.[12] The year 1891 was to be one of Jones's busiest, and he
was to maintain for the next decade an average of two plays a year,
becoming the preeminent exponent of "society drama." The passing
of the American Copyright Act in 1891 cleared the way for the publication of his plays, and Jones made full use of the opportunity. It
allowed him to reach the wider reading public he so desperately
wanted to influence while guaranteeing him a secure and continuing
financial return. At the same time, Beerbohm Tree's production of
The Dancing Girl at the Haymarket Theatre was an immense success.
In London it ran for 310 nights and received a New York premiere
in August of the same year with Jones himself present. It was on this

voyage that he met Brander Matthews who was to remain a lifelong friend. Matthews's position as professor of English and comparative literature at Columbia University was to be extremely influential in assuring Jones a continuing American popularity.[13]

On his return to England he embarked on a vitriolic condemnation of the position of the Victorian actor/manager in the pages of the *Pall Mall Gazette* (13 and 15 August 1891). We have seen how the Victorian popular dramatist depended upon the goodwill of a powerful actor or actress in order to reach an audience and make a living. None of the dramatists we have so far considered were able to write exclusively for the stage. Jones was in a position to do so and resented the compromises he had been compelled to make. To demonstrate his beliefs he went into management for himself and produced *The Crusaders* in November of 1891. Neither the furniture and sets by William Morris nor his own artistic integrity were enough to counteract the newspaper and audience hostility. The venture was a disaster and Jones suffered a personal financial loss of over 4,000 pounds.[14]

In January of 1893 Jones began his collaboration with Charles Wyndham, whose combination of romantic charm and astute worldliness were not dissimilar to the performance style of Squire Bancroft. Wyndham and George Alexander, with whom Jones was to associate the following year, were to influence considerably Jones's writing for the society audiences of their theaters, the Criterion and the St. James's respectively. In June, Jones's first political paper brought him to the serious attention of George Bernard Shaw. In "Middleman and Parasites" he expressed considerable sympathy for the working classes.[15] It was, however, the product of an essentially romantic view, an extension of the position he had taken in *The Middleman*. The lower classes represented, on the one hand, an exploited group, at the mercy of those who fed off their efforts, while, on the other, they formed the basis of the popular audience, the raising of whose consciousness Jones saw as his mission. In fact, Jones's personal attitude to the lower classes was at considerable variance with this. His daughter has pointed out that fundamentally he had a great dislike of lower classes, by which he meant lower middle classes. With them he identified the prejudice and narrow-mindedness that he had encountered as a boy. His success in the rarified circles of upper-class society made him increasingly elitist and antidemocratic, despite an early flirtation with socialism, until after 1914 he became an uncompromising reactionary.[16]

In September 1893, while Pinero's *The Second Mrs. Tanqueray* was the most discussed play on the West End, Beerbohm Tree mounted a lavish staging of Jones's only attempt at verse tragedy, *The Tempter.* He had spent over a year writing it and was greatly depressed by its failure. Even Shaw found the verse "a model of speakability,"[17] but such sentiments by eminent critics were not enough to dissuade Tree from withdrawing it after seventy nights. It was after all a literary freak that ran counter to the audience's expectations of Jones. More acceptable were the two plays of the following year: *The Masqueraders* with George Alexander and Mrs. Patrick Campbell, and *The Case of Rebellious Susan* with Charles Wyndham and his wife Mary Moore.

Because Shaw's evaluation raises issues that are central to Jones's writing at this stage and to his subsequent career, it is worth quoting from his letter to Jones on reading a copy of *The Masqueraders:* "The comedy is of course first rate: you have never appreciated yourself fully in that department, or you would have given us more in the way of unmixed thorough-paced comedy. The rest I forgive you for, though I believe you faked up that atrocious nurse for the express purpose of infuriating me. And there is such a lot to be done on the stage with the real hospital nurse. My real soldier in *Arms and the Man* would not have been in it if you had risen to the occasion. Every one of that woman's allusions to duty elicited a howl of rage from me. She morally outrages my tenderest sensibilities. . . ."[18]

Jones is undoubtedly at his best in comedy, but moral indignation and a desire to expose emotional fraudulence constantly bring him into confrontation with his audience's tolerance. Because he could not bring himself to challenge this, he would not only drift away in time from Shaw, but he would also compromise his own position. But this was in the future. The two plays of 1894 reflected accurately the preoccupations of the leisured class who went to the Criterion and the St. James's theaters. Of the two *The Case of Rebellious Susan* appeared the more revolutionary, setting up the premise that a woman has an equal right to contemplate adultery as a man. Despite this it ran for 164 nights in London and in the following December at the Lyceum in New York. It would be further revived by Wyndham in 1901 and 1910.[19]

In 1895 Jones consolidated his position as the foremost champion of English playwriting by publishing his first collection of essays and articles under the title *The Renascence of English Drama.* It was typical of him that he should have deliberately placed himself in a position of vulnerability. The publication enabled his critics to disparage his plays by now comparing them with his published policy. Nevertheless, the book was a major document that gave the Victorian dramatist a standing and a pedigree. The critics, however, had considerable ammunition to fire at Jones. His four plays between May 1895 and March 1897 were all failures. With the exception of *The Physician* (March 1897), they are concerned with imposters (*The Rogue's Comedy,* 1896), the double standards of morality (*The Triumph of the Philistines,* 1895), and passion and duty (*Michael and his Lost Angel,* 1896). Of these he felt deepest about the failure of *Michael and his Lost Angel,* which closed after ten performances. His feelings were intensified by the death of his eldest son Philip while the play was running, but his principal grievance was at the action of Johnston Forbes-Robertson in withdrawing the play too precipitately. It demonstrated clearly to him that his suspicions about actor/managers were fully justified.

In October 1897 Charles Wyndham produced Jones's most successful and enduring play, *The Liars,* significantly, in the light of Shaw's estimation, a comedy. On the evidence of his biographer, Jones himself thought little of the play,[20] perhaps because comedy he found easier to write. "Was it the Puritan in him," asks Richard Cordell,[21] "holding more precious the work effected with difficulty, and depreciating that which was accomplished with more pleasure than labor? And the Puritan undervaluing those plays shorn of serious admonishments and ethical implications?" That he had caught the spirit of the times was obvious as measured by the production's 291-night run in London and the comparison with Sheridan's *School for Scandal* made by the *New York Journal*[22] at its successful opening in New York in September 1898. It is also evident that Jones was closer to his audience than to his critics. The former were entrenched conservatives, the latter, including as they did A. B. Walkley and William Archer, believed in change and scrupulous moral logic. Their weight was behind the experiments of Jacob Grein's Independent Theatre rather than an author who appeared to be catering to a mass of well-heeled dilettantes. But for the moment Jones was right and they were wrong. The success of *The Manoeuvres of Jane* in October 1898, in the teeth of universally poor critical responses, seemed to prove this. If there was a casualty as a result of the conflict between Jones and the critics, it was the relationship with Shaw, who now found himself more and more at variance with someone who appeared to shirk the responsibilities that he himself saw with tunnel-vision clarity.

Despite his popular appeal, Jones was to wait until late 1900 for his next success. Two plays, *Carnac Sahib* and *The Lackey's Carnival,* despite Beerbohm Tree's performance in the first, failed, both productions dogged by unusually difficult rehearsals compounded by the presence of an unusually intolerant author. But *Mrs. Dane's Defence* in October brought together the Wyndhams and Jones in a serious quasi-courtroom drama. The response was unequivocally warm, even if critics congratulated the actors rather than the dramatist. It was destined to be one of his last successes. Despite grudging admiration for plays like *Whitewashing Julia* (1903) and *The Hypocrites* (1907), it was not until 1908 with *Dolly Reforming Herself* that he would surprise audiences again.

The period from 1901 until his death in 1929 is characterized by an increasing distance between Jones and his contemporaries: "the last twenty wonderful years of increasing success and happiness were over, and during the remainder of his life he was constantly worried about money matters; his nervous breakdowns were more frequent, while his general health grew worse and worse."[23]

He devoted himself to combatting censorship and, as World War 1 loomed, to political issues. His one happy moment in the years before 1914 seems to have been the conferral of an honorary degree by Harvard University in 1907 for his services to "the revival of English Drama and its reunion with English literature."[24] As he grew older, and especially after major cancer surgery in 1912, his views became more extreme and, at the same time, narrow. His last collection of theatrical essays appeared as *The Foundations of a National Drama* in 1913 and thereafter his writings were almost exclusively political. With an eye jaundiced by his audience's desertion and "genuinely appalled by the sacrifice of national defence to liberal ideology,"[25] he launched into bitter attacks on the socialism of Shaw and H. G. Wells during and after the war. His often irrational opposition to Shaw intensified in the 1920s, a part of that "creeping paralysis of outlook which gradually cut him off from new ideas and the new audience."[26]

The death of his wife in 1924 left Jones inconsolable. Two further serious operations in 1926 rendered him virtually immobile. The last production that Henry Arthur Jones was to see was his play *The Lie,* which had had its New York premiere in 1914. It was produced in London by Lewis Casson with Sybil Thorndike in October 1923. It was a nostalgic success as audiences rose to acclaim an almost forgotten playwright. Jones died on 7 January 1929.

Formative Years: Experiments with Melodrama

Although Jones had had five plays produced before *The Silver King,* both he and his biographers divide his artistic life into three distinct sections: from *The Silver King* in 1882 to *The Middleman* in 1889, from *Judah* in 1890 to *Mrs. Dane's Defence* in 1900, and from the beginning of the Edwardian era to his death in 1929. We need concern ourselves principally with the first two sections, because his best work was contained within the Victorian period. After 1900 Jones's appeal to popular audiences would decline as his own interests turned to social and political issues.

We have seen in considering the work of Jerrold and Taylor the emergence of particular forms of melodrama. With these Jones was familiar. He was especially impressed by melodrama's insistence on a strong plot and swayed emotionally by its idealism and absolute values. His work notes reveal how he felt a study of melodrama might benefit an aspiring playwright: "a knowledge of melodrama gives a sinewy and vertebrate frame to the work of a young dramatist and chastens him from the vice of substituting his own 'ideas' for a plot."[27] He was further influenced by the example of the Bancrofts and the developments in domestic realism that explored the workings of commercial life as Taylor had done in *The Ticket of Leave Man,* or the problems of career and homelife as H. J. Byron had done in *Cyril's Success.* Stylistically these developments were heavily indebted to French models, and their success was measured in terms of familiarity to known situations and adherence to the ideals of Victorian home life.[28] The Bancrofts had shown the appropriateness of an intimate acting style within the narrow parameters of their Robertsonian inheritance. They had further established a principle of artistic unity between actor/manager and dramatist and when they moved from the Prince of Wales Theatre to the Haymarket in 1880 they brought these elements into the heartland of the fashionable West End.

The Silver King. Jones felt he needed the collaboration of Henry Herman in the writing of *The Silver King,* a measure perhaps of the young playwright's stylistic insecurity. Its immense popularity can be attributed to a number of factors, not the least being the performances of Wilson Barrett as Denver and Willard as the suave villain, Skinner. Barrett had a glowing spirituality that gave his roles a kind of religious fervor that he would later put to good effect in plays like *The Sign of the Cross*. Willard was a versatile actor equally at home with understated villainy, a quality developed by actors like Alfred Wigan, and obsessed genius of the kind he was later to portray in Jones's *The Middleman*. The characters therefore possessed a complexity by virtue of their performers. There was the added attraction of a plot centered entirely upon the hero's mistaken belief in his own guilt. It suggested a melodrama in which character plays a more important role than mere narrative. Finally, though the play is structured formally into five acts, it is made up of seventeen scenes that dissolve filmically into one another. This gives the play a breathless immediacy and a sense of ruthless logic particularly appropriate in a story of pursuit and revenge.

Act 1 is made up of three expositionary scenes, the first of which takes place in the skittle alley of "The Wheatsheaf," a Clerkenwell hotel. As we saw in *The Ticket of Leave Man* and in *Society*, the public house is a useful location. It allows the dramatist to move people from different walks of life on and off the stage with little motivation other than the wish to have a drink. The act introduces the disconsolate Denver, a compulsive gambler, bitter at his losses in the Derby which, he realizes, will ruin him and his family. There is the villain, Skinner, in "faultless evening dress" (*CH*, 1:10), and his henchman Coombe, who plan to rob the premises of Ware, a rich jeweler. They will use Ware's clerk Corkett to break in. Ware is also a sometime rival for Denver's wife and delights in reminding the conscience-stricken Denver of his inadequacy. Finally, there is the detective Baxter, who is on the trail of Skinner whom he suspects of involvement in a string of jewel robberies.

The second scene introduces Denver's faithful servant, Jaikes, who tries to maintain a watchful eye on his master. The third scene brings all the protagonists to Ware's premises: the thieves engaged in robbing Ware's safe and Denver, drunk and irrationally jealous, determined to have it out with Ware. Skinner, however, chloroforms Denver, and shoots the returning Ware with Denver's revolver. When he recovers consciousness, Denver is convinced that in his stupor he has managed to shoot Ware.

Act 2 immediately plots the consequences of the actions as Denver stays one step ahead of his pursuer, Baxter. Denver, assisted by his wife Nelly and his servant Jaikes, disguises himself as a sailor. Nelly urges him to give the impression he is leaving the country and Jaikes gives him his savings. Indebted to both, Denver tears himself away as Baxter is about to enter and arrest him.

The pace is relentlessly maintained in the following scene which is set in a railway ticket office full of bustling crowds of passengers passing through to the station platforms. Jones punctuates it with sly humor as first-class passengers are escorted obsequiously to their carriages and third-class passengers are given short shrift by a pompous inspector. Denver buys a newspaper which immediately shows that the murder is making headline news and rushes for his train. Again Baxter arrives too late but manages to send off a telegram to stop the train before it arrives at its Liverpool destination.

The third scene involves a change of pace and an unexpected setting. Three men sit lazily on the porch of a country inn. One of them, Parkyn the parish clerk, has commandeered the only morning newspaper and refuses to give it up. Because he is a self-important little man who likes to hear the sound of his own voice, the only way the other two can find out the news is to have Parkyn read it out aloud. The news is an account of Denver's apparent crime. It is a relaxed country atmosphere broken by the appearance of Denver, travel stained and limping as a result of leaping off his train. The last scene of the act begins with a music cue. It serves to emphasize a certain artificiality for the first time, but deliberately so, as Denver is alone and must convey to the audience his inner emotional state. This soliloquy also contains Jones's most quoted and memorable line, "O God! put back thy universe and give me yesterday!" (*CH,* 1:41). Denver discovers by reading the newspapers delivered later that day that the very train from which he jumped was involved in a derailment. Believed to be dead, he now has the opportunity to begin a new life and to free his wife from any social stigma. Heaven has indeed answered his prayer.

Jones's plays cover a long period between acts and in this play there is a gap of three and a half years between acts 2 and 3. First Jones shows us the state of the "opposition." Skinner is revelling in the lap of luxury, undetected and secure, except for his wife Olive, to whom he has confided his crime. She is his voice of conscience. The other potential weakness in Skinner's armor is the presence of Corkett, who has become a petty criminal and arrives at Skinner's house fresh out of prison and demanding consideration for his silence. But the long arm of coincidence so necessary to melodrama now insures that Skinner is to remain insulated no longer. His tenant whom he proposes to evict is none other than Nelly. She has a sick child, and it is only with the intercession of Olive that she is allowed to stay. But this is a decision Skinner immediately reverses when Coombe informs him that she is Denver's widow.

Nelly and the faithful Jaikes are in dire financial straits. To reinforce the pathos in scene 2 Jones clears the stage and the audience hears the voices of children singing a hymn to Mercy, Repentance, Pardon, and Peace. As they do this Denver enters, "his hair is almost white, and his face worn, his manner grave and subdued" (CH, 1:57). It is the appearance of an ascetic saint who has arrived just in time. He is able to give his daughter Cissy, who does not recognize him, money for the outstanding rent and to reveal himself to the faithful Jaikes. Denver has become a wealthy man through silver mining in Nevada but, like the Count of Monte Cristo, he must keep his identity hidden. With the money given by Cissy's mysterious benefactor, Nelly is able to thwart Coombe who has come to evict her.

This act is the most traditionally melodramatic in the play, and is the moment of greatest desperation for the weak. When Denver appears, there is little sense of an heroic entry. His need to keep his identity secret removes the possibility of a tearful reunion and this deliberate omission fails to realize the audience's dramatic expectations. Jones skillfully manipulates the concluding moments of the act. Coombe is about to evict Nelly, Denver cannot intervene, Cissy has gone to search for her mother while clutching the money that Denver has given her, and it is only in the last few seconds that she appears and thwarts Coombe's intent.

Act 4 begins the process of revelation. First, Denver in his disguise as "John Franklin" is brought face to face with Baxter: "I've seen you somewhere before" (CH, 1:70). For Denver justice and his own conscience are now making exposure inevitable. He can tolerate no longer the pressure of his own guilt which tortures him at night as it does Hamlet, or Mathias in The Bells. He can put off the inevitable no longer and at the end of scene 2 he reveals his true identity to Nelly. What now remains is for Denver to establish Skinner's guilt before Baxter can apprehend him. Once more Denver disguises himself and worms himself into the confidence of Skinner's gang. The cracks in their solidarity that started to appear in the previous act have now become evident as they start to exploit one another. Predictably it is Corkett who reveals to a hidden Denver that he is innocent of Ware's murder. "Denver, no longer able to restrain himself, leaps up with a terrific scream of joy" (*CH,* 1:95) and reveals himself to the immobilized criminals.

Act 5, however, is not merely a collection of summary resolutions. The protagonists, Denver and Skinner, must necessarily confront one another and Baxter must find the means to convict Skinner. It is now Skinner's turn to make for a train and escape. Because Corkett is a greedy and maladjusted young man, he tries to break in to Skinner's villa and steal some of Skinner's ill-gotten gains, and it is there that Baxter is able to intercept him. Corkett proves more than willing to turn informer. The last scene brings Skinner and Denver face to face as Skinner offers to trade silence for silence. Denver, however, has made peace with himself and his family and is quite willing to place himself in the hands of the police. But Baxter already has the evidence he needs and enters to arrest Skinner and finally to exculpate Denver who sinks to his knees: "Home at last!" (*CH,* 1:109).

The play has all the fervid emotionalism of melodrama and it is couched in colorful and effective language. Jones furthermore is able to tell a good story and keep the audience guessing as to how the resolution will be contrived. The contrivance itself is logical and proceeds from either the necessity of the story or the inner drives of the characters. Obviously, Jones was interested in the extent to which individuals are able to mold events. Even if Denver's fate depends upon circumstances like the train accident or his discovery of wealth in America, Jones is more interested in how he will respond to them. Denver is himself an unusual hero: a drunken wastrel with a driving self-loathing, which will insure that he will change. It is therefore totally acceptable that when he reappears it is not as a plutocrat but as a saint. Skinner similarly is an unusual villain. He is sophisticated and not the personification of cruelty. His downfall comes about through his associates and his own determination to retain a social respectability. The combination of the characters' contradictory traits, the effective use of poetic diction, the deliberate avoidance of extraneous sensation, and Jones's ability to structure a story were enough to satisfy both an audience looking for diverting narrative and a critic looking for literary texture. Matthew Arnold saw in Jones a new voice in English dramatic literature and Wilson Barrett saw in the play the elevation of melodrama to the region of natural tragedy.[29]

Saints and Sinners. Closer to Jones's real interests were subjects based on his own experience and his most indelible experiences were those concerned with religion, in particular the narrow-minded

religious attitudes of small communities. He was able to use this subject matter and strike a blow for the right of the dramatist to depict
contemporary religious life on stage in the teeth of the censor's objections with *Saints and Sinners*. It opened in September 1884 at the
Vaudeville Theatre with Willard playing the leading role of Jacob
Fletcher. Reactions were hostile, in particular to the quotations of
Scripture, and a press discussion began that culminated in Jones's
"Religion and the Stage" (*Nineteenth Century*, January 1885), a plea
for the stage's right to be uncompromising. The play ran for 182
nights and proved immensely enduring.

As in *The Silver King*, the first act comprises one scene, set in the
study of a nonconformist minister, Jacob Fletcher. His living is supplied by erratic pew rent payments and the patronage of a few busi-
nessmen, and his chapel is the refuge for the flotsam of the country
town of Steepleford. He is a kindly man accustomed to forgive the
members of his poor congregation. But he is also scrupulously honest
and is quite prepared to thwart his deacon, Hoggard, when he comes
to him with a plan to misappropriate an estate of which Fletcher is
trustee. Hoggard is a powerful local businessman, sanctimonious on
Sundays and ruthlessly grasping during the remainder of the week.
Steepleford is a world of hard-nosed local politics and respectable fa-
cades totally unsuited to the temperament of Letty, Jacob's daughter.
Though she is devoted to her father, she desperately wants them to
leave and explore a world that seems so full of excitement. In this
mood she can hardly be satisfied with the attentions of George Kingsmill, the young farmer who has been hopelessly in love with her for
years. He now plans to seek his fortune in Australia in order to get
away from agrarian failure and his misplaced love. She is much more
attracted to Captain Fanshawe, the wealthy son of the local squire,
who sees in her an exciting local conquest. Letty understands the conflict between duty and her yearning for excitement but can only
halfheartedly fend him off when Fanshawe arrives to propose an assignation. Jacob enters the room, however, and banishes Fanshawe from
the house.

The act exhibits a curious mixture of unusual characterization and
highly conventional attitudes. The dilapidation of the setting, the
worn furniture, and the matter-of-factness of the conversation about
pew rents and local business complement the originality of the theme
of a Dissenting minister tyrannized by hypocritical members of his
congregation.[30] Even Letty's need to escape rings true, since it is clear
that it is only loyalty to her father that keeps her at Steepleford. The

intrusion of Fanshawe, however, insures that the major issues will be subordinated to the story of Letty's seduction at the hands of an aristocratic villain, and its consequences.

The second act charts the process of seduction as Fanshawe manipulates Letty away from a Sunday school picnic to a railway station and onto a London bound train. She cannot withstand a man who sees himself as determined by heredity and environment to be evil, and whose mission it is to corrupt as many women as possible. It remains for Lot Burden, Hoggard's foreman and a secret ally of Jacob's, to inform him that his daughter has gone. A deeply hurt Jacob and a furious George determine to go to London and find Letty. While act 1 had a decidedly modern feel to it, this act seems much more old fashioned. Perhaps the only interesting development lies in Jones's depiction of passion.

The first scene in act 3 takes place a month later in Jacob Fletcher's sitting room. There have been no traces of Letty. Hoggard and his fellow deacon, Prabble, are congratulating themselves at having Jacob at their mercy. Not only do they suspect that Letty's absence is due to moral delinquency but they intend to withhold their pew rents unless Jacob uses his position from the pulpit to advance their commercial interests. A letter from Letty arrives, postmarked Torquay, a fashionably discreet seaside resort, in which she begs her father's forgiveness and writes of proposed marriage to Fanshawe. Jacob immediately leaves to rescue her, followed by a determined George. The second scene in Fanshawe's villa reveals him to be in a predicament not dissimilar to that of George D'Alroy in *Caste*. He must tell Letty that, as a military man, he has been posted to India. Paradoxically, for the first time he is assailed by pangs of conscience. He finds himself to be in love with Letty whose purity has affected him, and yet he cannot marry her. He is still married to an alcoholic wife he has long since forgotten. Again, despite her despair, Letty is swept away by the urgency of Fanshawe's passion and agrees to accompany him to India as his mistress. At this point her father enters full of forgiveness. It is Christ confronting Mary Magdalen:

JACOB: Listen, my dear. I have come to take you from this place and make you a good and happy girl again.

LETTY: I can never be good and happy again. I must be wicked and miserable. Yes, I must. I have chosen my path—I must go on.[31]

Hers is the voice of melodrama and its unyielding Pauline Christianity, insisting that the wages of sin are death. But Jones is prepared to resist this, at least temporarily. She is to be saved and taken back into the bosom of a forgiving family.

What remains is the assessment of these principled actions in terms of their contemporary social context. Jones immediately presents us in the play with those to whom Jacob is answerable: Hoggard and Prabble clutching hymn books and Bible, and the Parridges, a family of country laborers, rigid in their Sunday best clothes and their pious morality. It is hardly a forgiving environment, so it is little wonder that Jacob and Letty feel exposed. As the church service is about to begin, Hoggard confronts Jacob in his vestry and reveals that Letty's escapade is known to him. He, however, will keep silent provided that Jacob will allow Hoggard to misappropriate the estate that was the subject of discussion in act 1. Jacob refuses, and in a climactic scene tells the congregation of Letty's seduction and resigns his ministry. It is the best act in the play. The characterizing of the small businessman is savage and personally felt.

The last act takes place four years later. Letty has become a nursing angel to the poor during an outbreak of plague; Jacob has been hounded from one short-lived incumbency to the next by Hoggard; and together with their servant Lydia, they live in abject poverty on the outskirts of Steepleford. The coincidences of a sentimental melodrama now become obtrusive. Fanshawe has providentially died in India; Hoggard is being sought for fraud, and suddenly arrives in Jacob's hovel begging for protection from the pursuers whom he has ruined. Jacob distracts them and gives Hoggard his last piece of bread. Prabble enters to ask Jacob back to his ministry, together with a raise in salary, and it appears that all will end happily at last. But it is not to be.

We should consider at this point the implications raised by the play's alternate endings, since they reveal much about the pressures under which Jones labored. If we look at the printed 1891 text we will see that the play ends with the death of Letty. The acted version ended with her recovery and marriage to her fiance, George Kingsmill, providentially returned from Australia. The preface to the printed version makes it clear that the pathetic ending was as Jones originally conceived it and that it was restored at the advice of Matthew Arnold.[32] Jones, however, was persuaded by Clement Scott that, in performance, the audience's belief in natural justice would be affronted and that this would result in box office failure.[33] Jones's apology for this in the printed edition is illuminating: "I did this with some reluctance, but I reflected that on the whole the final *dénouement* was not of such vital consequence as the presentation of the picture of English religious life. I do not think I shall be harshly judged by those who understand what have been the inner conditions of writing for the English stage and the concessions demanded by the public until quite recently" (xxiii).

To suggest that the importance of subject and character can excuse any maladroitness of plot is a piece of legerdemain devised after the fact. But to suggest that in 1884 the playwright was at the mercy of manager and audience is no more than a statement of fact. To do him justice, however, Jones saw his primary task was to force audiences to reject the complacency of outlook that the plays of Robertson had tacitly accepted.[34] The second task was to raise the status of the drama through character drawing. It is therefore natural that in *Saints and Sinners* Jones should concentrate on originality of characterization and a conscious avoidance of the stereotype. Thus, in the printed version Letty lives only long enough to see George Kingsmill returned, rich and ready to marry her. She dies with the resoundingly bitter line: "Oh you Christians, will you never learn to forgive?" (115). It gives the last act a strong element of "natural tragedy." Just as Jacob is restored to his position and George returns in triumph, Letty dies a martyr, revered by the community for her good works, and numbered among the saints of the play's title.

The Middleman. In August of 1889 Jones produced what the *Times* called "by far the most original and literary play of the year" (28 August). This was *The Middleman* which opened at the Shaftesbury on 27 August with Willard in the central role of Blenkarn, the idealistic potter. It marks the last development in Jones's attempts to pour new wine into the older bottles of melodrama, and is an important precursor of the English social plays of Galsworthy and even Shaw.[35] The play was later criticized for a sentimental and muddled treatment of capital and labor, but, as Jones was to argue, the play "is not so much a fight between labor and capital as a fight between grasping commercialism and inventive genius."[36] Though this conflict is worked out in highly personal terms between Chandler, the exploitative middleman, and Blenkarn, it shows Jones moving away, already evident in *Saints and Sinners,* from a drama based on plot, to a drama based on a combination of character and social criticism.

The play opens with Chandler the proprietor of the Tatlow Porcelain works addressing a crowd whom he hopes will support his parliamentary candidature. He is "a smug, fat, prosperous looking man of fifty, with the manners of an upper class commercial man" (CH, 1:117). He is a successful Hoggard surrounded by toadying manager and press agent (Todd), local reporter (Daneper), aristocratic sponsors (the Umfravilles), and a less than enthusiastic son (Julian). The aristocratic Umfravilles feel a profound contempt for Chandler but are constrained by a genteel poverty that they hope will end when Julian marries their daughter, Felicia. They are recognizable portraits of deracinated gentry preparing for a marriage of convenience with commerce. Julian is a version of Captain Fanshawe who is off to Africa before settling down to complement his father's desire for respectability. He is also genuinely in love with Mary Blenkarn.

When Blenkarn enters, he is the picture of the obsessed artist: "a keen, pale, thin man, with bent form, sharp features, restless, absent, distracted manner" (CH, 1:128). He is totally oblivious to everything in his determination to rediscover the art of Tatlow china. He is followed by his younger daughter, Nancy, and his assistant Jesse. He and Nancy are the humorous foils to Julian Chandler and Cyrus's older daughter, Mary. Despite the suggestion that Mary is pregnant by him, Julian is forced to leave England by his father, to retain a respectable facade and the support of the Umfravilles. Cyrus is too preoccupied to be even aware that a passionate relationship exists and is puzzled by Mary's collapse at the end of the act when Julian, with brass band playing and villagers cheering, is packed off to Africa and unknown hazards.

It is an interesting beginning to the play. Jones's techniques have developed considerably, especially in the casual integration of exposition with action. There are conventional elements: Mary, the "poor companion," Julian, the monied seducer, and the "low" comic elements of Jesse and impossibly old and deaf rustics. On the other hand, the portraits of Chandler and Cyrus Blenkarn are convincing ones. Chandler's "villainy" and Blenkarn's monomania are the products of social situation, on the one hand, and artistic temperament, on the other. They are both too self-centered to see people except from their own myopic points of view.

Act 2 takes place in Cyrus's house set near the kilns of the pottery works. It is visited by the Chandlers and the Umfravilles on a tour of their estates. It becomes obvious that there will be a falling out between Chandler and his manager, Todd, as soon as Cyrus discovers his firing process. Jesse demonstrates an unusual hardheadedness as he tries unsuccessfully to make Cyrus aware of his exploitation by the Chandlers. He is equally unsuccessful in his suit with Nancy, who sees little substance in him. Mary comes to see her father to try to make him understand her situation. She has decided to leave the area before her condition becomes too apparent. Cyrus genuinely dotes on her and promises her a life of happiness when he discovers his process. But inadvertently he hardens her resolve as he compares death favorably to moral disgrace and hurries back to his workshop. It is left to Jesse to inform Cyrus of Mary's liaison with Julian, and her departure is confirmed in a letter she leaves for her father. In a climactic scene at the end of the act Cyrus, completely distraught, confronts Chandler and demands that Julian be recalled to marry his disgraced daughter. Chandler wriggles uncomfortably as Cyrus asks him repeatedly "But you won't send for him?" (*CH*, 1:165), and eventually he walks out. On stage by himself, Cyrus, like an Old Testament prophet, calls down the wrath of heaven upon Chandler: "Give him and his dearest into my keeping! Make them clay in my hands that I may shape and mould them as I choose, and melt them like wax in the fire of my revenge!" (*CH*, 1:165). That Cyrus should use the imagery of the potter to frame the terms of his revenge suggests that, far from abandoning his quest, Cyrus will devote himself to its achievement with white-hot passion.

The third act shows this process in action. It takes place in a shed with kilns burning, remnants of coal, a truckle bed, and the flickering fires of yet more kilns burning outside in neighboring factories. It is a vision of the Inferno, with Cyrus's hair, now white, his ragged clothes and feverishly determined face reflected in the glowing fires (*CH*, 1:166). Mary has now been reported dead and Cyrus lives only to humiliate the Chandlers. He now no longer works for them and he retains around him his exhausted helpers, Nancy and Jesse. When Cyrus finally pulls out specimens from one of his cooling kilns, he discovers that his efforts have been rewarded. Among the spoiled specimens stands a perfect example of the chinaware he has been trying to rediscover. The act ends with a hysterical outburst of triumph. Cyrus's faith in his own technical prowess and his refusal to be daunted by providential velleities have been vindicated.

The play might well have ended here. Obviously Cyrus has trumphed over adversity. Nevertheless, the demands of melodrama have not been fully met. It is not enough for justice to be implied; it must be seen to be done. Act 4 is structured around a series of

dramatic reversals. The Chandlers are discovered leaving the Tatlow
Hall which they had usurped from the Umfravilles. They are penniless and are forced to beg Todd, now Cyrus's managing agent, for
assistance. The Umfravilles arrive to rub salt into the wound by telling Chandler that they can no longer entertain the possibility of their
daughter's marriage to Julian, who is due back from Africa at any
moment. Cyrus arrives completely changed. He is the new owner of
Tatlow Hall and quickly banishes the fawning Umfravilles. Jesse and
Nancy now enjoy a relationship completely reversed from that which
we have so far seen. Like Mrs. Mildmay in *Still Waters Run Deep*, she
is meek and compliant, he is masterful and confident as befits Cyrus's
new partner. At this point, Cyrus, calling on Mary's memory, decides
that forgiveness is the most telling form of revenge, and appoints
Chandler to be his undermanager. But his spirit of forgiveness is
sorely tested as Julian returns, a conquering hero from abroad. He
enters accompanied by the bands and cheering with which he left in
act 1. The final reversal occurs as Julian reveals that Mary is not dead
at all, and that he has brought her back as his wife: "Cyrus cannot
believe his eyes" (*CH*, 1:195). Even by 1894 such a coincidence was
too theatrical to be other than old fashioned.

But *The Middleman* marks an important stage in Jones's development. He regarded his apprenticeship to melodrama as now at an
end. He had prepared the way for a literary theater encompassing new
thematic directions, and being above all, English rather than French.
The reception given to the first authentic English production of *A
Doll's House* at the Novelty Theatre in June 1889, and the moves afoot
to form an independent theater based on the model of Antoine's "Free
Theatre" in Paris, suggested that there was an intellectual audience
waiting for its dramatic spokesman. But Jones saw little in Ibsen that
would attract more than a coterie of the avant-garde. He himself was
committed to elevating the native drama and its broad-based but
conservative patrons. It was this society, embarking on "a period of
analysis, of general, restless inquiry,"[37] to which he might address
himself.

The 1890s: The Serious Plays and the Depiction of Truth

Judah. Though it was through *The Dancing Girl* in 1891 that
Jones would come to be numbered among the ranks of the Society
Dramatists, it is in *Judah* that we can see him looking forward rather

than backward for the first time.[38] There is a growing confidence in the selection of his themes and characters. The absence of soliloquies and asides suggests that Jones may have at last subscribed to the realist's dogma of authorial noninterference. In retrospect, the play becomes a manifesto of ideas and attitudes to which he would adhere for the remainder of his creative life. Foremost among these is Jones's preoccupation with falsehood, both individual and social. The preoccupation is pervasive, stemming from his austere Puritan background rather than from any Ibsen influence. The corrosive effects of falsehood are constantly referred to in the titles of his plays: *The Masqueraders, The Tempter, The Liars, The Hypocrites, The Lie.* It is further reflected in the characters he selects: those who insist upon truth and those who shrink from it. To these kinds of characters Jones adds representatives of current intellectual and social movements: the new feminism, the aesthetic movement, rationalism, and the aristocratic patronage of fads. In *Judah* these representatives gave the impression of topically and immediately recognizable relevance. Binding these elements together was Jones's moral earnestness that at best would give his serious plays an invigorating passion. At worst, it would emphasize his blinkered narrowness of outlook.

When the play opened at the Shaftesbury Theatre in May 1890, it had once again Willard playing the main part of Judah Llewellyn. He is a passionate young clergyman in love with Vashti Dethic, a spiritual healer, who is also mysteriously effective. To him, she is a miracle worker whose virtues he is prepared to praise from his Non-Conformist pulpit. She has been invited to Asgarby Castle to try to heal the sick daughter of Lord Asgarby, who in turn is prepared to do anything for his only child. But there are those for whom faith and good deeds are not enough. Professor Jopp, a Rationalist, "keen, alert, intellectual; bald, very high forehead . . . genial Voltaire type of face" (*CH,* 1:201), who has written an article on "The Scientific Conception of Truth;" his daughter, Sophie, "a dogmatic, supercilious, incisive young lady, with eye glass and short hair" (*CH,* 1:206), a less than subtle cartoon of the New Woman. To balance these are Mr. and Mrs. Prall, and their son Juxon. The Pralls are a new version of the Chandlers. They are independently wealthy but have made a reputation from publishing accounts of Vashti's cures for credulous readers. Juxon, on the other hand, is a young poseur, dismissive of his parents' ingenuousness but financially dependent upon them. He is "a thin, wizened, old young man, spectacles, sharp features; knows everything" whose philosophy is encapsulated in "the experience of my entire life has convinced me that my own personal observation is the only instrument whose results are perfectly satisfying and convincing" (*CH*, 1:206–7). Against a combination such as this, acceptance of the irrational is hardly possible. Finally, to compound the difficulty, Jones introduces Vashti's father and personal manager, "a suave, furtive, sallow, oily man of about fifty, with a touch of the manner of a second rate platform orator" (*CH*, 1:210).

If the play were about the conflict in contemporary society between reason and emotion or unreason, then such a conflict would have already been resolved in terms of the stage directions alone. But as the play's title implies, the focus of Jones's attention is elsewhere. We have seen in *Saints and Sinners* through the changing relationship between Fanshawe and Letty, something of Jones's interest in passion and its effects. Melodrama traditionally charts the progress of love through the character of the heroine. Jones's unusual departure, again a conscious dramatic reversal, is to chart this progress through his male characters, in this case the character of Judah who confuses faith with a passionate, adoring love for Vashti. When Vashti challenges Jopp to prove that she is a fraud by agreeing to a complete fast for three weeks as a virtual prisoner in Asgarby Castle, Judah rounds on the disbelievers: "your own lips shall be the witness of her truth and goodness to all the world" (*CH*, 1:225).

Though the first act has strong characters and well-motivated action, Jones's emancipation from undisguised melodrama is incomplete. His stage directions betray an intrusive desire to leave no uncertainty in the minds of the audience about his characters. Jones's tendency toward explicitness is extended into act 2. Again the audience is deliberately made aware that Vashti's virtual imprisonment has been broached by her father using a duplicate key to her room in the castle. There is no possibility of a miracle. The principal interest of the act, however, lies in the love scenes between Judah and Vashti and the intentionally jarring proposal scene between Juxon Prall and Sophie Jopp.

The final act brings about the cleansing by fire. Lady Eve, Asgarby's daughter, appears to have been cured by Vashti and in gratitude proposes to build a new church for Judah and to donate a living to him as a wedding present. It is one year later. But Judah is possessed by the demons of his own conscience. At the same time his love for Vashti is strong and protective, a heady combination of passion and guilt. Even if the deception were to remain hidden, Judah's rejection of the church building, "it's built on lies" (*CH*, 1:259), would insure eventual self-exposure. Thus the mechanics of discovery—Jopp's unearthing of the locksmith who supplied the duplicate key to Vashti's father, and his threat to have Vashti imprisoned—are rendered less important than the inner motivations of the characters. Even Jopp finds there is less to gain in the exposure than he thought when confronted by the irrational hope on the faces of Eve and her father. His only satisfaction comes from forcing Vashti's father to emigrate hurriedly. It remains for Judah and Vashti to purge themselves publicly, like Jacob and Letty. Unlike the earlier play, however, confession is immediately followed by absolution as Jopp and Asgarby persuade them of their friendship and urge them to stay in the community. Judah accepts with a line that might have come from Ibsen's *Pillars of the Community:* "Yes, we will build our new church with our lives, and its foundation shall be the truth" (*CH,* 1:278).

It is a very satisfying play even if the second act tended to become bogged down with moonlit atmosphere and evening dressed conspirators trying to trap an imposter. The potential weakness in the play lies in Jones's heavy-handed satire and his refusal to allow the audience to make up its own mind. The first shows a fine ability to write amusing lines but a coarse appreciation of social issues, while the second betrays a terror of overestimating his audience's intelligence. Nevertheless, what is undeniable, and would provoke the admiration of his sternest critics, is Jones's ability to tell an exciting story.

Society drama. Though George Rowell dates the era of society drama from the first production of Pinero's *The Second Mrs. Tanqueray* by George Alexander in 1893, it is more appropriate to date the era from the beginning of his management of the St. James's Theatre in 1891, and Tree's production of *The Dancing Girl* which opened at the Haymarket Theatre on 15 January in the same year.[39] Society drama of the 1890s resulted from the efforts of actor/managers to attract a fashionable audience to the theater, an attraction the Bancrofts had started with conspicuous success at the Prince of Wales Theatre in the 1860s. It was quite natural, therefore, that this audience should wish to see its own milieu and attitudes depicted on stage. Nevertheless, actor/managers were aware that aristocratic audiences would never fill theaters. Thus society drama came to mean plays reflecting the milieu of high life and its sumptuousness, but using situations and themes recognizable to a broad spectrum of theatergoers.

Because the late Victorian audience felt itself to be enlightened and progressive, a modicum of social or moral controversy was acceptable. But the basis of broad popular appeal insured society drama's essential conservatism. Some dramatists chafed at this restriction, while others were prepared to compromise by modifying their dramatic structure to accord with the carefully guarded image that actor/managers had of themselves, or by pandering to a belief in inevitable moral regeneration and earthly rewards just as tenaciously held by audiences. The general ambivalence about morality came into sharpest focus when plays concentrated on "a woman with a past" or "a fallen woman," and society dramas were often identified with these themes. Though they suggested the serious investigation of a social or moral issue, the plays, in fact, were glossed over with a kind of Robertsonian idealism and an appeal to an audience's prejudice.[40]

Jones's best work displayed an ambivalent attitude. He was prepared in a bitter public exchange to attack the stranglehold of the actor/managers on audience taste and the playwright's freedom, while at the same time to applaud the increasing discrimination of theater audiences. His personal attitudes toward sex and morality were highly conservative. In principle he would have subscribed to a belief in a single standard of morality applicable to both men and women. But in practice, he was evolutionary and cautious rather than revolutionary and uncompromising. He believed that the departure of a woman from bourgeois morality brought in its train far more disastrous consequences than that of a man, and this belief informs all his dramatic writing.

The Dancing Girl.   *The Dancing Girl* is no exception to Jones's basic moral and social stance. In the story of Drusilla Ives who from a demure Quaker becomes a "feminine reincarnation of Paganism" at the beck and call of the dissolute Duke of Guisebury, and Sybil Crake, who though crippled, rescues him from despairing suicide, "Victorian audiences applauded the awarding of the fine young girl to the *roué* and complacently accepted as poetic justice the death of the dancing girl."[41]

The play contrasts two worlds, the Island of St. Endellion populated by hard working Quakers who are fishermen and seafarers, and the "smart" world of London, urban and, by definition, indolent. Straddling the two are Drusilla, the daughter of David Ives, an elder of the chapel, and the Duke of Guisebury, who owns the island and has been an absentee landlord for the last eighteen years. Drusilla left the island to take up a domestic position in London, but has become "Diana Valrose," a Society Isadora Duncan, and the mistress of Guisebury. In a thematic twist, however, Jones makes Guisebury the exploited and Drusilla the exploiter. The Duke, furthermore, is about to be ruined and is in the throes of indecision about his future. His infatuation for Drusilla prevents him from severing his connection, and at the same time this crisis makes him realize the benefits of tranquillity on St. Endellion and his own inadequacies as a landlord.

When in act 2 Guisebury decides to leave London's high society, Drusilla in turn abandons him. He responds to her callousness by hosting a farewell party. The third act takes place in the hall and on the staircase of Guisebury's house in St. James's Square, the very center of London's social occasions. Guests enter in evening dress and exit to rooms filled with the ring of champagne glasses and music. As Drusilla passes into an adjoining room to put the finishing touches to her dress for dancing, she and Guisebury part. He reveals that he has sold his properties to pay his debts before leaving England. Her response is characteristically flippant: "Then I shall go to America— or into a convent. . . . The Catholic is such an artistic religion. No harmoniums. I think I should like to try it for three months" (*CH*, 1:332). Guisebury indulges himself in a long soliloquy about the need for absolute serenity, a tendency toward philosophizing that critics found too glib. But Jones comes into his own with the depiction of the fashionable guests and their genteel hypocrisy. They mount the stairs, talking of Guisebury's flagrancy and the presence of the notorious dancing girl. They are quite prepared to ogle Drusilla, but when her father comes and denounces her as a harlot and calls the wrath of God down upon her, they scuttle hysterically about looking for their wraps and trying to dissociate themselves from the makings of a scandal. It is the high point of the act: "The evolutions of the fashionable crowd in this scene are a marvel of stage management; the Meiningers could not have manoeuvred better."[42] The theatrical organization to which A. B. Walkley here draws attention is matched by Jones's dramatic organization of the act's conclusion. As the stage empties and the lights are turned off, Guisebury stands alone and produces a bottle of poison. This is the exit he had planned all along. But as he is about to take the contents, Sybil, the crippled daughter of the Duke's agent and manager, enters quietly and without any words takes the poison away from him. Again in Walkley's summation: "The scene passes in dead silence, and is one of those triumphs of theatrical effect which reveals the born dramatist."

The last act returns to St. Endellion and, like the last act of *The Middleman,* is the least satisfactory. It is also untheatrical but mercifully short: Drusilla has died in New Orleans; the breakwater, due to Crake's managerial efficiency, will be built; Drusilla's father forgives Guisebury; and Sybil will continue to care for the Duke, who has returned to the island to cleanse himself. All critics were scathing about the act's deficiencies and labored resolution. Without it, by the end of act 3, "Mr. Henry Arthur Jones's work, though giving us the very worst side of human nature, would have given us one of its truest pictures. It showed us the depravity of life, but it also showed us how a good woman can by persistent efforts win back a weak frail man to a better life."[43]

Even before the run of *The Dancing Girl,* Jones had decided to go into management for himself. He had to test out personally whether the dramatist/manager could replace the actor/manager, and hired the Avenue Theatre for his play *The Crusaders.* It was a failure, the reasons for which we will consider when we examine some of Jones's comedies, although it is through his comedies that he was to maintain his popular appeal. *The Bauble Shop* in January 1893 is only significant insofar as it brought together Jones and Charles Wyndham, whose talent had been for light, romantic comedy but who was looking for vehicles that would allow him to modify his style to suit his middle age. *The Bauble Shop* is a sentimental drama set in the political arena. Its hero is the Prime Minister who, it is suggested, has compromised himself with a young girl. His career is ruined but he marries the girl, Jessie, whom he has innocently been visiting. Jones was far too conservative to consider political satire, and the play was simply written to Wyndham's order, peopled with the elegant, aristocratic world that would increasingly dominate Jones's plays.

The Tempter.   More interestingly, Jones had been engaged for over a year in writing a new play in a form new to him. It would be still part of his search for the expression of truth and would demonstrate yet again an alternative to the attempts of the new naturalism "to ally dramatic art with the realistic portraiture of disease, and decadence, and physical degradation."[44] It would also incorporate his love for Shakespeare in its form by mingling blank verse with prose in a quasi-historical fourteenth-century setting. *The Tempter* opened on 20 September 1893 at the Haymarket Theatre with Beerbohm Tree playing the title role. It was, like his exercise in theater management, a courageous probing of his belief in the new audience's developing taste and of his grasp of popular theater.

The attitudes and style of the play stem from an essentially modern viewpoint. The choice of a fourteenth-century context allowed Jones a degree of objectivity. It was a recognizably Chaucerian world of *The Canterbury Tales*—as popularized and "illustrated" by nineteenth-century genre painters.[45] It was, therefore, nationalistically English. Finally, it offered a starring role for Tree in which the manipulative power of an actor/manager could be translated into the machinations of a supernatural puppeteer. Tree, too, undoubtedly must have felt that the central role of the Tempter could give him the opportunity of rivaling Irving's performance as Mephistopheles.

If we extract the figure of the Tempter (Devil) from the play, we are left with a narrative about Prince Leon of Auvergne who is journeying to England from France to marry, for political and dynastic reasons, his childhood friend, Lady Avis of Rougemont. She is accompanying her father on a pilgrimage to Canterbury together with her cousin, Lady Isobel of Carmayne. They are all to meet in Canterbury where the marriage will take place and Lady Isobel will enter a convent. Unfortunately, Leon falls in love with Isobel and seduces her. He is persuaded subsequently that she has deliberately organized the seduction in order to supplant her cousin. She, in turn, is persuaded to believe that he has used her as an idle conquest, and, overcome with shame, stabs him. Too late they both realize their mistakes and as the litter carrying the dying Leon enters the great doors of Canterbury Cathedral, she kills herself in an attempt at expiation. The two lovers are then carried in for the last rites of absolution. The play, however, is dominated by the figure of the Devil, who has no other motivation than an irrational malevolence toward the human race.

The play is called a tragedy. But the essence of tragedy is contained in acts of human volition that are, all too late, brought into conflict with divine will, unforeseen circumstances, or even, if we subscribe to Arthur Miller, financial fluctuations. The irreducible minimum, however, is the belief on the part of the protagonists that they are in control of their destiny, a belief that is subsequently tested and found to be groundless. On this admittedly literary rather than theatrical criterion, the play falls down badly. It is the Devil who suggests to the characters not only their actions but also their lines. The characters accept without question his interpretation of their motives toward one another. When Leon protests at the Devil's suggestion that Isobel has contrived her own seduction and seems to be about to assert his independence, it only requires the Devil to say, "I wish you joy of Lady Isobel," for him to lose any sense of purpose: "Yes, yes, I will have joy of her. That word / Restores me to myself" (*CH,* 2:163). The actions are thus rendered motiveless.

Jones makes it clear in his prologue to the play that Chaucer's England and nineteenth-century England are in some respects interchangeable. Chaucer's world was prettier and romantic, unsullied by "wan faced railway herds" and "the muddy ferment . . . of industrial war." While fourteenth-century men battled with the Devil for their souls, nineteenth-century men battled "with darkness, taint of blood, necessity, / Fate, chance, or—what?" (CH, 2:96). In other words, heredity, environment, and the pressure of philosophical determinism. Jones in the course of the play shows determinism to be triumphant and human aspirations to be misguided and ultimately pointless. This may be an honest reflection of Jones's fundamental pessimism about nineteenth-century society. But drama cannot exist when human conflict is rendered pointless by arbitrary intervention. To an audience dedicated to upward mobility and social progress, the play's implied philosophy of human immobility except through death would have proved intolerable. Socialists like Archer condemned the play roundly, and theater critics sensed the play's "accidental" quality and rightly blamed the Tempter as "a loquacious busybody" who "hampers and hinders (his human folk) amazingly—seeing where his interest lies, and how prone they are to damn themselves—and the marvel is that he is not by one and all consigned to hell, instead of vice versa."[46]

Michael and His Lost Angel.   In order to regain his audience Jones increasingly moved toward comedy. He did not in fact return to serious drama until *Michael and His Lost Angel* in 1896. It opened simultaneously in London and New York on 15 January and closed in both locations within eleven days. Rehearsals in London were plagued with difficulties. Johnston Forbes-Robertson, Mrs. Patrick Campbell, and Jones disagreed continuously about the title (Forbes-Robertson felt that "lost angel" might be taken to mean "prostitute"), about the church scenes (Mrs. Patrick Campbell found them embarrassing), and with the delivery of lines (Jones insisted on interfering). A matter of days before the opening Mrs. Patrick Campbell was replaced by Marion Terry and the play was received with notices that clearly polarized the critical community. But Jones's reputation as a serious writer rests largely on this play and the approval of it accorded by its readers rather than viewers. Its lack of theatrical success was due to Forbes-Robertson's fainthearted reaction when confronted by the possibility of religious controversy.

Jones took the decision badly. The play was conceived as a prose tragedy, and he had spent much time and labor on it. There were no asides, and his natural narrative exuberance had been restrained so that minor plots were excluded. The theme was one about which Jones felt deeply: the conflict between passion and duty, intellect and emotion. Among the few critics who were not detractors was Shaw who wrote a lengthy appraisal in the *Saturday Review*, 18 January 1896: "The melancholy truth of the matter is that the English stage got a good play, and was completely and ignominiously beaten by it."[47]

The reasons that Shaw suggests for this defeat are illuminating. First he found fault in Forbes-Robertson's and Marion Terry's playing. In the character of the minister, Michael Feversham, the "calmness," "spirituality," and "strength of character" (*CH*, 3:8) are facets of Judah, Cyrus Blenkarn, and Jacob Fletcher. He is fired by a passion for purity and appears beyond temptation: "a rapturous faith in the gladness of an open and contrite heart," in Shaw's words. Forbes-Robertson, however, insisted on a doomed spiritual joylessness from the start. Michael's self-erected pedestal begins to crumble when he comes into contact with Audrie Lesden, a rich widow of thirty, who amuses herself by giving to charities. Michael to her is a charity who is to be cajoled out of his seriousness and capriciously tempted. At the same time, she is perverse and impulsive. She is therefore a mixture of Drusilla Ives and Letty Fletcher. Marion Terry was "inveterately amiable" but was unable to move beyond that.

In the course of the play Audrie and Michael find themselves alone on his island retreat and confess their love for one another. Perfectly motivated coincidence insures that she must remain the night with him. To keep up appearances they construct an elaborate series of lies which they find exciting. They feel no sense of guilt. But this is shattered when Audrie's husband is revealed to be not only alive but in the town and when the father of the girl whom Michael forced to make a public confession of moral delinquency in church in act 1 reveals that he knows Michael's secret. Shaw liked particularly the absence of sexual shame but found the subsequent dramatic engineering implausible. Shaw would have preferred Michael to brazen out any consequences in the name of personal principle. But this would have necessitated a change in Jones's makeup. It is wholly characteristic of Jones that act 4 should take place in the chancel of Michael's church, and that Michael should confess to his congregation publicly. It is just as characteristic that Jones should have built his situation on the theatrical model of *Saints and Sinners,* reinforcing the precedent and extending its emotional impact. Furthermore, unlike the figure of the

Devil in *The Tempter,* in this play Audrie, who tempts the self-confident ascetic, is unquestionably a human being.

The last act takes place in a monastery in Italy where Michael has found consolation in Roman Catholicism. To this mountain eyrie comes a dying Audrie, seeking and obtaining a final belated glimpse of happiness. There can be no real explanation for this other than "the fact that Audrie is dying of nothing but the need for making the audience cry." There can be little of pity or fear felt for a character who is simply satisfying a social dictate that the wages of sin are death. The play, however, remains Jones's most succinct statement on the conflict between duty and desire as seen through the filter of Victorian conservatism. The play's run was too short to allow any estimate to be made about its possible impact. It was, however, received very favorably by a literary readership. At the end of his life Jones was able to say, *"Michael* has done more for my reputation than any success I've ever had."[48]

From *The Physician* to *Carnac Sahib.* Between 1896 and 1900 Jones wrote three more serious dramas: *The Physician* in 1897, *Carnac Sahib* in 1899, and his most memorable theatrical tour de force, *Mrs. Dane's Defence* in 1900. For the rest, he concentrated on comedy. *The Physician* was written with Wyndham in mind. He played an elegant Harley Street physician who is consulted by a young girl on behalf of her alcoholic boy friend. In a commonplace of melodrama, he finds that he has to weigh between professional duty and his personal interest when he himself falls in love with the girl. In the end, the alcoholic conveniently dies and the conflict is resolved. As critics have observed, the play is the prototype for Shaw's *The Doctor's Dilemma* which he wrote in 1906. Both Shaw and William Archer were highly complimentary about Jones's ability to tell a story even though they both felt that Wyndham's Dr. Lewin Carey was a purely romantic conception. "Does one . . . find," asked Archer, "eminent nerve specialists buttonholing their colleagues to bewail their lack of 'faith,' and bemoaning to maidens in white muslin the inapplicability of the microscope to metaphysics?"[49]

With *Carnac Sahib* the failure was complete. It opened at Beerbohm Tree's new Her Majesty's Theatre in April 1899. The action takes place in India during an insurrection. There are alarums and excursions as soldiers move from one position of siege to another. But the play's real mechanism is the competition between Carnac and his adjutant, Syrret, over Olive Arnison, a provocative woman who enjoys blood and the romantic notion of chivalry. That she is married merely adds to her attractiveness. The play is a costumed melodrama whose setting was studiously researched by Jones. He demonstrated, however, little interest in his characters. The play's failure must be attributed to this and to Tree's lack of commitment as well. His performance gave the play a cynical detachment that communicated itself to the audiences. *The Lackey's Carnival* tried to be different. A play about masters and servants within an aristocratic household, it took its viewpoint from that of a power hungry valet seeking to exert his influence by exposing the household secrets. It again was a failure, rehearsals dogged by Jones's increasing irascibility with actors.[50]

Mrs. Dane's Defence. Two weeks after the opening of *The Lackey's Carnival,* Jones was to retrieve his reputation with both critics and audiences when Wyndham opened *Mrs. Dane's Defence* with himself as Sir Daniel Carteret and Lena Ashwell as Mrs. Dane. It ran for 209 nights and was to be revived in 1902, 1906, and 1912. Even such an unlikely critic as Jacob Grein, the founder of the Independent Theatre, was impressed by the "consummate skill" with which Jones could write scenes of "colossal effect."[51] The play also brings into clear focus the merits and demerits of Jones as a serious dramatist.

Jones was recognized as a preeminent storyteller. As such he was ideally suited to plot a detective story that is the structural basis of this play. Lionel (Lal), the adopted son of Sir Daniel Carteret, has fallen in love with and wishes to marry Mrs. Dane, a twenty-eight-year-old widow living among the aristocracy of a country town. She is a center of local attention as men find her irresistible. She thus becomes the focus of gossip when she is mistakenly identified as a Miss Hindemarsh, "the other woman" in the breakup of a marriage that resulted in the wife's suicide and the husband's madness of a few year's before. But rumor is not to be squashed and Mrs. Bulsom-Porter, insecure about her husband's affections, is determined to leave no stone unturned. A private detective is hired. Although he is prepared to give Mrs. Dane the benefit of the doubt, Sir Daniel is determined that his adopted son's marriage will be a secure one. He reveals that Lal is the son of a woman with whom he had a passionate affair some years before and who is now dead. Mrs. Dane appears to be simply the center of malicious gossip. But Jones cannot help giving the game away. From her first entrance she watches people "a little furtively," reacts "showing a little alarm" to innocent questions, and paces "in anxious deliberation" when alone (*CH,* 3:189–91). By the end of act

2, however, the game is over bar the public humiliation. Mrs. Dane can show Lal "a radiant, smiling face," but "the moment he has gone she utters a sharp cry, followed by a long groan of despair, sits down on sofa with a white, drawn, haggard face, wringing her hands" (*CH*, 3:222). But by dint of bribing the private detective, Fendick, who denies to Sir Daniel that she bears any resemblance to a Miss Hindemarsh, she is able to have a momentary triumph. Mrs. Bulsom-Porter is forced to consider making a public apology.

The moment of truth takes place in act 3. Sir Daniel cross-examines Mrs. Dane gently but firmly. He is, after all, not a villain but a man seeking to safeguard his family's reputation. As the noose tightens she becomes more and more the frightened animal and the scene culminates with Sir Daniel's "I say you're lying! You are Felicia Hindemarsh!" (*CH*, 3:253). The forthcoming marriage to Lal is broken off and she is banished to Devonshire and the child she has fostered out. In act 4, Sir Daniel proposes to Lady Eastney, in whose residence the play began, and Lal, after a suitable period of emotional exhaustion, the play suggests will marry his "suitable" Scottish girl friend. Mrs. Dane is driven out of society by "the hard law that we didn't make . . . that is above us all, made for us all, that we can't escape from, that we must keep or perish" (*CH*, 3:272).

The play's conclusion is as bleakly a deterministic vision of social immobility as that in *The Tempter*. Act 3 showed that Jones was a clever playwright: "but, alas! there is no home with us for the drama of life undefiled by considerations of exchequer. And thus Mr. Jones had to be content with pleasing himself in one act only, and the exigencies of the system in all the others." Grein's conclusion is an appropriate one. When Jones's theatrical mechanism ran down, his seriousness and moral earnestness were revealed to be in the service of atrophied ideals. The pressure on a reforming dramatist had insured that by 1900 compromise had now become custom. Jones may have intended at the beginning of his career to be a reforming dramatist. By 1900, however, his zeal had been affected by the compromises he had been compelled to make.

The 1890s: The Comedies and Social Satire

The Crusaders.   The comedies of the 1890s begin with *The Crusaders* with which Jones tried to prove that actor/managers were dispensable. He failed not because of managerial ineptitude but because the play was structurally uncertain and unfocused. As a satire of an entire social group, Richard Cordell finds it more powerful than Shaw's *Widowers Houses*.[52] William Archer, in his preface to the published play, found the intellectual basis—an examination of social idealism—a genuinely dramatic one: "The banner of Social Reform serves as a rallying point for all that is noblest and basest, wisest and foolishest, in the world of today. . . . This movement is in truth as dramatic an element in the life of the nineteenth century as was the Crusades in that of the thirteenth."[53] The problems came when Jones tried to reconcile the aims of social satire with those of dramatic intrigue and emotional involvement. The result was a confusion between fantasy and reality that resulted in the play becoming not a dissection of the present but rather, as Archer carefully worded it, "a fairy tale of the possible future."

The world Jones portrays is an upper-class one, using up its spare time and energies in the support of fashionable causes: the creation of a pollution free London, free love, and the rehabilitation of the poor. He peoples it with freakish proponents and their wealthy patrons: Philos Ingarfield, the guru of the London Reformation League, and his enthusiastic supporter, Una, who plays Sonya to his Uncle Vanya; the bored widow, Cynthia, with whom Philos is in love; Lord Burnham, the League's political patron and the play's raisonneur; Burnham's nephew, Dick, who together with his wife practices the modern marriage of ostentatious independence from one another. The ideas of the League are as impractical as their proponents: establishing a colony of indigents in Costa Rica and a colony of seamstresses growing roses in suburban London. Act 1 promises to be a savage comedy of manners, but the play soon disintegrates into a tale of love and intrigue in which Philos and Dick vie with each other for the affection of Cynthia.

It is an uneasy play hovering between scathing satire and drawing-room intrigue. This complicates the audience's reactions, particularly as the characters satirized evoke recognition and objective derision while the sympathetic characters suggest at the very least the need for understanding. The character of Philos falls between the two stools. Jones set himself a difficult task with this character. His silliness and unrealistic acceptance of those who batten upon him hardly prepares the audience for his important role in the intrigue. Dick too is not a bumbling silly ass but a determined seducer quite prepared to allow Philos to take responsibility for his actions. By contrast, the minor characters are cartoons, sketched economically and surely. The result is that the play's unity is fractured by illogical character development and by the juxtaposition of farcical behavior with serious emotional crises. Meanwhile, its audience is left to flounder amid the complicated plot devices.

Jones, however, was undeterred by the play's failure. The combination of romance with satire had worked well in *Judah* and he was determined to try again. In *The Dancing Girl* he had been able to grasp the intonations of a smug social world and had shown up its hypocritical attitudes. Worldly raisonneurs and passionate idealists made for good dramatic conflicts, provided that they offered satisfying parts to an actor/manager. Both dramatic conflict and satisfying parts had been wholly absent from *The Crusaders*. He redressed the balance in his new play *The Masqueraders*, which he offered to George Alexander in 1894.

The Masqueraders.   Whether the play ought to be considered as a comedy is questionable. Its claim rests with the depiction of the milieu, and that only in the first two acts: "in these . . . Mr. Jones has painted a large canvas of social comedy; and from this large canvas the play derives its title."[54] As in *The Crusaders*, the action is narrowly focused in the last two on the battle between David Remon and Sir Brice Skene for the love and possession of Dulcie Larondie. The reviews admitted the presence of the satirical elements but were unanimous in labeling the play a romance.

Dulcie, the object of the men's attention, is related as a character to Drusilla Ives. She works in a fashionable country hotel populated by professional gamblers and aristocrats. To her it is a tantalizing glimpse of the lights of London. Among her admirers are Sir Brice, a dangerous but dashing professional gambler, and David Remon, an astronomer and mountaineer who is looking for new worlds to explore. Her wish comes true when Sir Brice, after winning a kiss from her in a bar room auction, offers publicly to marry her and raise her to his station.

The result of this impulsive misalliance is a predictable one. After three and a half years, and one child, Dulcie, now Lady Skene, is taking sleeping draughts and desperately trying to cover up the repulsive antisocial behavior of a husband whom she despises. Her reception room is filled with witty scandalmongers whose lines are as self-consciously clever as those of Wilde. Her only real friend is Remon, now a famous and wealthy astronomer. By act 3, however, the humor to be elicited out of the vagaries of smart society has evaporated. The play assumes the hues of melodrama: a violent mix of primary colors. Dulcie is only persuaded by her sister, Helen, to remain with Skene. It is to Helen's arid view of marriage that Shaw so objected. The act culminates in an electrifying scene in which Remon challenges Skene to gamble his wife and child for Remon's entire fortune. Remon wins and sweeps Dulcie and the child away.

At this stage the play might have ended. Even the critics felt this to be the case. Structurally it would have been satisfying with the same device of a calculated gamble used to free Dulcie which had been used to imprison her in act 1. Brice is patently a villain who has received his just deserts. The world of the masqueraders has been revealed, through the agency of David, to be a sham, and Dulcie has seen the error of her social ways. But Jones refuses to end on this note. Helen persuades Remon and Dulcie to part from one another and he goes off on an African expedition from which he may not return.

The Case of Rebellious Susan. *The Case of Rebellious Susan* continued the successful association with Wyndham, which they had started in *The Bauble Shop* in 1893. The opening did not come about without some difficulties. Wyndham was quite prepared to have implied a certain suggestiveness, provided that, in the final analysis, there was no sexual or moral ambiguity. His reputation at the Criterion Theatre had been made on civilized farces by Burnand or Byron, and coffee and elaborate programs for his patrons. And he was not about to lose this support.[55] He wrote at length to Jones urging him to modify the character of Susan Harabin so that there would be no suggestion of impropriety in a play whose theme is a woman's determination to exercise the same sexual rights as a man. Jones, to his credit, refused, and had enough dramatic weight to carry the day.[56]

Wyndham played the part of the middle-aged, charming raisonneur Sir Richard Kato, a dramatic type that he would duplicate as Sir Christopher Deering in *The Liars,* and as Sir Daniel Carteret in *Mrs. Dane's Defence.* In the mouth of each Jones places society's point of view and his own conviction that social defiance was to be equated with social disaster. What prevented these characters from becoming smugly sententious was Wyndham's charm and elegance. When the play opened finally in October 1894, many of the press notices reflected a far more conservative reaction than that of the audiences that filled the Criterion for 164 nights.

The play's narrative structure is a very simple one. Susan is made aware that her husband has had an affair, and determines to do likewise. While on a trip to Egypt with her friend, Mrs. Quesnel, she meets Lucien Edensor and they have an affair. Coincidently, he is the son of an old friend of Sir Richard Kato, Susan's uncle. When they return to England, they intend to carry on the relationship, and it takes all of Sir Richard's skill as a jurist to thwart their intentions. Eventually Lucien is sent off to a government post in New Zealand and Susan and her husband are reconciled with the promise of a villa in Cannes and diamonds from Bond Street. It is both a bribe and Jones's cure for the collapse of matrimonial romance.

The character of Susan herself is full of life, a quality she shares with her other uncle, Admiral Sir Joseph Darby. He is an old sea dog, sentimental about his wife's virtues and overindulgent with champagne. By contrast, Susan's husband is morose and ineffectual. He is hardly worth the effort of cuckolding, but the characterization strengthens Susan's position and makes society's efforts to bring them together all the more intolerable. Ultimately, however, it is Susan's terror of discovery, riding uneasily on her impulsive desire for revenge, that loads the dice against her. Appearances, suggests Jones, is a universal intrusion as important to Mayfair society as it is to suburban Clapham. With this his audience would have agreed, however much it might have condoned Susan's avowed intentions.

The play marks a sure advance in the writing of comedy for Jones.[57] There is little sentimentality in his treatment of the situation, although the introduction of an Indian summer relationship between Sir Richard and Mrs. Quesnel in act 3 is contrived and unnecessary. It acknowledged, however, Wyndham's claim to be still a matinee idol, an image that Jones was to complement with Beatrice in *The Liars* and Lady Eastney in *Mrs. Dane's Defence*. The sureness is also to be seen in his ability to dispense with formal exposition. The whole premise of the play is clearly defined in the first few lines. Admiral Darby's wife enters and asks the first footman, "Where is Lady Susan now?" to which he replies, "Upstairs in her sitting room, my lady." She then asks, "Where is Mr. Harabin?" and the reply is, "Downstairs in the library, my lady" (*CH,* 2:275). Their marital contretemps and the suggestion of a difference in social class between them is as clearly to be read as the emblems in a William Orchardson society painting.

The Triumph of the Philistines and *The Rogue's Comedy.* The period between this play and Jones's next essay in "high comedy" was marked by two differing exercises in comic writing. In May 1895, George Alexander produced *The Triumph of the Philistines,* Jones's most savage identification of Puritanism with small-town bigotry and crass commercialism. Dramatically a return to satire of a whole stratum of society, it was condemned critically as pessimistic. But Shaw found much in it to admire: "the attack is not the usual attack of the stage moralist: it is courageous, uncompromising, made with sharp weapons, and left without the slightest attempt to run away at the end."[58] The second attempt was in *The Rogue's Comedy* which brought Jones and Willard together again. In this he played Bailey Prothero, a male version of Vashti Dethic, but translated into a specious fortune teller who swindles a credulous aristocracy. In the end Prothero and his wife abandon their prey when it appears as though their practices are to be exposed by a young barrister, George Lambert, who turns out to be the son they had abandoned years before. The play's universal appeal is that of *The Sting* in which gullible people, who think they are shrewd, are shown up to be less clever than "the sting's" perpetrators. The play is quite free of moralizing and sentiment. Prothero is a capable and likable rogue who has used the greedy, inbred aristocrats for his own ends. But they in turn have profited materially as well, so that their discomfiture is relative only. They are Victorian versions of predators like Corvino and Corbaccio, and indeed there is a distinct resemblance between Prothero and Volpone. It is not surprising that American audiences responded to the world of high finance in the play more readily than the English.

The Liars. In *The Liars,* which Jones wrote to replace *The Physician* in October 1897, we come to the play generally regarded as his greatest achievement. Cordell, Clayton Hamilton, and even the sometimes harsh Marjorie Northend are unequivocal in their praise of the play as a flawless comedy of manners. Jones in retrospect recognized its similarity to the structure of Molière's *The Misanthrope,* though its situation is fundamentally different. Unlike Susan Harabin, Jessica Nepean has no quarrel with her husband other than that he is boring and possessive. Her head has been turned by Edward Falkner, arrived from Africa a national hero in the fight against slave trading. Falkner believes himself to be in love with her, but she is sufficiently realistic to try to warn him off. Even when the raisonneur, Sir

Christopher, describes the social disasters that lie in wait for him, Falkner cannot be dissuaded from taking up Jessica's suggestion that they have a clandestine meeting. He refuses to return to Africa despite an urgent plea from the Colonial Office to do so. Unlike Lucien he will not be as easily persuaded to put duty first.

The second act sets up the intrigue as Falkner arranges a French dinner for two in a private room of a country hotel. It is a disaster as all Jessica's friends arrive unexpectedly and she receives a telegram announcing the return of her husband Gilbert to London. William Archer found the haphazard entry of the characters in this act irritating. In his review he goes to great lengths to argue the inconsistency of the fiction that Jessica and her friends create. But he misses the point. The second act is an elaborately absurd joke, an anglicized scene from Feydeau or Nestroy. Its exact mechanical quality assures us of that, just as the exact mechanical entries of all the characters in act 3 is emphasized by making them come in through the same door at the back of the stage.

The title of the play refers directly to act 3. Each character is persuaded by a delightfully contrite Jessica to support her fiction that she dined with her friend Dolly Coke. Even Sir Christopher agrees to turn a lie into "a sort of idealized and essential truth" (*CH*, 3:145). Gilbert refuses to believe the story and is about to attack Falkner physically when finally Jessica asks him to tell her husband the truth. He tells the company: "She is guiltless. Be sure of that. And now you've got the truth, and be damned to you" and storms out (*CH*, 3:162).

The final act takes place in the drawing room of Sir Christopher's flat. He is to go to Africa and wishes to persuade Falkner to go with him. In this play the raisonneur is provided with Beatrice Ebernoe as his romantic foil. She agrees to marry him when he returns a soldier hero. The real business of the act, however, is to impose Sir Christopher's social attitude upon the protagonists. He succeeds and as a now uxorious Gilbert takes Jessica to the Savoy for dinner, Sir Christopher and Beatrice remain to comfort Falkner in preparation for their departure to Africa in the morning.

The act is less trying than many of Jones's attempts to reconcile a dramatic structure in act 4 with the conclusion of a sermon. But Shaw was right when he described "its pious theology and its absolute conceptions of duty belong to a passionately anticomedic conception. . . . Its observations could only have been made today; its idealism might have been made yesterday; its reflections might have been made a long time ago. . . . It is surely immoral for an Englishman to keep two establishments, much more three."[59] It is fitting, however, that we should conclude our examination of the work of Henry Arthur Jones with the play which, together with *Mrs. Dane's Defence,* marks the apogee of his career.

Postscript

In the years following 1900, Jones continued to write comedies, and though he had modest successes with *Whitewashing Julia* in 1903, *Joseph Entangled* in 1904, *Dolly Reforming Herself* in 1908, and *Mary Goes First* with Marie Tempest in 1913, the gap between Jones and his audience was widening. Critics like Archer rapidly grew impatient with plays that seemed to be merely self-plagiaristic in theme and characterization. Jones's reputation, however, remained high in the United States, and it is therefore apposite that a final evaluation should come from a letter that Jones wrote to his American admirer and editor, Clayton Hamilton. Jones in personal appraisals of his work was often disarmingly honest. Writing to Hamilton who was about to publish his collection, he says: "I am sadly conscious that I have not worked always upon my highest levels. That has been impossible in the conditions that the English theatre has imposed upon me. I think, however, that I may claim that I have always done the best work that there was a good chance of offering to the public. I think that my plays, taken as a whole, will give a truthful picture of English life and character from the year 1885 to 1915. I have drawn more English types in these years than any other English dramatist."[60] With this estimate Walkley, Shaw, Archer, and Max Beerbohm would have concurred.

Chapter Six
Conclusion

The four dramatists we have considered wrote between them over 250 plays, and yet their collective works comprise merely a small fraction of nineteenth-century dramatic writing. All of them resented and were forced in some cases to accept the humiliating position the dramatist occupied in his society that obliged him to remain at the beck and call of theater managers or egocentric actors. All of them aspired to quality but were hampered by the constant demand for quantity. If there is a modern parallel, it is the position of the screenwriter in television today at the beck and call of the channel executive, the producers, and the consumers. This parallel can be extended to include a comparison between the thematic concerns and attitudes expressed in the plays to which we have referred and those of television drama. There is nothing in the costumed historical plays, the crime melodrama, the plays about money and social status, or the illustrations of the mores of high society that suggests other than a direct continuum between nineteenth-century popular drama and that of today. There is also little to suggest that there been any material change in our appreciation in the last hundred years of character types or exotic locations. Even the conditions of nineteenth-century theater have a modern parallel in television viewing. Until late in the nineteenth century, theatergoing was an informal affair into which was integrated the business of eating, drinking, and conversation.

A study of the plays and their contexts reveals not only modern parallels but also the complexity of Victorian society. Nothing can be further removed from the truth than the largely unsubstantiated claim for monolithic Victorianism. The plays clearly reveal the fundamental insecurities of people living in a world of constant struggle: the struggle to be recognized, the struggle to cope with the new technology, the struggle to adjust to upward social mobility, the struggle to maintain personal integrity in an increasingly materialistic world. The plays are thus just as important as documents of social history as they are examples of developing and changing dramatic forms. Even if the solutions that the plays offer are unadventurous and are intended to satisfy the cautious optimism of the many rather than radical aspirations of the few, the plays consistently demonstrate a perhaps overzealous awareness of the marketplace. We can be sure, therefore, that the plays reflect both the problems and solutions, tempered by wish fulfillment, that were understood by a broad spectrum of nineteenth-century society. When the playwrights failed, their failures sprang more often than not from misjudgment of market demand rather than from lapses in their own creative ability.

We have seen that the nineteenth century was an age of performers. These performers moved easily round the English-speaking world and the plays formed part of their personal baggage. Though the playwrights may have resented their dependence upon flattering an actor's ego, the success of their plays demanded it. The themes and concerns of the plays may have accurately reflected those of any English emigrant or English-speaking urban dweller, but, ultimately, the plays depended on the portability and universality of the actor's talent. When these elements combined in the theater, the result was a union between performer and spectator that twentieth-century theater has rarely attained.

Notes and References

Preface

1. David Mayer, "Towards a Definition of Popular Threatre," in *Western Popular Theatre,* ed. D. Mayer and K. Richards (London: Methuen, 1977), 264.

Chapter One

1. Allardyce Nicoll, *A History of English Drama 1660–1900,* vols. 4–5 (Cambridge, 1959–60), 4:331–33, 5:439–40, 592–94, 546–47. This work by Nicoll is hereafter cited as *HED.*
2. Quoted in ibid., 4:11–12.
3. Exemplified in the dramatized confrontation between the illegitimate and legitimate dramas in Planchés *The Drama's Levée; or, A Peep at the Past;* see ibid., 4:150.
4. On the poets and the theater, George Rowell, *The Victorian Theatre* 2d ed. (Cambridge, 1978), 32–38.
5. On nineteenth century taste for spectacle, Michael Booth, *Victorian Spectacular Theatre 1850–1910* (London, 1981), 1–29.
6. Leigh Hunt, *Critical Essays on the Performers of the London Theatres:* quoted in *HED,* 4:50.
7. On actors, managers, and authors, see *HED,* 4:47–57, 5:49–72.
8. Michael Booth, *English Melodrama* (London, 1965), 13–39, and James Smith, *Melodrama* (London, 1973), passim.
9. See the preface to the edition in Michael Booth, *English Plays of the Nineteenth Century* (London, 1969–73), 1:31–34. This work hereafter cited as *EPNC.*
10. Quoted in *HED,* 4:114.
11. Booth, *English Melodrama* 174–75. Booth gives further examples of the lengths to which dramatists and managers went to demonstrate the latest technological marvels on stage.
12. Ibid., 163.
13. See Booth's introduction to this play in *EPNC,* 1:75.
14. On comic acting in the early nineteenth century, see *EPNC,* 3:145.
15. Booth analyzes carefully the compatibility between seriousness of purpose and farcical technique in *EPNC,* 4:10–15.
16. Ibid., 5:2. This section is much indebted to Booth's introduction to this volume.

17. "Illustrated Interviews: No. VI—Sir Augustus Harris," *Strand Magazine,* December 1891, 561; quoted in Booth, *Victorian Spectacular Theatre,* 86.

18. J. R. Planché, *Recollections and Reflections;* quoted in ibid., 11.

19. Ibid., 38.

Chapter Two

1. W. Blanchard Jerrold, *The Life and Remains of Douglas Jerrold* (London, 1859), 241.

2. On its history and Jerrold's wry account of these years, Walter Jerrold, *Douglas Jerrold: Dramatist and Wit* (London, 1914), 1:44–45.

3. Jerrold, *Life and Remains,* 79; and E. B. Watson, *Sheridan to Robertson* (Cambridge, Mass., 1926), 355.

4. Christopher Murray, *Robert William Elliston, Manager* (London: Society for Theatre Research, 1975), 128–34.

5. *Dramatic Magazine,* 1 February 1830, 25.

6. See Walter Jerrold, *Douglas Jerrold and "Punch"* (London: Macmillan, 1910).

7. *HED,* 4:185.

8. Clement Scott, *The Drama of Yesterday and Today* (London, 1899), 1:253–60.

9. James Hannay, "Douglas Jerrold," *Atlantic Monthly* 1 (November 1857):4, 6; and *Living Age* 53 (1857):315–16.

10. B. Harrison, *Drink and the Victorians: The Temperance Question 1815–1872* (London: Faber, 1971), 37–55.

11. Jerrold provided the paradigm for W. H. Smith's American temperance play *The Drunkard; or, The Fallen Saved* (1844)—though with a happy ending—T. P. Taylor's *The Bottle* (1847), and Charles Reade's *Drink* (1879).

12. Murray, *Robert William Elliston,* 53.

13. See *Dramatic Magazine,* 1 May 1829, 79, for a critical reaction.

14. Quoted from a letter in Jerrold, *Douglas Jerrold,* 1:10.

15. *Dramatic Magazine,* 1 August 1829, 172; *Athenaeum,* 2 December 1829, 761; ibid., 16 December 1829, 794.

16. Reference is to Cumberland's *Minor Theatre* (London, n.d.), 11:59; hereafer this work is cited as *C.*

17. On the interaction between politics, economic conditions, and the theater, see Clive Barker, "The Chartists, Theatre Reform and Research," and Robin Estill, *"The Factory Lad:* Melodrama as Propaganda," *Theatre Quarterly* 1, no. 4 (October–December 1971):3, 22.

18. See *Times,* 12 July 1830; *Examiner,* 25 July 1830, 468.

19. For the historical basis of the play, G. E. Manwairing and B. Dobree, *The Floating Republic* (London: Cassell, 1966).

20. Michael Booth, "The Metropolis on Stage," in *The Victorian City: Images and Realities,* ed. H. J. Dyos and M. Wolff, vol. 1 (London: Routledge, 1973), 215–17.

21. On the nineteeth-century "realization" of paintings, see Martin Meisel, *Realizations* (Princeton: Princeton University Press, 1983), 147–53.

22. References are *Selections from the Modern Dramatists,* ed. G. H. Lewes (Leipzig: Brockhaus, 1867); 142; hereafer cited as *L.*

23. From the *Figaro in London*; quoted in Jerrold, *Douglas Jerrold,* 1:214.

24. *Times* and *Age* reviews are quoted in J. R. Stephens, *The Censorship of English Drama 1824-1901* (Cambridge: Cambridge University Press, 1980), 54.

25. Sally Vernon, "Trouble up at t'Mill: the Rise and Decline of the Factory Play in the 1830s and 1840s," *Victorian Studies* 20 (Winter 1977):120–32.

26. On *The Hazard of the Die,* see *Athenaeum,* 21 February 1835, 154. On *The Painter of Ghent,* see *Athenaeum,* 7 May 1836, 332 and *New Monthly Magazine,* n.s., 47 (May 1836):110. On *The Mother,* see *Morning Chronicle,* 1 June 1838.

27. *Athenaeum,* 28 February 1835, 383.

28. Scott, *The Drama of Yesterday and Today,* 1:92–97, and introduction to the edition in *Nineteenth Century British Drama,* ed. Leonard Ashley (Glenview, Ill.: Scott, Foresman, 1967), 193.

29. *The Writings of Douglas Jerrold* (London, 1853–54), 7:4; hereafter this work is cited as *W.*

30. G. H. Lewes, *On Actors and Acting* (London: Smith Elder, 1875), 85–87.

31. *Dramatic and Musical Review,* 17 September 1842, 295.

32. Jerrold, *Life and Remains of Douglas Jerrold,* 170.

33. Hannay, "Douglas Jerrold," 6.

34. *Athenaeum,* 14 October 1854, 1236.

Chapter Three

1. Quoted in Winton Tolles, *Tom Taylor and the Victorian Drama* (New York, 1940), 199.

2. "In Memoriam," *Macmillan's Magazine* 47 (August 1880):298.

3. As he himself describes in "'Some Personal Reminiscences of Alfred Wigan," *Theatre,* 1 January 1879, 411.

4. Tolles, *Tom Taylor,* 28–29.

5. Stephens, L., and Lee, S., eds., *Dictionary of National Biography,* vol. 19 (London, 1921), 473.

6. For their collaboration, see Tolles, *Tom Taylor,* 83, 92–93.

7. John Oldcastle, "Bundles of Rue," *Magazine of Art* 4 (1881):66.

8. Tolles, *Tom Taylor*, 188.

9. On Ellen Terry's and Taylor's relationship see Terry's *The Story of My Life* (London, 1908), 107–19.

10. Tolles, *Tom Taylor*, 218.

11. Stephens and Lee, eds., *Dictionary of National Biography*, 19:473.

12. Tolles, *Tom Taylor*, 248.

13. Terry, *The Story of My Life*, 117.

14. *Macmillan's Magazine*, August 1880, 298.

15. Tolles, *Tom Taylor*, 67–69.

16. Quoted in *EPNC*, 3:22.

17. Quoted in Tolles, *Tom Taylor*, 65.

18. Ibid., 129.

19. References are to French's Minor Drama edition (London, n.d.), 7; hereafter cited as *F*.

20. *Times*, 7 March 1854.

21. Tolles, *Tom Taylor*, 128.

22. Quoted in *EPNC*, 4:10.

23. Tolles discusses Taylor's burlesques in *Tom Taylor*, chap. 3.

24. On the historical figures see H. Barton Baker, *Our Old Actors* (London: Bentley, 1881), 221–27, 227–31.

25. References are to the edition in G. Rowell's *Nineteenth Century Plays* (London, 1972), 127; hereafter cited as *R*.

26. Henry Morley, *Journal of a London Playgoer* (London, 1891), 49.

27. Lewes's review is in the *Leader*, 27 November 1852; reprinted in *Victorian Dramatic Criticism*, ed. G. Rowell (London, 1971), 262–63.

28. See also *Athenaeum*, 27 November 1852, 1304.

29. On the history of the play's transmission see T. Edgar Pemberton, *A Memoir of Edward Askew Sothern* (London: Bentley, 1890), 155–60.

30. A. Clapp and G. Edgett, *Plays of the Present* (New York: Dunlop Society, 1902), 203.

31. References are to the edition in J. O. Bailey's *British Plays of the Nineteenth Century* (New York, 1966), 200.

32. For Sothern's textual distortions see Pemberton, *Memoir*, 42–44.

33. *Times*, 24 February 1860.

34. *EPNC*, 3:244.

35. John Coleman, *Plays and Playwrights I have known* (London, 1888), 2:138.

36. On the history of the play see Clapp and Edgett, *Plays of the Present*, 260–65.

37. References are to French's Acting Edition (London, n.d.), 39; hereafter cited as *F*.

38. *HED*, 5:100, and *Times*, 16 May 1855.

39. Tolles, *Tom Taylor*, 148.

40. See also *Athenaeum*, 6 June 1863, 753.
41. *Times*, 6 March 1865. See also *Athenaeum*, 11 March 1865, 355.
42. See the *Times*, 22 June 1869.
43. *Times*, 18 October 1853.
44. References in the section are all to Tom Taylor's *Historical Dramas* (London, 1877); hereafter cited as *H.*
45. Morley, *Journal of a London Playgoer*, 200–201.

Chapter Four

1. A complete account of Robertson's life can be found in his son's memoir in *The Principal Dramatic Works of Thomas William Robertson* (London, 1889). Quotations from his plays are from this edition, hereafter cited as *PDW.*
2. Mr. and Mrs. Bancroft, *On and Off the Stage.* (London, 1891), 82.
3. Watson, *Sheridan to Robertson*, 404.
4. William Archer, *The Old Drama and the New* (London, 1923), 258.
5. William Tydeman, *Plays by Tom Robertson* (Cambridge, 1982), 14.
6. Scott, *The Drama of Yesterday and Today*, 1:506
7. Auguste Filon, *The English Stage* (New York, 1970), 118.
8. *Times*, 19 September 1866.
9. Scott, *Drama of Yesterday and Today*, 510.
10. T. E. Pemberton, *The Life and Writings of T. W. Robertson* (London, 1893), 1:87.
11. Archer, *The Old Drama and the New*, 260.
12. Michael Booth, *Six Plays* (London, 1980), xvii.
13. Robertson was to use this device again in *M.P.*, in which an auction scene suggested to the *Times*'s reviewer R. Martineau's *The Last Day in the Old Home*, and in *War*, in which the Colonel and Oscar, the romantic hero, are asked to "form the picture from Horace Vernet's *Retreat from Moscow* (*PDW*, 766). See Meisel, *Realizations*, 356–59.
14. Tydeman, *Plays*, 19 and n. 17.
15. Michael Booth et al., eds., *The Revels History of Drama in English;* vol. 6 (London, 1975), 253.
16. G. B. Shaw, *Dramatic Opinions and Essays*, vol. 1 (London: Constable, 1924), 281.
17. A. Booth, ed., Tennyson, *Lady Clara Vere de Vere*, ll.55–6; and *PDW*, 84.
18. *Revels History of Drama in English*, 254.
19. Booth, *Six Plays*, xviii.
20. *Daily Telegraph*, 9 January 1899.
21. Maynard Savin, *Thomas William Robertson: His Plays and Stagecraft* (Providence, 1950), 103.

Chapter Five

1. Richard Cordell, *Henry Arthur Jones and the Modern Drama* (New York, 1968), 72.

2. Clayton Hamilton, ed., *Representative Plays by Henry Arthur Jones* (Boston, 1925), 1:xxvi; hereafter cited as *CH*.

3. Doris Arthur Jones, *The Life and Letters of Henry Arthur Jones* (London, 1930), 58.

4. Cf. Henry Arthur Jones, *The Renascence of the English Drama* (London, 1895), 1–24; hereafter cited as *RED*.

5. Even Jones later apologized for his jejune attempt to modify Ibsen in the introduction to Filon's *The English Stage*, 13.

6. E. A. Willard was not available to take the role despite Russell Jackson in *Plays by Henry Arthur Jones* (Cambridge, 1982), 30.

7. See Jones's "Religion and the Stage," *Nineteenth Century*, January 1885.

8. "First Night Judgments of Plays," in *RED*, 56.

9. Jackson, *Plays*, 9.

10. Quoted in *CH*, 1:xli.

11. Jones, *Life and Letters*, 108.

12. Ibid., 110.

13. Ibid., 114f.

14. Ibid., 123.

15. *New Review*, June 1893.

16. Jones, *Life and Letters*, 127–30.

17. In a letter written to Jones in 1898 and quoted in ibid., 152.

18. Shaw to Jones, 11 June 1894; in ibid., 156.

19. Ibid., 167.

20. Ibid., 188.

21. Cordell, *Henry Arthur Jones*, 237.

22. Jones, *Life and Letters*, 186.

23. Ibid., 218.

24. Ibid., 236.

25. Jackson, *Plays*, 23.

26. Rowell, *The Victorian Theatre*, 125.

27. Cordell, *Henry Arthur Jones*, 37.

28. Of the contemporary spectator Thomas Purnell writes, "Resemblance to what he is acquainted with is the measure of excellence" (*Dramatists of the Present Day*, 80).

29. Matthew Arnold in the *Pall Mall Gazette* quoted in Jones, *Life and Letters*, 62.

30. Archer, *The Old Drama and the New*, 295.

31. Jones, *Saints and Sinners* (London: Macmillan, 1891), 69; hereafter cited in the text by page number.

32. See also Arnold's to Jones, 23 December 1884; quoted in *CH*, xl, and in Jones, *Life and Letters*, 93.

33. Clement Scott's attitudes toward the theater were conservative in the extreme: "[We go to the play] . . .to believe in hope, in faith, in purity, in honour, in nobility of aim and steadfastness of purpose. We must enforce the good, without showing the bad" (*Theatre*, April 1897, 208).

34. "The Dramatic Outlook" (1884), in *RED*, 165.

35. Marjorie Northend, "Henry Arthur Jones and the Development of the Modern English Drama," *Review of English Studies* 18 (1942):455.

36. Cordell, *Henry Arthur Jones*, 50.

37. In the opinion of Pinero, "The Modern Drama," *Theatre*, June 1895, 348.

38. Filon, *The English Stage*, 244.

39. Rowell, *The Victorian Theatre*, 103.

40. In the *Pall Mall Gazette*, 13 and 15 August 1891; and in "The Science of the Drama," *New Review*, July 1891 (in *RED*, 93).

41. Cordell, *Henry Arthur Jones*, 86.

42. A. B. Walkley, *Playhouse Impressions* (London: Fisher Unwin, 1892), 130.

43. *Theatre*, 1 February 1891.

44. "The Future of English Drama," *New Review*, August 1893; in *RED*, 129.

45. That Jones approved of the "illustrated" style of Shakespearean production is shown in his *Nineteenth Century* article of October 1893; quoted in Booth, *Victorian Spectacular Theatre 1850-1910*, 31.

46. *Theatre*, 1 November 1893, 283.

47. References to Shaw's review are from *Our Theatre in the Nineties*, (London, 1932), 2:14–21.

48. Jones, *Life and Letters*, 180.

49. William Archer, *Theatrical World of 1897* (New York: Blom, 1969) 87, and Shaw's review of 3 April 1897 (in *Our Theatres in the Nineties*, 3:96).

50. See Max Beerbohm's review in *Around Theatres* (London: Hart-Davis, 1953), 104.

51. J. T. Grein's review in his collected *Dramatic Criticism 1900-1901, 1902;* reprinted in Rowell, ed., *Victorian Dramatic Criticism*, 246.

52. Cordell, *Henry Arthur Jones*, 94.

53. William Archer, preface to *The Crusaders* (London: Macmillan, 1892), vii.

54. *CH*, 2:xiv.

55. For an account of Wyndham's career, see George Rowell, "Wyndham of Wyndham's," in *The Theatrical Manager in England and America*, ed. J. W. Donohue (Princeton: Princeton University Press, 1971), 189–213.

56. Wyndham's illuminating letter to Jones is reproduced in Jones, *Life and Letters,* 163–67.

57. See William Archer's review in the *World,* 10 October 1894; in *Victorian Dramatic Criticism,* ed. Rowell, 267.

58. Shaw's review of 18 May 1895 is in *Our Theatres in the Nineties,* 3:123.

59. Shaw review of 9 October 1897 is in *Our Theatres in the Nineties,* 3:212.

60. Quoted in *CH,* 4:xx.

Selected Bibliography

The plays of Jerrold, Taylor, and Robertson were all published in either *Cumberland's Minor Drama* or *Lacy's Acting Editions*. These are often difficult to locate or are inaccessible to the ordinary reader. Jones's plays were published singly by Macmillan & Co., London, from 1891. All playtexts referred to in this study, however, may be read in microcard format in *English and American Drama of the Nineteenth Century*, edited by A. Nicoll and G. Freedley (New York: Readex Microprint Corp., 1965–).

General Secondary Sources

1. Bibliographies

Arnott, J. F., and **Robinson, J. W.**, eds. *English Theatrical Literature 1559–1900*. London: Society for Theatre Research, 1970. Definitive source for primary and secondary material written within the period.

Conolly, L. W., and **Wearing, J. P.**, eds. *English Drama and Theatre 1800–1900: A Guide to Information Sources*. Detroit: Gale, 1978. Good recent resource tool.

2. Theater History and Dramatic Forms

Archer, William. *The Old Drama and the New*. London: Heinemann, 1923. An opponent of Victorian drama as represented by Robertson, Albery, and Grundy.

Baker, H. Barton. *The London Stage: Its History and Traditions*. 2 vols. London: Allen, 1889. Best contemporary account.

Booth, Michael R. *English Melodrama*, London: Herbert Jenkins, 1965. A useful catalog of the different kinds of melodrama.

————. *Prefaces to English Nineteenth Century Theatre*. Manchester: Manchester University Press, n.d. Collected from his five-volume edition of nineteenth-century plays. The best historical account of principal dramatic forms.

————. *Victorian Spectacular Theatre 1850–1910*. London: Routledge & Kegan Paul, 1981. Detailed account of the visual nature of Victorian theater.

————, et al., eds. *The Revels History of Drama in English*. Vol. 6, *1750–1880*. London: Methuen, 1975. A good overview with illustrations of actors, audiences, and playhouses.

Filon, A. *The English Stage.* 1897. Reprint, New York: Kennikat Press, 1970. Curiously malicious but refreshing outsider's look at the English drama.

Hunt, Hugh, et al., eds. *The Revels History of Drama in English.* Vol. 7, *1880 to the Present Day.* London: Methuen, 1978. Not as good as the earlier volume.

Nicoll, Allardyce. *A History of English Drama 1660–1900.* Vols. 4–5. Cambridge: Cambridge University Press, 1959–60. The standard history to which all scholars are indebted. Particularly useful as a source book.

Rowell, George. *The Victorian Theatre 1792–1914.* 2d ed. Cambridge: Cambridge University Press, 1978. Better on the latter part of the century then the earlier. Good source of bibliographical material.

————, ed. *Victorian Dramatic Criticism.* London: Methuen, 1971. Representative collection of critical responses to performers, plays, and audiences from Hazlitt to Beerbohm, Shaw, and Walkley.

Scott, Clement. *The Drama of Yesterday and Today.* London: Macmillan, 1899. Biased, conservative Victorian doyen of theater criticism. Essential reading.

Smith, James. *Melodrama.* Critical Idiom series. London: Methuen, 1973. Concise and readable but simplistic.

Watson E. B. *Sheridan to Robertson,* Cambridge, Mass.: Harvard University Press, 1926. Still the most sensible and penetrating account of London theater until the 1860s.

Individual Authors

DOUGLAS JERROLD

1. Collections of Plays

Booth, Michael, ed. *English Plays of the Nineteeth Century.* London: Oxford University Press, 1969–73. Vol. 1, *Black Eyed Susan;* vol. 4, *Mr. Paul Pry.*

Writing of Douglas Jerrold. London: Bradbury & Evans, 1853–54. Vol. 7, *Bubbles of the Day, Retired from Business, St. Cupid; or, Dorothy's Fortune, Time Works Wonders, The Prisoner of War, and The Catspaw;* vol. 8, *The Rent Day, Nell Gwynne, The Wedding Gown, Schoolfellows, Doves in a Cage, The Painter of Ghent, and Blacked Eyed Susan.*

2. Secondary Sources

Booth, Michael, et al., eds. *The Revels History of Drama in English.* Vol. 6, chap. 1. Particularly useful for Jerrold's audiences.

Horne, R. H. *A New Spirit of the Age.* 2 vols. London: Smith, Elder, 1844. Interesting comments on Jerrold's achievements by a contemporary critic.

Jerrold, W. Blanchard. *The Life and Remains of Douglas Jerrold.* London: Bentley, 1859. Rather sentimental and anecdotal account of his father's life.

Jerrold, Walter. *Douglas Jerrold: Dramatist and Wit.* London: Hodder & Stoughton, 1914. Jerrold's grandson's sensible and detached account of his grandfather's life. Particularly good for relating Jerrold's plays to their theatrical context.

Kelly, R. M. *Douglas Jerrold.* New York: Twayne, 1972. Useful for connections between Jerrold's plays and his journalistic career.

Nicoll, Allardyce. *A History of English Drama 1600–1900.* Vol. 4. For a list of Jerrold's plays and performance dates see 331–33.

TOM TAYLOR

1. Collections of Plays

Bailey, J. O., ed. *British Plays of the Nineteenth Century.* New York: Odyssey Press, 1966. Includes *Our American Cousin.*

Booth, Michael, ed. *English Plays of the Nineteenth Century.* vols. 1–5 London: Oxford University Press, 1969–73. Vol. 2, *The Ticket of Leave Man;* vol. 3, *New Men and Old Acres.*

Historical Dramas. London: Chatto & Windus, 1877. Includes *Lady Clancarty, Plot and Passion, The Fool's Revenge, Arkwright's Wife, Twixt Axe and Crown, Ann Boleyn,* and *Jeanne D'Arc.*

Rowell, George, ed. *Nineteenth Century Plays.* London: Oxford University Press, 1972. Includes *Masks and Faces.*

2. Articles

"Mr. Phelps and *The Fool's Revenge.*" *Theatre,* 1 December 1878, 338–44.

"Some Reminiscences of Alfred Wigan." *Theatre,* 1 January 1879, 410–18.

3. Criticism

The Theatre in England: Some of its Shortcomings and Possibilities. London: British & Colonial Pubishing House, 1871.

4. Secondary Sources

Coleman, John. *Plays and Playwrights I have Known.* 2 vols. London: Chatto & Windus, 1888. One of the main sources of biographical material. Not very discriminating.

Morley, Henry. *Journal of a London Playgoer, 1851–56.* London: Routledge, 1891. Useful for a critical reaction to Taylor's plays.

Nicoll, Allardyce. *A History of English Drama.* Vol. 4. For a list of Taylor's plays and their performance dates see 592–94.

Q [Thomas Purnell]. *Dramatists of the Present Day.* London: Chapman & Hall, 1871. Critical disenchantment with Taylor.

Stephens L., and **Lee, S.**, eds. *Dictionary of National Biography.* Vol. 19. London: Oxford University Press, 1921. S.v. "Taylor." Basic biographical source. Some factual errors.

Terry, Ellen. *The Story of My Life.* London: Hutchinson, 1908. Best account of Taylor, the social man.

Tolles, Winton. *Tom Taylor and the Victorian Drama.* New York: Columbia University Press, 1940. Still the only full-length appreciation of Taylor's work. Balanced and authoritative.

THOMAS WILLIAM ROBERTSON

1. Collections of Plays

Booth, Michael, ed. *Six Plays.* London: Amber Lane Press, 1980. Includes *Society, Ours, Caste, Progress, School,* and *Birth.*

The Principal Dramatic Works of Thomas William Robertson. With a memoir by his son. London: Sampson Low, 1889. Vol. 1, *Birth, Breach of Promise, Caste, David Garrick, Dreams, Home, Ladies' Battle,* and *M.P.;* vol. 2, *The Nightingale, Ours, Play, Progress, Row in the House, School, Society,* and *War.*

Rowell, George, ed. *Nineteenth Century Plays.* Includes *Caste.*

Tydeman, William, ed. **Plays by Tom Robertson.** Cambridge: Cambridge University Press, 1982. Includes *Society, Birth,* and *School.*

2. Secondary Sources

Bancroft, Mr. and Mrs. *On and Off the Stage.* London: Bentley, 1891. The best account of the collaboration between Robertson and the Prince of Wales company.

Pemberton, T. E. *The Life and Writings of T. W. Robertson.* London: Bentley, 1893. Affectionate and anecdotal. Includes a parody by Gilbert of a Robertson play.

Savin, Maynard. *Thomas William Robertson: His Plays and Stagecraft.* Providence: Brown University Press, 1950. A good full-length appreciation but uncritical.

Watson, E. B. *Sheridan to Robertson.* Chaps. 17–18. Particularly good for Robertson's staging innovations.

HENRY ARTHUR JONES

1. Collections of Plays

Booth, Michael, ed. *English Plays of the Nineteenth Century.* Vol. 2, *Mrs. Dane's Defence.*

Hamilton, Clayton, ed. *Representative Plays by Henry Arthur Jones.* Boston: Little Brown, 1925. Vol. 1, *The Silver King, The Middleman, Judah,* and

The Dancing Girl; vol. 2, *The Crusaders, The Tempter, The Masqueraders,* and *The Case of Rebellious Susan;* vol. 3, *Michael and his Lost Angel, The Liars, Mrs. Dane's Defence,* and *The Hypocrites;* vol. 4, *Dolly Reforming Herself, The Divine Gift, Mary Goes First,* and *The Goal, Grace Mary.*

Jackson, Russell, ed. *Plays by Henry Arthur Jones.* Cambridge: Cambridge University Press, 1982. Includes *The Silver King, The Case of Rebellious Susan,* and *The Liars.*

2. Collections of Articles
The Renascence of the English Drama. London: Macmillan, 1895.
Foundations of a National Drama. London: Chapman & Hall, 1913.

3. Secondary Sources
Bettany, W. Lewis. "The Drama of Modern England, as Viewed by Mr. H. A. Jones." *Theatre,* 1 October 1893, 203–9. A savage criticism of Jones's dramatic principles and his position in contemporary theater.

Cordell, Richard. *Henry Arthur Jones and the Modern Drama.* 1932. Reprint. New York: Kennikat Press, 1968. Still the best, balanced appreciation of Jones and his work.

Jones, Doris Arthur. *The Life and Letters of Henry Arthur Jones.* London: Gollancz, 1930. The standard biographical work, particularly useful for Jones's correspondence.

Nicoll, Allardyce. *A History of English Drama 1660–1900.* Vol. 5, chap. 5. Relates Jones to other dramatists of the 1880s.

Northend, Marjorie. "Henry Arthur Jones and the Development of the Modern English Drama." *Review of English Studies* 18 (October 1942):448–63. Less than enthusiastic but good introduction to Jones's dramatic connections with Galsworthy, Shaw, etc.

Rowell, George. *The Victorian Theatre 1792–1914.* Good overview of "society drama" and actor/managers with whom Jones worked.

Shaw, G. B. *Our Theatres in the Nineties.* 3 vols. London: Constable, 1932. Brilliant accounts of Jones's plays.

Index

DATE DUE

GAYLORD			PRINTED IN U.S.A.